teach
yourself

globalization

teach ®
yourself

globalization
keith suter

For UK order enquiries: please contact Bookpoint Ltd, 130 Milton Park, Abingdon, Oxon OX14 4SB. Telephone: +44 (0) 1235 827720. Fax: +44 (0) 1235 400454. Lines are open 09.00–17.00, Monday to Saturday, with a 24-hour message answering service. Details about our titles and how to order are available at www.teachyourself.co.uk

For US order enquiries: please contact McGraw-Hill Customer Services, PO Box 545, Blacklick, OH 43004-0545, USA. Telephone: 1-800-722-4726. Fax: 1-614-755-5645.

For Canada order enquiries: please contact McGraw-Hill Ryerson Ltd, 300 Water St, Whitby, Ontario L1N 9B6, Canada. Telephone: 905 430 5000. Fax: 905 430 5020.

Long renowned as the authoritative source for self-guided learning – with more than 50 million copies sold worldwide – the **teach yourself** series includes over 500 titles in the fields of languages, crafts, hobbies, business, computing and education.

British Library Cataloguing in Publication Data: a catalogue record for this title is available from the British Library.

Library of Congress Catalog Card Number: on file.

First published in UK 2006 by Hodder Education, 338 Euston Road, London NW1 3BH.

First published in US 2006 by The McGraw-Hill Companies, Inc.

This edition published 2006.

The **teach yourself** name is a registered trade mark of Hodder Headline.

Copyright © 2006 Keith Suter

Typeset by Transet Limited, Coventry, England.
Printed in Great Britain for Hodder Education, a division of Hodder Headline, 338 Euston Road, London NW1 3BH, by Cox & Wyman Ltd, Reading, Berkshire.

The publisher has used its best endeavours to ensure that the URLs for external websites referred to in this book are correct and active at the time of going to press. However, the publisher and the author have no responsibility for the websites and can make no guarantee that a site will remain live or that the content will remain relevant, decent or appropriate.

Hodder Headline's policy is to use papers that are natural, renewable and recyclable products and made from wood grown in sustainable forests. The logging and manufacturing processes are expected to conform to the environmental regulations of the country of origin.

Impression number   10 9 8 7 6 5 4 3 2
Year   2010 2009 2008 2007

contents

01	**the hinge of history: the new global order**	**1**
	introduction	2
	new centres of world power	5
	assessing globalization	9
	the end of the Europeanization of the globe	9
	the end of the Cold War	13
	conclusion	16
02	**rise of the old world order: era of nation-states**	**17**
	introduction	18
	the basic unit of international politics	18
	European system before 1648	19
	characteristics of the nation-state	22
	ambiguities of the Westphalian system	23
	European impact on Africa	28
	conclusion	31
03	**problems with the nation-state system**	**33**
	introduction	34
	diplomacy	34
	localization	38
	the importance of new technology	40
	conclusion	44
04	**individual governments and global problems**	**45**
	introduction	46
	plagues and infectious diseases	46
	pollution	49
	crime	53

mass movement of peoples 60

conclusion 63

05 **the United Nations** **65**

introduction 66

the League of Nations 66

composition of the UN 67

assessment of the UN 72

conclusion 78

06 **the European Union and other
organizations** **80**

introduction 81

the European Union (EU) 81

the Commonwealth 85

Group of 8 (G8) 87

Association of South East Asian
Nations (ASEAN) 89

the Bank of International Settlements 91

the future of national governments 96

conclusion 97

07 **transnational corporations** **98**

introduction 99

evolution of the corporation 99

the global economy 101

global impact 105

conclusion 107

08 **transnational corporations' challenge to
governmental power** **108**

introduction 109

education of a president 109

the rise and fall of governments in
economic policy 110

merchant power 111

Adam Smith and the role of the market 112

John Maynard Keynes and the role of
government 114

the market returns 119

conclusion 122

09 **consuming passions** **123**
introduction 124
consumerism as a new idea 124
sophisticated marketing 126
the situation in developing countries 129
the rise of free trade 130
is the 'good life' killing us? 134
is the pace of life too fast? 135
conclusion 144
10 **people power: nongovernmental**
  organizations **145**
introduction 146
the size of NGOs 146
NGOs and the decline of national party
  politics 147
characteristics of NGOs 147
four case studies 153
conclusion 160
11 **how NGOs challenge governmental power** **161**
introduction 162
NGO pressure on national governments 162
four case studies 164
conclusion 174
12 **how NGOs challenge the power of**
  transnational corporations **175**
introduction 176
putting justice into business 176
boycotts 177
ethical purchasing 180
shareholder activism 181
conclusion 185
13 **the reaction against globalization** **187**
introduction 188
religious fundamentalism 188
white male rage 195
the global justice movement 198

globalization in novels   203
conclusion   205
14 globalization cannot be reversed   207
introduction   208
globalization is here to stay   208
government has been reinvented   209
the value of nationalism in sport   210
trade knits the world together   211
conclusion   214
15 making the most of the new era   216
introduction   217
uniting the people   217
world federalism   218
the continuing debate   221
the idea continues   225
refusal to change   225
conclusion   226
glossary   229
abbreviations   230
taking it further   232
index   234

Acknowledgements

The author would like to thank all those at Hodder Education, particularly Lisa Grey and Barbara Smith.

01

the hinge of history: the new global order

This chapter will cover:
- the definition of 'globalization'
- new centres of world power
- how Europeanization impacted on the world
- ways in which globalization helped end the Cold War
- whether globalization is good or bad.

Introduction

The process of globalization is one of the most important developments affecting the world in the last few decades. It is encouraging – if not forcing – us to look differently at the world. We are moving into an era where the national boundaries that were very important to us are far less so.

A child growing up soon acquires an awareness of national boundaries. He or she has a nationality, a sense of national identity and learns at least one language. The person lives in his or her own nation-state, as part of the worldwide system of nation-states. The adult person pays taxes to the national government, has the opportunity to vote for national politicians and may serve in the national defence forces. That person will look to the national government to provide educational and welfare services, defend the country from attacks by foreign governments and preserve the special qualities of the particular nation-state. That person expects national leaders to look after their country's interests.

However, that era is ending. This chapter provides an overview of the process of globalization and how new centres of power – rather than national governments – set the pace of events. First, 'cooperative power' refers to the way in which national governments are obliged to work together on common issues through organizations, such as the United Nations (UN), to solve common problems. Second, 'corporate power' refers to the increasing economic and social influence of transnational corporations (such as Coca-Cola, McDonald's and Shell). Third, 'people power' refers to the organizations through which ordinary people seek to influence politics outside the political party process. This chapter also contains an historical overview of the rise and fall of Europe's domination of the globe and a case study of how globalization helped end the Cold War.

Globalization defined

'Globalization' means the erosion of national boundaries and the reduced significance of national governments. We are moving from a world with borders to one without. No one knows what the future holds – but we do know that it will be different from today.

National governments are a comparatively new idea. International lawyers date them from 1648, the end of the

Thirty Years' War in Europe and the 'Peace of Westphalia' (hence the name of the present world order: 'Westphalian system'). Prior to that time people in Europe lived in small tribes or clans, possibly as part of a large empire.

No one suddenly decided in 1648 to create the Westphalian system. Indeed the date is somewhat arbitrary. Some countries are older, such as England, Spain and Portugal. By contrast, Germany seems to redraw its boundaries every generation or so (the last time being in 1991).

It is only with the benefit of hindsight that people can see that around the seventeenth century a new world order had been created. Peoples (nations) were now to be governed by 'states', hence the title of 'nation-states' (as distinct from, say, the previous 'city-states'). Another term for nation-state is 'country'.

As Europeans colonized the world, so they took this system with them. The UN currently has 192 nation-state members. If President Bush is successful with his Middle East 'roadmap for peace', then Palestine will also join the UN as a nation-state. Montenegro (which in 2006 broke away from Serbia) is the most recent member.

The nation-state system is now so prevalent that it is seen as the norm in world politics. But national governments are no longer so relevant to world politics. If a person from outer space landed on Earth and said, 'Take me to your leader', to whom would we take the person? Tony Blair? Gordon Brown? George Bush? Bill Gates? Rupert Murdoch?

The current world order is ending but there is no clear replacement for it. The old order has been based on nation-states (or countries) with centralized national governments. The old order has worn well but it is nearly worn out. The process of globalization is now the most important factor in world politics.

Main characteristics of globalization

There are eight features of globalization to note:

- The new era is 'global', rather than 'international'. The concept of 'international' regards the nation-state as the basic component of world affairs, so that all that happens at the planetary level is a form of interaction between nation-states or national governments. This is no longer the case. There are other non-state actors on the world stage, most notably transnational corporations, intergovernmental organizations (particularly the United Nations and European Union), and nongovernmental organizations (such as the women's, peace and environment movements).

- Globalization is more than just a matter of economics (which is often the focal point of anti-globalization demonstrations). Globalization means that global change is running ahead of governments' ability to manage it. Economics is only a part of that process. This book also deals with other matters such as war, crime, environment and health. Therefore, while there is an examination of the growth and impact of transnational corporations, this book takes in many other factors in order to get a fuller picture of globalization.

- The anti-globalization protesters are as much part of the globalization process as the people and organizations they criticize. For example, they use the internet, modern media and other sophisticated communications techniques so that their messages cross borders.

- Globalization challenges the traditional academic disciplines. The study of history at school level, for example, used to be the study of kings and queens and other 'great people', particularly the wars they fought. Now we need also note factors such as economics, environment, diseases, plagues and climate change as factors shaping history. In the study of international relations, there is the traditional 'realist' view of the world – politics is seen as a ceaseless competition by states, especially through military power. Globalization means that national governments are no longer the only players in the global power struggle and that military power is not the only tool.

- Globalization is not just a form of 'Americanization'. It is not simply the imposition of American values on the rest of the world. Indeed, the US is itself undergoing stresses due to globalization, for example, the loss of manufacturing jobs to cheaper workplaces, such as those in China and India. As many as one-third of the annual US tax returns are now done in India.

- The process of globalization is not some dark sinister conspiracy organized by a group of transnational corporations or some group of ill-motivated individuals or secret organizations wishing to take over the world. It is simply another evolution in world's affairs. However, it has not been well communicated to the general public.

- The reduction in national government power is creating a vacuum at the global level that is not being filled by any supranational organization. There is no clear replacement for the existing world order – or even an agreed mechanism for creating one.
- The process of globalization is not reversible. It is not possible to reinvent the era of nation-states. It is more a matter of coming to terms with the new era and seeing how we are to cope with it. Therefore, there has to be a search for a new order rather than waste time trying to patch up the system of nation-states. Countries will remain in existence in one form or another but the process of globalization means that national governments will have to share their power with three other forms of power.

Globalization is not going to go away. It is the main game in town. The anti-globalization demonstrations are useful as a way of drawing attention to the importance of globalization. They have encouraged some attention (albeit not enough) on the massive transformation through which the world has passed but much more education is required.

New centres of world power

Cooperative power

Governments increasingly have to work together on common problems. Diseases, pollution and climate change do not recognize national boundaries. They have no respect for human-made lines on maps and force national governments to work through intergovernmental organizations such as the UN and European Union (EU). Until the expansion of the UN's peacekeeping work in the early 1990s, about 80 per cent of the UN's expenditure was on economic and social cooperation.

By this means, countries and individuals can gradually see the benefits of mutual cooperation and so create a sustained ethos of cooperation. This is done out of the public eye, with little publicity and political controversy. For example, even during the Cold War, the US and Soviet Union and their respective allies were working together on various projects – smallpox was eradicated by the World Health Organization (this was based on a Soviet proposal and the project was headed by an American); the International Telecommunications Union (ITU) oversaw the creation of the global telephone dialling service based on numbers (rather than letters) leading to ISD (international subscriber dialling); the ITU also oversaw the conference process by which radio and television airwaves were apportioned out; the International Maritime Organization created a common bill of lading for merchant marine vessels; and the World Meteorological Organization created a global network for exchanging data on weather patterns. These are just some examples.

These were all unexciting developments (compared with mass media interest in war and the arms race) but were matters that were easily taken for granted and whose benefits have had a lasting significance. The Cold War has come and gone but the contribution of the less glamorous functional cooperation remains. Indeed, with the Cold War now gone, there are now far more opportunities to trade across national lines or to telephone across them.

Corporate power

Transnational corporations (TNCs) are becoming increasingly important. They are now the major driving forces in economic policy. Transnational corporations can, for example, move jobs offshore in search of cheaper workers and fewer unions.

A transnational corporation is one that engages in foreign direct investment and owns (or controls) activities in more than one country. Transnational corporations are now the main global economic force and have eroded the notion of a national economy; there is now only a global one. Transnational corporations sprawl across national political boundaries. They can change character to maximize profits. For example, if a government tries to protect its own industries by keeping out imports, they will try to buy local companies and so produce goods within that country.

Transnational corporations have evolved through four stages. From about 1895 to 1945, there was the emergence and consolidation of oligopolies (a small number of large corporations dominating a market) in key sectors in north America, western Europe and Japan. In the second stage, from 1946 to the mid-1960s, transnational corporations rose to their position of prominence. For example, they were responsible for roughly 80 per cent of the global trade conducted outside the communist bloc.

In the next transnational stage, from the mid-1960s to the 1990s, corporations have consolidated their dominance. For instance, there have been mergers across national boundaries and there has been a rise in the significance of non-US corporations, such as additional Japanese and western European ones.

The last stage is the current process of consolidation with the ending of the Cold War and the opening up of the former Soviet bloc to transnational corporations. China is also more willing to have foreign corporations invest in it. There is a new oilrush by the corporations into the countries that were largely off-limits during the Cold War. These countries include Kazakhstan, the Russian Arctic Circle, China's Tarim Basin and the waters off Vietnam. These countries strive to develop their resources and earn hard currency. Former communist countries are also opening up to the capital, technology and management skills that international oil firms offer.

Virtually the entire globe is now within reach of the corporations. Even Libya is now ending its international isolation because it has cooperated with the trial of the alleged criminals involved in the December 1988 Lockerbie Pan-Am aircraft bombing. Foreign oil corporations want to resume exploration.

Another development that fosters globalization is that the corporations are staffed by a form of global 'civil service', rather than 'national' personnel. Corporations have been far more successful than the UN in encouraging their staff to see themselves as global workers rather than ones with national loyalties. The corporations have been able to create a commitment to a single, unified global mission that transcends nationalistic feelings by individual staff. As an example, a person does not think that they are working for a Japanese car manufacturer trying to build and sell its products in the US. Instead, such a person works for Honda or Nissan or Toyota.

The telecommunications revolution means that workers can be employed in cheap labour areas to do data processing for an entire corporation, such as where a New York insurance corporation has located all its data processing in Ireland. This also takes advantage of the time zone differences because the New York office can offer an overnight service: the paperwork is being processed in Ireland, ready for a cheque to be collected the following day New York time. A US airline company has located its booking system in Jamaica. British Telecom has relocated some of its administration, finance, personnel and customer service operations to Australia; while the northern hemisphere sleeps, Australian staff work on software development, fixing problems that occurred during the day in the European and UK network. A company in Wellington, New Zealand, is exploiting the time zones to create a niche market in translating documents in foreign languages. The documents are sent by email from Europe and translated overnight in Wellington so that they can be ready for the following day.

To conclude, transnational corporations are themselves becoming global entities. In the 1950s, transnational corporations were widely regarded as a peculiarly US form of business organization. By the early 1990s, every industrialized country provided a base for a considerable number of transnational corporations that, collectively, were becoming the dominant form of organization responsible for the international exchange of goods and services.

People power

The mobilization of people power is mainly done through nongovernmental organizations (NGOs), such as Amnesty International, women's movement, peace movement, Greenpeace, Humane Society International and Rotary International. They enable people to work together across national lines for the betterment of humankind.

NGOs are the most important way of mobilizing public opinion and focusing attention on a problem. The 1972 UN Conference on the Environment arose largely from the way in which NGOs argued that there was an environmental crisis, such as the Club of Rome report on the *Limits to Growth* (the biggest selling environment book in world history). NGOs acted and governments reacted. Similarly, NGOs publicized the Brundtland Report on the environment and development and so encouraged governments and the UN to create the 1992 Conference on Environment and Development (UNCED). Environmental NGOs remain active in, for example, opposing the resumption of commercial whaling (banned in 1986 but which the Japanese are trying to revive) and encouraging support of the 1997 Kyoto Protocol on climate change.

NGOs, then, are a growing force in global politics. They are adept at attracting media coverage, they appeal to people who are disenchanted with the usual party political process and they provide a sense of vision and continuity that outlasts the short-term perspective of governments.

Assessing globalization

Is globalization good or bad? This question is difficult to answer because the question is so broad. Some aspects of globalization may be good and some may be bad. This is a bit like asking if 'weather' is good or bad. A farmer may want rain but a person planning a picnic in the park may not.

This means that some anti-globalization demonstrators are not quite correct. Globalization is often defined by demonstrators as simply an economic matter yet economics is only part of the process. To focus on economics is therefore to get a distorted picture of the full magnitude of the changes. Globalization refers to the declining power of national governments generally – and not just in economics.

Due to the fact that national boundaries are not as important as they once were, we need to learn to live in an era when national governments, though still present and still collecting taxation revenue, will not be the main drivers of change.

The end of the Europeanization of the globe

The rise of globalization has coincided with the end of an era of 500 years of world history. This has been a unique period during which Europeans dominated the world. They took their nation-state model with them. When they gave their colonies independence, they left the model in place.

Exploration and exploitation

European domination of the globe began with two of Europe's oldest nation-states, Spain and Portugal. Other nation-states followed suit, such as the Netherlands, France, UK, Belgium, Italy and Germany. The Europeans sailed to all parts of the globe in search of commodities like gold, silver and spices. Thriving original civilizations were destroyed and European citizens and values were imposed. Colonialism transported rivalries between the colonial powers to other parts of the globe. The victims of colonialism were drawn into struggles about which they knew nothing. They were often recruited into European forces to fight for European causes.

Decolonization

The world since 1945 has been transformed. In 1945, the UN had 51 members – now it has 192. Most of this growth has come from the winding up of empires. This transformation – one of the greatest changes in the twentieth century – has come about for four reasons:

1 Colonial peoples rebelled against their masters. Japan's entry into World War II by defeating western countries – especially the 1942 capture of Singapore – showed that Europeans were not always destined to win. Japan may have eventually lost the war but its example stayed in the minds of Asian peoples. They had seen a non-European country defeat – at least initially – one of the world's greatest countries.

2 The communications revolution – then in its initial stages – meant that ideas on resisting colonialism could be broadcast around the world.

3 The imperial powers had been weakened by the fighting among themselves. The UK, for example, emerged from World War II heavily in debt and unable to maintain the large military force that would be required to put down colonial rebellions.

4 The temper of the times had changed. In Europe there was less enthusiasm for maintaining the burden of the empire. Additionally, economists argued that the money to be made from colonies had already been gained and that continued imperialism would be a financial burden (and not a profitable investment).

Most of the territories that are left in some form of colonial status have very small populations. The world now has – as a percentage of total population – the smallest number of people under colonial rule for 500 years.

From colonies to nation-states

Seventy per cent of all the world's land borders have been created by Europeans.

As colonies have become independent so they have carried on with colonial borders. Unfortunately, the borders were established as a colonial convenience rather than as a result of European consultation with their colonial subjects. As an example, Europeans were fond of using rivers as national boundaries. However, rivers (especially in Africa) were often a form of highway, with people living either side of the road. Colonialism divided up tribes at the whim of the imperial pen. Thus, a patchwork of about 55 African nation-states has been imposed on over 200 tribes.

Many of the conflicts in Africa today are derived from the mismatch of borders and ethnic group. But the 'states' (political entities) cannot redraw their boundaries to fit their 'nations' (ethnic entities).

As far as we can tell, Africans governed themselves quite competently before the Europeans arrived. They generally enjoyed a unity of purpose and a system of mass participation that indicated a healthy distrust for power. By imposing inappropriate notions of nationalism and the nation-state on Africa's emerging élite, the Europeans set African people and institutions on the road to ruin from which they have still not recovered.

Permanent impact of Europeanization

The world has been permanently transformed by the process of Europeanization. Most territories cannot be 'ethnically cleansed' to revert back to their 'ethnically pure' condition – although some appalling attempts are being made. How are we to define 'Europe', especially in the context of the enlargement of the EU (formerly called the European Community)? Is Canada more 'European' (thanks to the British and French) than Albania, or is Brazil more European (thanks to Portugal) than Bulgaria? Canada and Brazil share western Europe's Greco-Roman Christian traditions.

Meanwhile, Europeans have moved around to seek employment – or they are recruited from countries that once had a labour shortage. Melbourne is the third largest 'Greek city' in the world and Australia has more Maltese than Malta does. People have inter-married and formed new relationships. Some of the new governments in the former Soviet republics would like to remove the Russians but the Russians (many of whom were transferred by Moscow against their will) have settled in the republics and have no families to go back to in Russia.

From about 1500 Europe was a continent of emigrants. The global Europeanization process was conducted by the mass transfer of people to the rest of the world. Europe is now a continent of *immigrants*. People, especially from the third world, try to gain a better life (or, as overseas students, wish to get a better education and then intermarry) in Europe. The Iron Curtain has gone but the west Europeans (and the US, Canada and Australia) have installed a glass curtain. Thanks to the mass media revolution, third world people can see on television the lifestyles in the west (or at least how they are portrayed) but they are denied entry because of the new curtain.

The fourth world

The 'fourth world' refers to the minority populations within nation-states.

With the UN being so successful in ending the *formal* system of colonialism, there is still the issue of 'internal colonization'. This means that independent countries have given poor treatment to the original inhabitants of the land.

There are problems in many countries. The UN estimates that there are 370 million indigenous people in at least 5,000 groups spread across the world in more than 70 countries.

Despite their diversity, they face similar problems. Most of India's tribal people live below the poverty line and the life expectancy of indigenous people in northern Russia is 18 years below the national average. Three decades ago the Brazilian government set aside a portion of land – the equivalent size of Portugal – for Indians to live on their own. Now gold and oil have been discovered on the land. Miners are invading it, killing the Indians and going after the resources.

However, the indigenous peoples are fighting back. The 500-year nightmare is coming to an end. First, they have survived. They will not perish. Their numbers are slowly increasing and they are learning the strength of networking, for example, the Inuit (wrongly called 'Eskimos') who live in northern Russia, Canada and Scandinavia are sharing their experiences – including how to lobby their governments and how to mobilize the mass media. In the US, there are now 600 Indian lawyers working for their people. They also have had their first senator.

They are also seeking economic compensation. The annual market of pharmaceutical products derived from medicinal plants discovered by indigenous peoples exceeds US$43 billion, but the profits are rarely shared with indigenous peoples. They are campaigning for their royalty payments.

To conclude, although the process of the Europeanization of the globe has itself stopped, we will be living with the consequences indefinitely. The new countries are trying to make a success of Westphalian national governance in an era of globalization.

The end of the Cold War

Revolutions go better with Coke

Another way of examining the impact of globalization is to see what it did to the Cold War. The Cold War was the central defining event for the period from 1945 to 1990. All major political decisions were made in the context of it. Even the political labels of first (pro-US), second (pro-USSR) and third (neutral) worlds were coined in the Cold War's context.

In the grand sweep of Westphalian history, the Cold War was very much a product of the Westphalian system. Here were two nation-states emerging onto the international scene as the main superpowers and so they had to go through a period of competition to see which would triumph over the other. Europe had been there before with the imperial rivalries between Spain and Portugal then France and the UK, and finally between the UK and Germany.

But while the two superpowers were so focused on their own arms race, a new global order started to emerge. One component of the post-Westphalian system is the power of transnational corporations. Media transnational corporations have the ability to shape political and social priorities. Global television coverage has created a new era of transparency. Stalin could get away with his mass murders because they were done out of the mass media spotlight. Gorbachev's USSR, by contrast, could not be so easily hidden. For example, the USSR's first nuclear disaster (in the Urals in 1957) was hidden from Soviet and foreign view for about two decades, whereas the April 1986 Chernobyl disaster was known within hours overseas and was well televised (including foreign satellite coverage).

Television's impact also includes – for better or worse – the development of a global consumer culture. This is currently based on such items as Coca-Cola, Big Macs and Madonna. The grass roots NGOs in eastern Europe, which campaigned for an end to the Cold War and the free movement of people throughout the continent, were partly motivated by the desire to gain access to the 'good things' in western life. Revolutions go better with Coke.

NGOs were a very important way of mobilizing public opinion to end the Cold War. Ordinary people were suddenly given the opportunity to change the flow of political events – especially when their work was publicized by the global mass media. As the Soviet bloc crumbled, the Reverend Laszlo Tokes was important for galvanizing public opinion against the Ceausescu regime in Romania. Tokes and his church congregation were in the Hungarian minority in western Romania (Transylvania). For years the discipline of the Warsaw Pact had stifled Hungarian resentment over the loss of Transylvania in 1918 and the mistreatment of its Hungarians by the Romanian regime but, as *glasnost* expanded the limits of political expression, the fate of Transylvania became a major issue in Hungary. Word of Tokes's plight leaked out to Hungary and, in July 1989, a Hungarian television crew managed to get to Tokes and film an interview. He spoke of his own situation and, more generally, about repression in Romania. The interview also made its way to Radio Free Europe, the BBC and other western radio stations that transmitted to Romania. Foreign broadcasts over Romania's borders, bypassing the state media, played a major role in the revolution and the Tokes interview was one of the first instances of the phenomenon.

Transnational corporations are helping to create a new global culture. The citizens of the USSR may have been militarily loyal to Moscow but their hearts were in Hollywood. Hollywood makes the best dreams.

The US had the wrong Cold War strategy

The US made a fundamental mistake in implementing its policy of 'containment'. It opposed the USSR on the USSR's own grounds rather than US grounds. A centrally planned economy can make weapons but it has much more difficulty in making consumer goods. It is itself the market for the first (and therefore knows what it wants) but its citizens are the market for the second. The USSR was able to compete with the US in the arms race (though the US probably overestimated the USSR's military strength) but it could not match the US in the production of goods. The USSR could build nuclear weapons and put people into space but it could not put food on the shelves.

Western Cold War politicians and conservative 'realist' scholars saw the arms race as the key component of the Cold War yet they ignored the everyday basics of life. Few predicted the collapse of the USSR from within. Soviet citizens were yearning for the 'good things in life' and recognized that the Soviet system could not produce Coke, Big Macs and Madonna. The Red Army could resist a NATO invasion into eastern Europe but not the televised transmission of *Dallas* and *Dynasty*.

Thus, while President Reagan regarded the USSR as the 'evil empire', transnational corporations saw its people as potential customers. Soviet citizens were disturbed by such presidential rhetoric – but still yearned for the American way of life. Now that the Cold War is over and the 'Iron Curtain' – made incidentally in France since east European barbed wire was not as rust-resistant – has been removed, the corporations are moving into eastern Europe.

NGOs also cut across national borders. Citizen diplomacy enabled US and Soviet citizens (such as those in peace groups) to meet and discuss the Cold War and ways of ending it. They focused on what united humankind rather than what divided it. NGOs in other walks of life enabled citizens to discuss, for example, scientific and cultural matters. There was never a Cold War at the South Pole – scientists either cooperated together or froze separately. Australia, the largest claimant to Antarctica, hosted as many Russian bases there as it did US military bases on the Australian mainland.

The UN also brought the US and USSR together. For example (as noted earlier), smallpox was eradicated, a global telephone dialling service was created based on numbers (rather than letters) leading to ISD (international subscriber dialling), and a global network was created for exchanging data on weather patterns. Thus, there was a growing sense of irrelevance of the Cold War. It froze governmental political relations between the US and USSR but the chill did not reach all areas of the lives of their respective civilians. Along with the growing importance of TNCs, NGOs and the UN, a new global agenda also emerged. The 'national security state' that emerged at the outset of the Cold War had a narrow military-dominated perception of national security. A broader definition of national security should include environmental concerns – the erosion of soils, the deterioration of the earth's basic biological systems and the depletion of oil reserves that now threaten the security of countries everywhere. Ultimately, these stresses will translate into social unrest and political instability. Military expenditure will do little to help protect the environment or solve these other problems.

To conclude, the Cold War was overtaken by events. It became an expensive irrelevance. It dominated global politics for almost half a century but eventually other concerns took priority.

Now it is necessary to address the issues the world should have addressed in 1945 – before it was diverted by the Cold War. The main focus of this book is on how the nation-state cannot cope with challenges presented by economics, diseases and the environment. A new global order is emerging.

Conclusion

Globalization is transforming the old system of nation-states. The system was invented in Europe and the Europeans took it with them when they colonized much of the rest of the globe between the late fifteenth and early twentieth century. We have become accustomed to national governments setting the pace of change and now we will have to get used to other centres of power. Because globalization is such a wide-ranging development, it is not possible to say whether it is good or bad. There certainly are some winners and losers.

Questions

1 How have you become aware of the globalization process in your life?
2 How does cooperative power affect your life?
3 How does corporate power affect your life?
4 How does people power affect your life?
5 Who are the winners and losers of globalization?

02

rise of the old world order: era of nation-states

This chapter will cover:
- the rise of the nation-state system
- the characteristics of the nation-state system
- the impact of Europe on Africa.

Introduction

This chapter deals with the old world order. It considers how people originally lived in local tribes or clans, with few connections with the outside world and how, beginning in Europe in 1648, a new political system gradually emerged, the nation-state. Right from the outset there were problems with the new system, such as the way that a 'people' or 'nation' may not live in the area ascribed to them. The most tragic example of this has been the African continent and so a case study of the European impact on Africa is included in this Chapter.

The basic unit of international politics

The nation-state (or 'country') is regarded as the basic unit of world politics. International lawyers call it the 'Westphalian system'. The name comes from the Peace of Westphalia of 1648, which meant the end of one of the longest and bloodiest wars in European history. Like the dating of the beginning and end of all 'eras', the precise use of this date is somewhat misleading. However, it is necessary to give some sort of date as the beginning of this era and so it might as well be 1648. The Peace of Westphalia marked the effective end of one form of political system and the beginning of a new one.

No one in Europe in 1648 suddenly realized that they were now living in a new era. Everyday life remained harsh; there were plagues and poverty and there was no guarantee that the peace at the end of the Thirty Years' War would last. Some of the components of the Westphalian system were in place before the key year of 1648 and many of them would arrive later.

All this is worth noting in the context of the globalization process. The world is now moving into a post-Westphalian era, with the globalization process creeping up on nation-states. It is not possible suddenly to declare that the Westphalian system has ended and that a new global order has taken its place. People living through such a momentous global change are the least equipped to detect the full extent of that change; historians will have to do that. All that can now be done is to identify some of the features of the change.

European system before 1648

Tribes, empire and the Church

Before nation-states were developed, Europeans lived in local tribes or clans (much as they did in other parts of the world before the Europeans colonized them). The European system of government for just over 1,000 years before 1648 was derived from the power of the Roman Catholic Church, which claimed to rule from the authority of God.

Christianity began as a persecuted minority religion on the fringe of the Roman Empire almost 2,000 years ago. In the fourth century it had become so popular that it became the official religion of the empire. Clergy acquired a senior status within the empire. The Church, as representing the established religion of the empire, became wealthy. Over the centuries, christian officials increased their power so that they provided much of the legal, political and bureaucratic underpinning of the empire.

The Church had its own single language (Latin), officials (including bishops, monks and nuns) and places of training. Its staff were mobile across Europe. In medieval society, the Christian commonwealth was hierarchically organized and subject to the authority of the Pope and the Holy Roman Empire. The Roman Catholic Church and its appointed representatives exercised centralized authority across the territorial boundaries of the different lands. The Church was the closest Europe (or the rest of the world) has come to a regional government for about 1,000 years. The EU is still a long way from having the power of the medieval Church.

The Church's officials were usually the only people who could read and write and so assisted with the empire's administration. The Church created a uniform system of rules based on its interpretation of the Bible. Thus, a person in, say, Ireland or Germany would both be subject to the same law of murder or robbery. The rules covered most aspects of life, including economic practice. For example, 'forestalling' means to stop an event from happening. The origin of the word goes back to this period, when the Church governed the hours of trade and forbade stallholders from opening early and so getting an advantage over the others. Everyone had to trade at the same time so there were no special arrangements to undercut the others. The Church also laid down rules on wages to look after the workers.

The Church introduced the world's first orphanages. The work began before the conversion of the Roman emperor. Under Roman law children had no rights and parents could throw babies away after birth if they did not want to keep them. Early Christians rescued dying babies from rubbish tips to look after them because they believed that all human life should be respected. After the fourth century, the Church also ran the first schools and hospitals in Europe. It developed its own local currencies and owned a lot of land. It also ran the world's first motels. Pilgrims and merchants travelled by road and monasteries and other religious buildings were built on major roads at a day's journey apart. This meant that pilgrims and merchants had somewhere safe to stay at night and did not risk thieves and wolves by sleeping in the forest or by the roadside.

Life in the Middle Ages

There was little notion of a 'national government' and life in the European Middle Ages was based on the region: the local market town with its trade privileges, the parish church and the manor, all flourishing, often with their own particular jurisdictions. People knew little about the outside world because most of them did little travelling. Emperors and kings did not always enjoy a happy relationship with the Church. Local rulers resented Church leaders having links outside their region back to Rome. There were demarcation disputes as to what were 'religious' and what were 'secular' matters and who could decide what.

Meanwhile, the Church's power was not completely absolute. There were often dissidents protesting against some of the Church's teachings or the corrupt behaviour of the clerics. But these were usually brutally suppressed. By the sixteenth century, however, Rome was caught between two forces. On the one hand, there were renewed criticisms of the corruption within the Church, and on the other, secular rulers were getting restless being controlled by Rome, especially because that centre was so far away. Political leaders used the religious turmoil to further their own viewpoints. On 31 October 1517 Martin Luther (professor of theology in the Saxon University of Wittenberg) nailed a paper of Ninety-Five Theses to the door of the Castle Church in that town criticizing the Church's corruption. This was later seen as the beginning of the Reformation movement, which would lead eventually to the drastic reduction of Rome's political and financial influence. The alternative form of Christianity to Catholicism was Protestantism (as a 'protest' against Catholic corruption and influence). The Protestant Reformation in England began as a political movement for national control over its way of life. King Henry VIII famously fell out with Rome over his desire for a divorce and to remarry but the real issue was that he wanted to run his own kingdom, without having to share power with the Catholic authorities. Divorce was a symptom of a much larger issue. He effectively formed his own national church, the Church of England.

The Catholic Church, starting in the 1540s, embarked on a campaign to stop the popularity of the Protestant movements throughout Europe. The ensuing disputes were not a clear-cut struggle between Protestants and Rome because some Catholic regions also liked the idea of greater autonomy from Rome. Meanwhile, the Protestants were united in their dislike of Rome but were often divided over other issues, such as loyalty to Martin Luther in Germany and to Calvin (based in Geneva).

These disputes reached a crescendo in Germany, where the Thirty Years' War began in 1618. This was the last of Europe's major religious wars. The people who took part in it were fighting not only for their own form of Christianity, but also for greater freedom and independence both in the way they were governed and in the way they earned their money by trading. Much of the fighting was done within Germany's boundaries by foreign armies. By 1648, there was a sense of exhaustion, especially by the Holy Roman Empire's forces. In per capita terms, more Germans were killed in that war than in the two world wars of the twentieth century.

Across half of western Europe the rebellion was completely successful. Even in those countries that rejected Protestantism as a religion, the Church was so shaken that as a political force it could no longer compete with the local ruler. The Peace of Westphalia, which in 1648 brought to an end the great Thirty Years' War of religion, marked the acceptance of the new political order in Europe.

The Peace of Westphalia acknowledged the development of independent, secular, sovereign states, no longer subject to the centralized authority of the pope or emperor. A new world order had been created.

Characteristics of the nation-state

The creation of nation-states was a deliberate effort. Nations (groups of people with a common sense of national identity) had to be controlled via a state (a system of government). This involved five developments: national consolidation of power; creation of national feelings of loyalty; erosion of the concept that there was a law above national rulers to which rulers were accountable; a system of national laws and the concept of national sovereign equality of all nation-states. These five developments ran together and reinforced one another. The following analysis is not in any order of priority: rather, it is an examination of the same process from five perspectives.

1 The national rulers had to consolidate themselves against domestic and foreign forces. Ruling houses had to quell internal unrest and rivals, as well as protect the country against foreign invaders. Rulers liked specific boundaries as markers for the extent of their rule and national boundaries became very important. National governments sought a monopoly of military power within their borders.

2 The governments had to manufacture loyalty to the nation-state. Each state evolved symbols (flag, anthem, historical figures and events, special holidays) to reinforce the consciousness of a specific and unique national identity. While its schoolchildren studied universal subjects such as mathematics, science and geography, other elements in the curriculum (especially history) had a national focus, just as teaching itself followed a national pattern. The national language steadily encroached on such regional tongues as Welsh (superseded by English) or Catalan (Spanish). Eventually most counties had one specific national language.

Creating national patriotism was important because national governments increasingly asked for more and more from their citizens. The states increased the demands they made on their people. They had to pay taxes and serve in the military.

3 The third development was, in theological terms, the erosion of the 'natural law'. The Catholic Church had claimed to rule from a divine mandate from God (natural law) but modern governments claimed to run their own affairs without reference to religion. Human reason replaced the theological principles that saw a divine force in the universe creating a uniform sense of justice and morality. The Treaty of Westphalia ended the medieval idea of a universal religious authority acting as the final arbiter in all things. Additionally,

some people found that they could live without any religion at all. There was a separation between 'church' and 'state' so the former had to keep out of the political affairs of the country.

The old system of law from Rome had been a unifying factor. It gave western Europe a standard system of morality. A person in England or Upper Saxony, for example, lived under similar laws of, say, murder, robbery and rape. The end of Rome's unifying control meant, then, that local legal systems treated the same acts differently in terms of punishment.

4 'Positivism' replaced the 'natural law'. Positive law was created by the national sovereign (king, parliament, etc.), and the nation-state was bound only by the laws it created or international treaties it agreed to accept. In theological terms, positivism ended the idea that rulers were ultimately accountable to God. Rulers themselves were at liberty to do what they decided was best for their countries. In international law terms, states could not be forced to accept any international treaty they did not like.

5 The concept of 'national sovereignty' evolved. The strong central ruler would make the laws and enforce them. Each ruler became an 'emperor' in his or her own nation-state, answerable to no one else. After the American and French Revolutions in the late eighteenth century, rulers became more accountable to the people. Thus 'popular sovereignty' saw the ruler as interpreting the wishes of the people. But it was still the ruler making the decisions – and not being answerable to anyone else outside the nation-state.

To sum up, the Treaty of Westphalia established the state system as the basis of world order. National governments enjoyed exclusive control over internal affairs and were the exclusive formal actors on an international level.

Ambiguities of the Westphalian system

The Westphalian system had problems right from the outset. These were derived from the ambiguities in four basic concepts. The Westphalian system is based on the assumption (or, more likely, the hope) that the boundaries of nations should coincide with the boundaries of states. The first two ambiguities were based on this defective assumption. The second two were derived from issues of legal and political control: sovereignty and self-determination.

Nation

The 'nation' part of the Westphalian system refers to a group of people who see themselves to be a particular group. The application of the definition, however, is often difficult. On the one hand, there is certainly something that provides a common bond. For instance, a tune – which is not necessarily the official national anthem – can bond a group of people. For example, *Waltzing Matilda*, which is for most of the world's population a pleasant piece of music, is for a particular group of people a special tune and they need only to hear a few bars to become misty eyed (especially if they are overseas at the time). Much the same could be said for other musical items such as *Jerusalem* (England) or Egypt's *Our Mother*. The element of self-definition is reinforced by reference to geography, language, hostility to neighbours and history.

On the other hand, the term nation can be unclear. Members of nations move around the globe. The British 'nation' runs into hundreds of millions of people, with members in such countries as the US, Canada, South Africa, Australia and New Zealand. Much the same could be said about the Irish, French, Chinese and Indians. These people have, for hundreds of years, been moving overseas to take up such positions as that of traders, administrators, clerks, educators, soldiers, health practitioners and missionaries. They have married and settled down, with their children thus having two sets of loyalties (and often two separate passports).

Then there is the problem of how nationality (or citizenship) is acquired. There is no universal principle that determines what the rights and duties of a citizen should be, or how one might become a citizen. For example, in France, the citizens are the inhabitants of French territory. There is a notion that being French is associated with French language and culture – and this can be acquired; immigrants and minorities can assimilate. Australian and US citizenships are acquired by residence in the countries and according to government criteria (which nowadays are based on the applicant's skills or the number of relatives already present in the country). By contrast, the German notion of citizenship is ethnic. Anyone of German ethnic origin can claim German citizenship. To become a Japanese citizen a person has to be born of people whose own parents were Japanese (which explains why Japanese–Koreans whose families have been resident in Japan for about a century still do not have full Japanese citizenship).

Lastly there is the much narrower definition of a nation often used by anthropologists. This refers to indigenous peoples. Therefore, a nation is a group of people with a strong cultural and political identity that is both self-defined and acknowledged by others, such as the indigenous peoples in Australia and New Zealand, and the 'First Nations' in the US and Canada.

State

A 'state' is an organization for governing a set piece of the earth's surface. The most obvious ambiguity is that nation and state rarely coincide. In contemporary terms, a way to solve this problem is by ethnic cleansing (killing or in other ways removing the other ethnic groups in a state's jurisdiction).

A second ambiguity is that a state may have changing boundaries. One example includes Germany, whose borders have been in flux for centuries. A neighbouring example is Poland, which is geographically in the centre of Europe, whose borders (as a result of Soviet pressure in the Allied negotiations in 1945) moved westward into eastern Germany, but which was referred to during the Cold War as being part of eastern Europe.

Ruthenia (or Carpathian Russia) is another example, with Uzhorod as its capital. It had been part of the Hungarian Monarchy but in 1920, when Czechoslovakia was created, it became a province of Czechoslovakia. Under pressure from Hitler, it was given back to Hungary in 1938. After World War II, it was annexed by the then USSR to become part of Soviet Ukraine. Within a generation, a citizen in the area would have had three very different nationalities.

A traditional joke is that a citizen of that territory dies and goes to heaven. He explains to St Peter: 'I am Hungarian. I was born in the Austro–Hungarian Empire; I lived for a time in Czechoslovakia; then I was in Hungary. Later I was in the Soviet Union and I died in Ukraine.' St Peter marvels at the amount of travelling the man has done. The dead man replies: 'On the contrary, this is the first journey out of my village.'

A third ambiguity is the existence of 'multinational' or 'multiethnic' states. European empires were, of course, multinational but so too were some countries. Switzerland, for example, has four official languages (German, French, Italian and Romansch) and shows how well a multinational state can flourish. But the collapse of the USSR and Yugoslavia show that multinational states have no guaranteed existence. Meanwhile, Canada has problems with its French-speaking minority. In 2006, the people of Montenegro voted to leave the federation along with Serbia. These were the remnants of one of the most multinational of east European states, Yugoslavia.

National sovereignty

What, in practical terms, does 'national sovereignty' actually mean? Right from the outset of the Westphalian system, nation-states did not lead solitary lives; they had to interact with other nation-states (for trade, defence pacts and wartime alliances, etc.). Thus, the practical meaning of sovereignty was always less than the grand claim of some form of national independence.

This means that a state may in law be independent but in reality is not. Since 1648 people have forfeited portions of their national sovereignty in order to acquire the benefits arising out of a cooperative relationship with other people. However, there is the question of just how far a country can go in trading off its sovereignty before it loses that sovereignty entirely. Constitutional independence is being surrendered in the interests of, for example, greater British cooperation within the EU.

Self-determination

Finally, there is the problem of how a nation can become recognized as a nation (and not just be seen as a dissident ethnic group). The idea of national self-determination assumes quite simply that the world is composed of separate, identifiable nations, and claims that these nations are, as such, each entitled to form a sovereign state. But it is not that simple in reality. Indeed, national self-determination can be a recipe for disorder and not of order.

The concept (though not the term) of self-determination has been around for thousands of years. One of the first leaders of a movement for self-determination was Moses leading the Hebrews out of Egypt. George Washington and his colleagues in the 1770s would also come into that category.

During the twentieth century, there were three phases of self-determination. The first phase was at the end of World War I, when US President Woodrow Wilson advocated the breaking up of the central European multiethnic empires into a series of homogenous, democratic nation-states, where people could choose, via referendum (plebiscites), where they wished to live. Wilson claimed that the unrest within the minority populations had contributed to the onset of World War I (such as the assassination in Sarajevo of Archduke Franz Ferdinand by the angry Serb Gavrilo Princip on 28 June 1914). Therefore, he argued, special attention ought to be given to protecting minority populations (especially by letting them have their own countries). The League of Nations was created partly to deal with the problems of self-determination of nationalities and gave minorities within the former Austro–Hungarian territories special rights (such as the right to petition the League with human rights complaints).

However, nations and states could not be made to coincide in the boundary redrawing after World War I. States were not homogenous. Allen Dulles (later head of the US Central Intelligence Agency) worked on the US delegation at the 1919 World War I Peace Conference redrawing the maps of eastern Europe. He was on the Czechoslovak Boundary Commission, along with a fellow American and a Frenchman. None of them had any detailed knowledge of eastern European history. They wanted to make the new nation-state of Czechoslovakia a geographically viable one and so, in addition to Bohemia and Moravia, they also included a considerable piece of German-speaking territory known as the Sudetenland. The Czechs were in a minority there, but it seemed to Dulles and his two colleagues that the Sudetenland gave Bohemia and its capital Prague a hinterland where any future German attack could be fought off. Ironically, it was over the Sudetenland that Adolf Hitler created the Munich crisis in 1938. Hitler used the alleged mistreatment of Germans in Czechoslovakia as an excuse to gain control over originally the western end of that country (via the 1938 Munich Agreement) and then later all of it. In September 1939 he used that excuse again to get control of Poland's northern coast – and this time provoked the UK and France into going to war to protect Polish territorial integrity. (After the end of the Cold War, Czechoslovakia broke into two separate countries.)

The second phase of self-determination took place after World War II, with the breakup of the European empires in Africa and Asia.

The third phase is now underway, with groups of people wishing to leave existing nation-states and form their own, hence the growth of local conflicts, as in Africa.

To sum up, what is so fascinating about the Westphalian system is not that it is now in collapse, but that it has lasted for so long. Right from the outset, there were – to say the least – some ambiguities in the system, but it proved to be very resilient.

However, as this book will show, in recent decades the system began running into severe problems. As a simple example, there is the issue of national currencies. Having one's own currency has traditionally been an important sign of national sovereignty. This was emphasized by its containing the portrait of the ruler or of the national mint. A traditional right of the nation-state was the exclusive sovereign power to determine the value of its own money. But some Latin American countries have now 'dollarized' their currencies, that is, taken the more stable US currency as their own (a matter over which the US itself has had no say). Meanwhile, the euro is the currency of 12 European states and the Vatican, San Merino and Monaco (as well as being used in Kosovo, Montenegro and Andorra).

European impact on Africa

Slaves and colonies

Africa has attracted European attention for about 500 years. For much of that time, the Europeans thought they were doing the Africans a favour but in many cases the colonial experience has been a disaster. There are many reasons why Africa is the world's only continent that is not making much economic progress – there are many home-grown issues of corruption, lack of human rights and a shortage of skills.

Europe is also partly responsible for some of Africa's problems. Africa has been the target of Europe's merchants, missionaries and misfits. The merchants went in search of trade and the missionaries went in search of converts to Christianity. The misfits were people who thought they could do better in Africa than in Europe (such as the young sons of rich landowners who did not expect to inherit the family property).

The Portuguese began the exploration process in the fifteenth century, with small ships that sailed cautiously around the African coastline. Gradually, their expeditions (beginning in 1434) got longer and more adventurous and in 1498 Vasco da Gama reached India. The Portuguese claimed locations on the African coast. They went in search of slaves, gold, ivory and spices.

The Spanish headed west in 1492 and reached the Americas. They were also looking for money and souls. The settlement of the Americas required slaves, such as for cultivation and mining. Very quickly the slave trade reached across the Atlantic and thriving African civilizations were wrecked. Arab traders rounded up slaves and got them to the coast, where they were shipped on European vessels to the Americas, both north and south.

Between about 1650 and 1900 at least 28 million Africans were forcibly removed from central and western Africa as slaves. This was one of the largest movements of peoples in history. A triangular trade was created. The slaves went across the Atlantic where they produced raw materials that were sent to Europe. These were then made into finished products, some of which were sold to slave traders to buy the next consignment of people to be sent to the Americas.

The slave trade disrupted African civilizations and has had a lasting impact. As an example, present-day west coast Benin was at the height of its influence in the fifteenth century, with a high standard of economic and cultural life. Much of that was destroyed by the slave trade. The slave trade is also the basis of the racial tensions in the US and elsewhere, where the descendants of the slaves still claim that they are badly treated – there are more young male Afro-Americans in prison than there are in university.

A second European impact was claiming African territory as colonies. The conquest was carried out slowly, without any overall grand plan. The Europeans nibbled at the coasts and gradually moved inland. They had little knowledge about what could await them and so they moved cautiously.

The Industrial Revolution, which began in Britain in about 1750, gave Europeans a powerful basis on which to invade Africa. The Europeans had inventions that underpinned their expeditions and they went looking for markets. For example, Africans had lived with mosquitoes bearing malaria for generations – some had even built up some resistance to them – but the Europeans died in great numbers. Once quinine was developed in the 1850s, Europeans could fight off malaria and so do more inland exploration.

The British invented the steam engine in 1804 and first used it to pull carriages in 1825. In 1853, the first railway track was laid in Egypt. In 1890 Dunlop produced the first rubber tyres, greatly improving the comfort of a bicycle ride and then later driving a car. Wild rubber grew in the Belgian Congo and so King Leopold of Belgium used his colony as the basis for producing rubber. Many Africans were killed (either through direct violence or from overwork) in this brutal exploitation. Other European imperial powers were shocked at the Belgian violence in the Congo.

The Europeans also improved their weapons. They had far more firepower than the Africans. On one occasion, during the 1898 Omdurman campaign (in which young Winston Churchill fought), the British beat a fanatical Islamic leader, with the death of 10,800 Sudanese and the loss of only 49 Britons.

Dividing up the continent

Eventually almost all of Africa went under European control. The two exceptions were Ethiopia (which fought off the invaders) and the west African country of Liberia, which had been bought by American anti-slave activists in the nineteenth century. They wanted to free the slaves but did not want them staying in the US and so sent them back to Africa.

The Europeans may have decided to claim Africa, but they had yet to agree on how the continent should be divided up between them. The most important conference to divide up Africa took place in Berlin between November 1884 and June 1885. By this time, probably as much as 80 per cent of Africa was still under traditional local control. However, the Europeans were getting ready for the final push across Africa – they needed to know where they should go. They were not worried about African opinion but they did want to avoid treading on the toes of fellow Europeans.

Germany had been united in 1870 and had beaten France, a major imperial power. It was now heading for great power status. It was also looking for colonies because that was a standard way for a European country to demonstrate its great power status. German Chancellor Otto von Bismarck decided to invite 13 countries to come to his capital to divide up Africa. The countries were: Austria–Hungary, Belgium, Britain, Denmark, France, Italy, the Netherlands, Portugal, Russia, Spain, Sweden–Norway (unified 1814–1905), Turkey and the US.

The leaders drew up lines on the map of a continent that was still largely unexplored. They ignored tribal, linguistic and traditional boundaries. No Africans were involved. The leaders did not think to get African advice. They assumed they knew best.

Eighty years later, when the colonies began their slow progress towards independence, the colonial boundaries were retained as the new national boundaries. The European mapmakers sliced through traditional areas and divided up families, while also amalgamating other areas. Fifty-five countries had been imposed on a continent that had about 1,500 languages.

Africa still lives with the impact of the Berlin Conference. Now, 120 years later, there are problems of maintaining national unity in many countries. There are many tribal and ethnic conflicts, for example in Rwanda a decade ago, the massacres with knives and machetes were carried out at a faster kill ratio than the Germans managed to do in the World War II holocaust.

All the African colonies are now free, but some things do not change. Africa is still aiding European and North African economic and social development. It pays back in bank loans more money than it receives in foreign aid. Many of the best school students get a university education overseas and never return home. Their medical doctors serve with distinction in the health services of Europe and North America. There are more doctors from Ghana working in the British health system than there are working in Ghana.

Conclusion

Europe has made many impacts on the world outside its borders. Two major ones have been the process of colonization itself (the world's most ambitious form of colonization) and the invention of the nation-state system (which it carried to the corners of the world). Africa remains permanently scarred by its European experience. The nation-state system has always had internal problems and these have continued to haunt the Westphalian system.

Questions

1 What makes you 'feel' that you are a national of your country? What are the symbols used to reinforce national identity?
2 How is nationality acquired in your country?
3 What does national sovereignty mean in practical terms?
4 What are some current self-determination struggles around the world?
5 What can be done to help Africa overcome the adverse impact of Europe's colonization?

03
problems with the nation-state system

This chapter will cover:
- how globalization has made diplomacy more difficult
- the rise of 'localization'
- how new technology reinforces the impact of globalization.

Introduction

One of the reasons why globalization seems so complex is that it is linked with other developments: either it affects those developments or it is affected by them. This chapter deals with three issues: how the practice of diplomacy has been made even more difficult by the process of globalization, how a reaction to globalization has been the rise of 'localization' where people are overwhelmed by the pace of change and how technology has itself reinforced the impact of globalization.

Diplomacy

Diplomacy and the Westphalian system

The roots of diplomacy are much older than the Westphalian system. For over 2,000 years, diplomatists (as they prefer to be called) have had a special protected status as representatives of their rulers in other lands. The Westphalian system built on those old traditions and developed the process of conference diplomacy, such as the 1815 Congress of Vienna. It laid down the rules that have existed largely unamended into this century.

Diplomatists have – until recent decades – tended to be recruited from the élite families of their countries since these were in the best position to assess intuitively how their rulers may react to particular proposals; communications were often difficult and so diplomatists had to have a great deal of discretion. Until recent decades, European diplomatists were white males, drawn from the upper class of their societies and who learned French (the language of diplomacy).

The diplomatic process was a straightforward one. For example, the Berlin Conference of 1884–5 brought together representatives of 14 states – roughly all the main states of Europe except Switzerland. It divided up much of Africa into 'spheres of influence' (the first time the phrase had been used in international conference diplomacy). It was agreed that in future any power that effectively occupied African territory, and duly notified the other powers, could thereby establish possession of it. This inaugurated the new era of colonialism. The diplomatists at the Berlin Conference shared many assumptions. They may have disagreed over which country should get what territory, but all agreed that it was the responsibility of élite white people to take European civilization into Africa for the benefit of the natives (and, of course, their own states).

Diplomacy is now much more complicated and more protracted. For instance, in the 1880s, much of Africa was divided up by the Berlin Conference in a few months, but the new UN Law of the Sea Treaty took 12 years to negotiate (with the US suddenly deciding at the end of the process to boycott the treaty's signing in 1982). It took another 12 years for the treaty to come into effect (November 1994).

This section looks at the reasons why Westphalian diplomacy is running into severe problems.

More nation-states

There are many more states involved. The UN – the world's largest intergovernmental organization and the centre of multilateral diplomacy – has a membership of 192, and the figure will increase as current states break up into smaller ones. Similarly, bilateral diplomacy is also more complicated. A century ago, a diplomatist could deal, for example, with the British government, whose views would cover those of the dominions and colonies within the Empire; now each state has to be contacted. In terms of sheer numbers alone, then, diplomacy is much more difficult – especially given the doctrine of sovereign equality, whereby each state is of no higher status (in international law terms) than any other.

More perspectives and priorities

There are different perspectives and priorities. African, Asian and Latin American countries have different ways of looking at the world's problems and they have introduced their own rituals.

Until the early 1990s, the most notable ritual at the UN and other major conferences was criticism of South Africa's apartheid racial policy – even if the gathering was not specifically devoted to that subject in particular or human rights in general. At the 1972 Stockholm UN Conference on the Human Environment, to take an extreme example, delegates from the developing world ensured that the Conference declaration on the environment contained, in the first principle, a criticism of 'apartheid, racial segregation, discrimination, colonial and other forms of oppression and foreign domination.'

The diplomatists themselves recognized that these acts had to be performed by delegations from the developing world, partly because if they failed to do so, this omission could be regarded as a subtle hint of a policy shift of some kind. Both the diplomatists who performed them and those that saw them performed (that is, mainly western delegates) knew their importance. They were more than just a recitation of, say, the prayers that are offered up at the beginning of each meeting of most western parliaments. They were less significant items of conference agendas – even though the media themselves regularly reported them more often than the substantive items.

They were part of the developing world's attempts to gradually alter the attitude of western governments by regularly criticizing South Africa. The developing world wanted to isolate South Africa diplomatically – that is, to use diplomatic means, rather than military ones to reduce South Africa's international standing. This paid off in the early 1990s, with the ending of racial discrimination and the holding of free elections. Arab states have used this method (with far less success) against Israel since 1973.

Sovereign equality of states

Another problem for modern diplomacy is the discrepancy between the doctrine of sovereign equality of states and the reality of international politics. Even a century ago, of course, some states were (so to speak) more 'equal' than others. But the discrepancy has become much wider in recent decades.

States vary in gross national product and population size from one end of the spectrum containing states like the US, Japan and China, along to 'microstates' in the Pacific and elsewhere that have a smaller national income and population than some British local government authorities. Fiji, for example, has a population of about 747,000 people and Western Samoa 158,000. Half the member-states of the Commonwealth have populations of fewer than a million people each and a quarter have fewer than 200,000.

Incidentally, one relic of the pre-Westphalian system is still very much in operation, albeit naturally greatly reduced; the Vatican City (Holy See) has a territory of 44 hectares (109 acres), a population of fewer than 3,000 (with few children) and no national anthem. But it does have a special 'observer' status at the UN, which it used to great effect in its criticism of family planning at the 1994 Cairo UN Conference on Population and Development.

However, each state has to be treated alike. According to the doctrine of sovereign equality, a visiting president of a small state is as important as a visit from a US president and so all diplomatic protocol, which has evolved over the centuries, has to apply.

Additionally, some states have limited scope for participation in diplomacy. They do not have the expertise required for many international conferences and projects. Some states sometimes even lack the staff to sit at the conference delegation spots.

Improvements in communications and transport

The improvement in communications and transport is another problem for modern diplomacy. A diplomatist travelling to the 1815 Congress of Vienna took the same time to go the distance as a Roman courier would have done almost 2,000 years earlier. He would have arrived with sufficient time to become refreshed and relaxed.

Aircraft have tempted political leaders – rather than diplomatists – to do the negotiations and they occasionally overdo the travelling. For example, in January 1992, US President Bush became sick at a dinner in Tokyo and publicly vomited over Japanese Prime Minister Kiichi Miyazawa. Journalists blamed the President's illness on his excessive travel.

The diplomatic service is a 500-year-old invention designed to make it unnecessary for kings, presidents, prime ministers and ministers to be everywhere at once. But politics is now a global drama of motion. The national media love the exhilaration of nomadic overseas statecraft. Additionally, foreign meetings mean that politicians can flee from domestic political turmoil. They often get treated better overseas than at home. In each case, there is a welcoming ceremony and applause that could not reasonably be expected at home. Communiqués are issued, often written in advance by others, telling imaginatively of the topics under discussion and the areas of agreement. All this travelling is pleasant for politicians and gives the mass media something to report (including colourful shots of other countries), but is of marginal use to their countries. Rarely is the destiny of a country determined by the close relations between the leaders (for example, Britain would have joined the US invasion of Iraq in 2003 no matter which person or party was in power).

Complexity of the global agenda

Finally, the diplomatic agenda is now much longer, requiring more staff and expertise than ever before. The British imperial 'head office' in Whitehall, which in 1901 governed at least one quarter of the world, consisted of one massive block built around a courtyard on the south side of Downing Street. However, as the empire shrank so the Foreign and Commonwealth Office (FCO) staff have increased in number. This is a reflection of the growing demands on government.

During the twentieth century, governments took over more and more aspects of the everyday life of their country's affairs. Governments (national and local) absorbed an ever increasing share of national wealth because they can do certain things better, such as the building and maintenance of water supply, roads, education, healthcare or defence. This is a sign of progress. When the population density is low, each house can have its own water supply (such as a rainwater tank) but as the density builds up, this becomes less practical. If the matter were left in private hands, the wealthy areas could afford to install an effective system – the poor could not. This would, sooner or later, lead to outbreaks of cholera, typhoid and other infectious diseases in the poorer areas. There would be the distinct possibility of the epidemic spilling over – that is, there would be a direct public health threat. Such epidemics lead to social and economic disruption, with the labour force becoming unreliable and streets becoming unsafe. Economic activities will be affected (as happened in 2006, with the growing concerns over avian 'flu). As national governments get drawn in more and more by such economic and social matters, so they have to share ideas across national boundaries or obtain global cooperation (to be examined in the next chapter).

Localization

National governments not only have to deal with global problems but there is often an emerging desire at the local level for more self-government. Therefore the Westphalian system is being eroded by both forces running across national boundaries and by the evolution of sub-national entities, globalization and localization. There has been the erosion of national borders across Europe that permits the emergence (or the re-emergence) of regional economic zones, which had been barred by national customs and tariff systems. As new trading relationships develop, the former ones fade: Slovenia trades increasingly with Austria and less with Serbia, Alsace-Lorraine becomes more integrated with Baden-Württemberg than with Paris, northern Italy develops closer links with Alpine states than with Calabria or Sicily. Individual American states, often frustrated by the lack of interest shown by the federal government, open their own 'missions' in Tokyo and Brussels in order to conduct investment and trade diplomacy. Russian cities like St Petersburg declare themselves free-trade zones in order to attract foreign investment.

There is a similar regional trend in the Pacific Northwest of the US. Regional economic interdependencies are now more important than political boundaries. In Seattle, Washington state, Japan is seen as a neighbour and valued trading partner, while New York and the East Coast are regarded as distant. There is also a regional economic community that has developed across the US–Canadian border among five American states and two Canadian provinces without the approval of either Washington DC or Ottawa.

Similarly, within nation-states, people, political power and economic wealth are not necessarily evenly distributed. Australia is a good example, with Western Australians and Tasmanians complaining about the way in which the country revolves around the Canberra–Sydney–Melbourne axis. Some Western Australians have argued that they would be better off forming their own nation-state. There was an attempted secession by Western Australia in the early 1930s when the state had been hit hard by the depression and some people argued that the state would do better on its own, rather than being governed by the distant Canberra. (Perth is the most isolated major city in the world.) A state referendum was held in 1933, with 138,653 voting for secession and 70,706 voting against. The leading secessionists departed for London late in 1934 with a petition 26 feet long. They were told that the Commonwealth parliament had to consent to Western Australia's secession – and this was obviously not forthcoming.

Looking more generally at the global process of urbanization, the world is becoming a planet of cities, which then overshadow small nation-states. In Latin America, for example, 75 per cent of Brazilians live in urban areas, one-third of Argentineans live in Buenos Aires and Mexico City has a population of about 23 million (over 20 per cent of the country's population).

The US is too large an economy to be dominated by any one city, but Los Angeles provides another challenge to the idea of the nation-state. Los Angeles is the world's second largest Hispanic city (after Mexico City). It is the main city of the western industrialized world still to be growing. Los Angeles is now the fifth biggest economy in the world – bigger than France in terms of GDP.

In terms of economic size, Los Angeles would deserve to be an important UN member-country in its own right – and would even be larger than most non-permanent members of the Security Council. But Los Angeles, under the current nation-state system will not get that right. This is in contrast with the UN's 184th member-nation that joined the organization in July 1993. Andorra, on the Pyrenees between France and Spain, has a population of about 47,000 people, living in an area of 453 square kilometres. In due course, it will be eligible for election to the Security Council.

The importance of new technology

Technology is a natural enemy of the nation-state

Technology is an important driving force in the globalization process. This is all the more the case with the world passing through a new technological revolution. The new industries include the following: micro-robotics (miniature robots built from atomic particles that could, among other things, unclog sclerotic arteries); machine translation (telephone switches and other devices that will provide real-time translation between people conversing in different languages); digital highways into the home that will offer instant access to the world's store of knowledge and entertainment; and urban underground automated distribution systems that will reduce traffic congestion. It also includes 'virtual' meeting rooms that will save people the wear and tear of air travel; bio-mimetic materials that will duplicate the wondrous properties of materials found in the living world; machines capable of emotion, inference and learning that will interact with human beings in entirely new ways; and bio-remediation (custom-designed organisms) that will help clean up the earth's environment.

This section will look only at the global impact of communications technology in the context of globalization.

Communications technology

Communications technology erodes the power that national governments have over what their citizens hear, read or watch – and their ability to communicate with the outside world. The control of information is a standard theme in many events in history. The rise of printing assisted the Protestant Reformation as European Christians were able to get access to their own copies of the Bible in their own language, which in turn led to the war of 1618–48. Governments have tried to censor information and issue propaganda; generals have tried to distort the accounts of their battles. Some novels are also based on this theme, such as George Orwell's *1984* (where the bending of truth is overt) and Aldous Huxley's *Brave New World* (where the media make people into comfortable consumers).

The internet is assisting the process of globalization. The internet was conceived in 1964 as a computer network that had thousands of links but no governing authority, on which messages travelled randomly. This was a response to US worries about the Cold War and the threat of a surprise nuclear attack. If the US were attacked and telephone lines were destroyed, US senior officers would need a system that could not be disrupted. Thus the internet evolved. It just kept growing and is a very fast way of sending messages.

Technological progress has made possible daily activities that would have been inconceivable only half a century ago. For example, it is possible to dial direct to almost every person in the world who has a telephone – without going through a local operator. The world's telephone numbering system has thus been standardized and coordinated. This, in turn, is linked to the major charge cards so that, a person in a foreign airport, without local currency, can make a telephone call via a public telephone, that can first access that person's charge card record in their own country and then clear that cardholder to make a telephone call. Another example is that a person in, say, London can make an airline booking on a domestic flight across the USA. Technology is thus helping to erode national boundaries.

Anyone in the world who has access to a computer screen may exchange messages with anyone else in the world, get information, news and entertainment, work and play, at minimal cost – and at no marginal cost for distance. Distance has become irrelevant. In practice (but not in actual telephone billing), an international telephone call is the same as a local call.

A casualty in the global reach of communications technology is national control over the mass media. The British Broadcasting Corporation (BBC) was the world's pioneer in radio and television and remains highly regarded for its news coverage. In the early days of radio in Britain, broadcasting was regarded as a medium of education rather than entertainment. The programmes were mostly 'highbrow' – whether audiences wanted them or not.

But the BBC was also among the first national broadcasters to be hit by transnational broadcasting. In the late 1950s, the BBC still maintained its tradition of highbrow broadcasting. However, a new generation of consumers was emerging – children born after World War II who had access to crystal sets and radios and whose parents were willing and able to buy this equipment for them. The youngsters wanted something more exciting. Since they could not get it from the BBC, they tuned to Radio Luxembourg, which broadcast pop music and cheery conversations from the continent to the UK. Later Radio Caroline was established off the UK's east coast on a 'pirate' ship beyond the UK's maritime jurisdiction.

The BBC surrendered. It changed some of its programming and introduced Radio 1. With the BBC changing its standards (some might say, lowering them), so the precedent was set for other countries to follow its example.

The biggest change of all has come in television broadcasting. For example, in June 1989, Chinese student demonstrators at Tiananmen Square held placards explaining their views in English (English was then hardly used in China). The students were not wanting to communicate with their fellow Chinese but with people outside China who were watching on television – at that very instant. Cable News Network (CNN) has since become a standard force in television, especially during crises such as the 1990–1 Gulf War and the 2003 US-led invasion of Iraq. In 1991 the CIA complained that President Bush was not reading his CIA reports – he replied that he preferred CNN which was 'live', while the CIA was a day late.

Conservative Islamic countries have endeavoured to restrict outside non-Islamic influences, but they are having more difficulty in the era of satellite broadcasting. Malaysia, for instance, has strict regulations on what may be broadcast. However, the country's rapidly growing middle class can afford satellite dishes and so draw down, among other things, material that is banned in Malaysia. One measure of control that some of these governments try to exercise is access to satellite dishes, since such dishes are essential to pick up the transmissions. However, it is only a matter of time until the broadcasting will be done directly into television antennas, so that television will be as easily available as radio is today. It is already possible to 'broadcast' throughout the internet (audio streaming) and so eventually people will be able to get good quality TV pictures through the same system.

Television can also set the political agenda, irrespective of whether or not governments are willing to get involved, as with Somalia in 1992. It was only after the media steadily bombarded western sensibilities with images of starving Somali children that the US and other governments stopped dithering and began to act and send in troops and food. Much the same could be said two years later in 1994, with the international response to helping the survivors of the Rwanda massacre. Similarly, Prime Minister Tony Blair's decision to send British troops into Sierra Leone in the late 1990s to help stop the rebellion, came partly as a reaction to the harrowing media images of children and babies having their hands cut off by the rebels challenging the government.

The era of transparency

The Soviet Union had an abrupt introduction to the new world of communications technology via the Chernobyl nuclear disaster in April 1986. Nuclear disasters are nothing new in the USSR, with a serious one in the Urals in the late 1950s being hushed up by both the USSR and the CIA (so as not to add to the western public's opposition to nuclear power). In April 1986, the USSR resorted to its old technique of refusing to comment and refusing to permit any foreign coverage of the Chernobyl disaster. This had worked for Stalin; it did not work for Gorbachev.

The French private enterprise SPOT satellite (Système Probatoire d'Observation de la Terre), which had been launched in February that year, flew over the site and sent back coverage of it – for a fee. Gorbachev, recognizing that he had a public relations disaster on his hands, eventually decided to be more cooperative and admit that the nuclear disaster was far worse than had been previously announced.

There is now a new era of transparency. SPOT has broken the US/Russian monopoly over spy satellites; what SPOT revealed about Chernobyl it can also reveal about US military installations (or those of anyone else) – for a fee. In due course, press agencies will acquire their own high-resolution satellites and acquire information on matters that governments would prefer to keep quiet. It is also in the interests of transnational corporations to acquire them so as, for example, to get a better idea of a country's natural resources.

More recently, the Google internet search facility has created 'a 3D interface to the planet', which enables people to zoom in on their neighbourhood from the sky. They can also get driving directions for schools, parks, restaurants and hotels.

Conclusion

The nation-state has some basic problems. Some (as seen in Chapter 02) come from within the nature of the nation-state itself. Others have come with the process of globalization, for example, trying to maintain diplomatic relations in an era of greater complexity and having to cope with the new technology. Meanwhile, citizens feel overwhelmed by the pace of change and so want to concentrate more on local matters. Therefore, a sense of national identity is declining in the face of global and local identities.

Questions

1 How has the practice of diplomacy been assisted (if at all) by the globalization process?
2 If people are to 'think globally and act locally', what is left to be done at national level?
3 To what extent (if at all) are you involved in political activities at national level?
4 What can be done to encourage governments to cope better with technological change?
5 To what extent are you conscious of the impact of technological change on your life?

04 individual governments and global problems

This chapter will cover:
- how plagues and diseases cross national boundaries
- how pollution crosses national boundaries
- how crime has gone global
- the mass movement of peoples.

Introduction

There are no national boundaries when the planet is viewed from outer space, but the existence of boundaries can undermine a national government's attempts to address global problems.

There are no 'national' solutions to global problems. The Westphalian system – the nation-state system – is based on national sovereignty, that is, each country governs itself and cannot be forced into accepting international obligations. Its internal affairs remain its own internal affairs and so it cannot be forced into accepting any international obligations regarding its own treatment of its citizens. But increasingly problems sprawl across national boundaries.

This chapter examines four clusters of global problems. National governments need to work through intergovernmental organizations to deal with them – known as 'cooperative power'. They either work together or they perish separately.

Most of the problems examined in this chapter are human made (or at least exacerbated by humans). There are other problems that also need cooperative power as a response, such as the international relief effort to assist the southeast Asian countries affected by the 26 December 2004 tsunami.

Plagues and infectious diseases

Rat power

Plagues and other diseases are not new. For example, rats have killed far more people throughout history than warfare. Bubonic plague is caused by the bacteria *Yersinia pestis*, which is carried by rats and the fleas that live on them. Rats are prolific breeders: a pair can create 15,000 descendants in one year. They thrive in cities – there are almost as many rats as there are people in New York. When an infected flea bites a human, it can transmit the disease. Pneumonic plague occurs when the disease spreads to the lungs and can be passed from human to human through the air by coughing or heavy breathing.

The death toll has been:

Disease	Date	Number of deaths
Bubonic plague (first pandemic)	AD 542	unknown
Bubonic plague (second pandemic)	1347–51	75 million worldwide
Bubonic plague (third pandemic)	19th century	20 million worldwide

The plague has not been eradicated from the planet. There was small outbreak in India in 1994.

Some other infectious diseases in the 20th century included:

Typhus (Russia)	1917–21	3 million
Influenza (pandemic)	1918–9	22 million

There is currently concern about the threat of avian 'flu.

Infectious diseases

The study of infectious diseases has gone through a major change. Half a century ago, no one had ever heard of Lyme or Legionnaire's disease, much less AIDS. Back in the 1970s, medical researchers were even boasting that humanity's victory over infectious disease was just a matter of time. The polio virus had been tamed by the Salk and Sabin vaccines; the smallpox virus was eradicated; the parasite that causes malaria was in retreat and the once deadly illnesses, including diphtheria, pertussis and tetanus were all in decline in developed countries. The first widespread use of antibiotics in the years following World War II had transformed the most terrifying diseases known to humanity – tuberculosis, syphilis, pneumonia, bacterial meningitis and even bubonic plague – into far less threatening illnesses. Providing they were detected in time they could probably be cured. The growing disease areas were ones of lifestyle, notably cancer (such as through smoking), obesity and heart disease.

Plagues and other contagious diseases are now bouncing back. The main explanation is the globalization of the planet. Since 1950 there have been major increases in international tourism. Increases in speed and the extent of human movements have been matched by the expansion of international business. Now no one is ever more than about 36 hours away from any disease outbreak.

Tuberculosis is returning. It has been around for about 8,000 years but was reduced after World War II because of medical progress. Medical authorities lowered their guard against it, thinking that it was on the way out. Research funds were cut back and public health programmes focussed on other issues. However, they should not have dropped their guard. *Mycobacterium tuberculosis* hopped on the modern transportation systems searching for new breeding grounds. It found them in the ghettoes of the western world. It also found them among the beneficiaries of advanced healthcare in rich countries, where cancer chemotherapy and organ transplants can depress natural immunities. It found them in eastern Europe, where people are now so overwhelmed by economic problems that they delay medical consultations. It found them among the weakened immune systems of the HIV infected.

Malaria

At least one million people die each year from malaria – only AIDS kills more people. About 500 million get infected. Malaria killed more Australian troops in the Pacific in World War II than the Japanese did. People in developed nations are now dying from malaria, which is principally a disease from the developing world.

The World Health Organization (WHO) has an annual research budget of only US$6 million for malaria. Transnational drug corporations estimate that a new drug would cost about US$100 million to research, test and register and, since no developing world country could afford to buy it, it is not profitable to develop it. Consequently, first world tourists are still using Chloroquine and Malopim on their exotic travels – and risk encountering mosquitos that are now resistant to them. Malaria is one of the world's major problems – but gets overshadowed by diseases and conditions that are far more prevalent in developed countries (such as blood pressure and heart attacks).

AIDS: the 'Kinshasa disease'

The major current plague is, of course, AIDS. The virus was first identified in 1981. By 1990, an estimated ten million people had been infected and by the end of 2004 the number had risen to 78 million. Of this total, 38 million died, while 39 million lived with the virus. Most victims are among the most productive young adults populations, therefore there are, especially in

Africa, fewer people to cultivate the fields and work in schools and factories. Additionally, as one person gets the virus, so another person must leave the workforce to stay at home to look after them. In many hospitals in eastern and southern Africa, a majority of the beds are now occupied by AIDS victims, thereby leaving less space for those with other illnesses. The epidemic is also creating AIDS orphans – by 2010 18.4 million children will have lost at least one parent to the disease.

Viruses are named after the place where they are first discovered, such as 'Hong Kong flu'. If the global medical community had been quicker in the detection of AIDS, it may now be known as the 'Kinshasa disease'. The Kinshasa Highway used to be a dirt track but it is now a modern highway, with one of the main travellers being HIV. The highway runs across central Africa from the Congo's Pointe-Noire to Tanzania's Mombassa and the breakout initially came from the rainforest in 1979.

Had the virus been noticed earlier it might have been named 'Kinshasa Highway', in honour of the fact that it passed along the Kinshasa Highway during its emergence from the African rainforest. The paving of the Kinshasa Highway has adversely affected many people, and turned out to be one of the most important events of the twentieth century. It has already cost over 38 million lives, with the likelihood that the ultimate number of human casualties will exceed the total number killed in World War II.

Diseases, whether global or just confined to a small locality, emphasize the individual's interdependence with their neighbours (be they across the street or across the planet). Diseases move from one person to another. Each person has a vested interest in the health of their neighbours. Thus, ironically, it is in the interest of rich people pay for the health costs of people who cannot afford vaccinations. To avoid doing so is a false economy.

Pollution

Human activity and the earth's environment

Pollution has also long crossed national boundaries. Nowadays, however, there is far more pollution and the impact on other countries is far worse. The four most well-known examples of this problem are: the so-called greenhouse effect, the hole in the ozone layer, acid rain and marine pollution.

The common factor is the role of *human activity*. This is a unique period in earth's evolution. For the first time, one species (humankind) has the ability to alter the global environment within the lifetime of an individual.

Greenhouse effect/climate change

The greenhouse effect is the term used for the alleged warming up of the globe due to human activity. The earth already has its own greenhouse effect and is kept warm because the air traps heat, as if under a pane of glass (such as cultivators of exotic flowers use in their garden greenhouses). Thus, certain gases in the atmosphere (such as water vapour and carbon dioxide) are more transparent to solar radiation than to thermal radiation. In other words, they permit the sun's heat to fall onto the earth but then prevent the heat from bouncing back into space. The heat is thus trapped on the planet. The greenhouse effect contributes to the miracle of life on earth. If it did not exist, then earth would be too cold to sustain life.

The problem, then, is not that there *is* a greenhouse effect but that humankind is tampering with earth's own inbuilt greenhouse effect by putting too much pollution into the atmosphere. There is a great deal of scientific consensus about there being some form of human-made greenhouse effect. The differences arise in assessing the size of the human-made impact and what the implications of this impact will be.

One impact is that there could be a rise in sea levels. This change would come about partly because of the melting of the polar icecaps, especially the ice in Antarctica. Antarctica – which is about the size of Australia – has over 90 per cent of the earth's supply of ice. Additionally, as water gets warmer, it expands, and so as the sea gets warmer sea levels rise. These developments could cause coastal flooding. A second impact would be change in climate. Overall, the temperature would get warmer, thereby changing, for example, patterns of agricultural cultivation. Since the tropics would increase in size, so traditional tropical diseases would become more dispersed.

Rising sea levels will erode the coasts of some countries and may even submerge others. The small island country of Kiribati is made up of 33 small atolls, none of which is more than 6.5 feet above the South Pacific. This may be the first country to disappear. Tuvalu, also in the South Pacific being another.

Among the challenges arising out of the speculation of climate change, is the problem that scientific evidence is still so unclear. But when that evidence becomes more precise in favour of there being some form of greenhouse effect, then it will be even harder to reverse the pollution going into the atmosphere. Governments are not geared up to thinking in the long term. Attention is focused on the time to the next election or palace coup. Economic problems, for instance, always seem more immediate and acute than environmental ones. Most national departments of the environment have only small budgets.

Hole in the ozone layer

These challenges are also seen in the context of the holes in the ozone layer. This is a separate problem from the greenhouse effect, although there is a common root: pollution. The ozone layer limits the amount of solar ultraviolet radiation reaching the earth. Such radiation causes skin cancer and cataracts, depresses the human immune system and reduces crop, animal and fish yields. Excessive exposure to the sun has always been a danger; the holes in the ozone layer merely add to that risk.

Chlorofluorocarbons and halons have been released into the atmosphere by the use of refrigerators, air conditioning systems, hamburger cartons, paint and hairsprays and fire extinguishers. These gases rise into the stratosphere, where they destroy the ozone molecules. The holes in the ozone layers have been appearing over the polar icecaps. There is speculation that the holes could get larger and so affect the much more populated areas of northern Europe, southern Latin America, South Africa and Australia.

Acid rain

Acid rain (more accurately 'acid air') comes from the emission of sulphur and nitrogen oxides by coal-fired power stations, heavy industry factories and motor vehicles. The chemicals undergo a change in the atmosphere and fall as sulphuric and nitric acid in rain, mist and snow. The acid rain kills forests and their wildlife and erodes ancient buildings, such as cathedrals, and modern concrete ones. The problem crosses national boundaries because the pollution is carried by the prevailing winds – for example, more than 50 per cent of Canada's airborne pollution originates in the US.

Marine pollution

Finally, there is the problem of marine pollution. The oceans are too easily taken for granted. All of the world's population – including people living a long way from the coast – depends on the oceans. They are the source of all life. Out of them stumbled the forebears of humankind; from them humankind draws living resources for food. They are the key factor in maintaining the oxygen/carbon dioxide balance in the atmosphere and maintain the stability of the earth's climate. They provide the medium for transport between continents as well as being a source of recreation and holidays.

The oceans are also the last legal frontier. Humankind continues to do to the oceans what it is now outlawing on land: using them as a refuse tip for non-biodegradable substances, for old chemical weapons and radioactive material and as a repository for fertilizers washed off the land. Unlike the rivers, which wash pollutants to the oceans, the oceans themselves have no outlet. In short, the muck stops here.

The sea was, for thousands of years, traditionally viewed as inexhaustible (no matter how many fish or whales were taken from the sea, there were always more left), limitless (a person could sail for years without necessarily retracing their route) and indestructible (could always absorb the garbage of humankind).

That view is changing. The sea is not inexhaustible. Some whales have been hunted to extinction and others have almost disappeared. Nevertheless the major whaling countries (notably Norway and Japan) now wish to end the global moratorium on whaling and resume their full hunting.

Our view of the sea as being limitless is also changing. The sea covers 70 per cent of the globe's surface but, compared with the diameter of the planet, is shallow. If the planet were reduced to the size of an egg, the total amount of water would be the size of a teardrop.

Finally, there is a fundamental unity in the composition of the sea, pollution that goes into it tends to stay there. There is nowhere else it can go. Ninety per cent of that pollution comes from the land, such as garbage and agricultural fertilizers. Thus, a person who lives well inland may still be contributing to the sea's destruction.

To conclude, pollution does not recognize national boundaries. Transnational pollution levels were small until recent decades and so governments attempted to solve national pollution problems by national means. Pollution has now gone global.

Winning battles but losing the war

It is possible to win battles but lose the war. In other words, there may be improvements in some areas but overall the environmental situation remains gloomy. As an example, all countries now have ministries for the environment and tougher environment legislation than existed at the time of the first UN Conference on the Human Environment in 1972 but there are still many major problems such as climate change and the exhaustion of non-renewable resources.

Many problems cannot be solved by national action alone and so governments benefit from working together. For example, no matter how good a government may be in looking after its own country's environment, this would be of little value if it is situated downwind of a dirty neighbour. Pollution recognizes neither national boundaries nor national sovereignty.

Crime

Crime goes global

As recently as the 1960s, the Japanese were not allowed to travel abroad for mere pleasure. Just a few years ago exit visas for those living in the Soviet Union, eastern Europe and China were rare. Now Czech criminals work the Italian Riviera, Chinese immigrants to America are trans-shipped through Hungary and South American drug lords recruit traffickers in Nigeria.

The new borderless era has brought a period of unparalleled prosperity to the world, as goods find new markets and people sell their skills to the highest bidder. However, when combined with the enormous profits to be made from crime, it has also created an unprecedented opportunity for evil.

Modern technology in the banking, communications and electronic sectors has provided criminals with new tools enabling them to steal millions of dollars and to launder their illicit profits across borders. During the 1980s, the profitability of the drug trade led to a situation where the 'narco-dollar' began to assume the economic significance of the 'petro-dollar' in the 1970s.

The development of computer and communications technology means that the electronic funds transfer systems can move billions of dollars around the globe in seconds. Faxes and cellular telephones can be encrypted, making it all but impossible to trace calls from them. Drug cartel planes flying north to the US have internal interceptors to plot radar and avoid US monitoring.

This section contains case studies of the Russian mafia, the global dimensions of the drugs trade and the problems involved in supervising banking.

Russian mafia

Violent crime in the old Soviet Union was a state-run affair (with the secret police and other law enforcement agencies being the main perpetrators). Life there was brutal but Soviet crime was hardly a global concern. Indeed, foreign tourists often thought it was more peaceful there than back in the western countries. They felt safe in the streets because everyone was being monitored.

However, there has been a collapse of strong central government in the former Soviet Union and in eastern Europe, with the rebirth of the individual profit motive. Russian mobsters now operate in about 50 countries (one-quarter of all the countries in the world).

The Russian mafia is a legacy from hundreds of years of the Czarist era and then the Soviet Union. Daily life was brutal under the czars and violence was a way of life. If the czars treated their subjects badly, then the subjects had few reservations stealing from their rulers. They had to, simply to survive.

The Soviet system could put a person into space but it could not put enough food into people's mouths. A criminal culture developed still more because people had to survive. Theft became a way of life. It was a way of coping with government rationing. A central committee in Moscow decided each year how many items should be produced. If the committee guessed right, then the consumers would be all right. But if the committee got it wrong and there was a shortage, a black market developed in those goods. Farm peasants stole food, workers stole goods and the products they made, doctors stole medicines and drivers stole petrol. All these items would be sold on the black market and so provided an additional source of income.

The culture of crime ran through all levels of the system. Managers employed 'phantom' workers to receive additional salaries. They would label some of their goods as 'rejects' and 'defective' as a way of retaining them for sale on the black market. Goods arriving in retail shops were set aside for customers who would be willing to pay extra for them. Workers and managers were in on the schemes and pocketed the money. It was the normal way of life. The items on the Soviet black market were ordinary goods. The Soviet system was not just catering for an illegal addiction in drugs or prostitution (which is where the black market exists in western countries). Everything had to be subjected to the black market. It was possibly the only way that some people could get those goods. In short, there was no rule of law. No one had confidence in an honest legal system or an honest police force.

Meanwhile, there was no scrutiny of what was happening. There was no free media in the Soviet Union. It was no good complaining to a newspaper or radio or television programme – no one would take up your case if it were likely to cause some embarrassment to the system.

The Soviet Union collapsed in 1991. Its criminal culture provided the foundations and training ground for the Russian mafia. Generations of Russians had been educated in the criminal culture and so the gangs had plenty of potential recruits. The recruits had few problems with their conscience – they knew from hard experience what they had to do to survive.

As the Soviet empire in eastern Europe collapsed, the troops were brought home and demobilized. They suddenly became unemployed, with no government plans for how they could enter civilian life. They just walked off their bases with as much military equipment as they could carry. The gangs are therefore well armed and their members are well trained. Protection rackets have become a way of life. Businesspeople are warned that they need to pay money to avoid their businesses suddenly catching fire or being somehow destroyed.

The mafia is able to make use of globalization and Russia is now friendly with western countries and so its citizens move into and out of western countries on legitimate visas. They can open bank accounts in other countries. They can hide their money overseas as legitimate customers.

The very poor are having a very bad time. They have lost out on the opportunities (both legal and illegal) to make money. Russia is the only developed country in world history to have declining life expectancy and, thus, a declining population. Life has become so grim that some people are giving up trying to live. Russia loses about half a million people a year. At this rate, it will be empty in a century or so.

In the meantime, the Russian mafia is flourishing both at home and abroad.

Drug trade

The global dimensions of the drug trade may be seen in various ways. The most obvious is that peasants grow coca bushes (which produce cocaine) and opium poppies (which produce heroin) to meet a foreign demand for them. Attempts to get peasants to grow alternative crops (such as potatoes in Bolivia) have usually failed because these are not as profitable as drugs. If there were no overseas demand, then the peasants would be obliged to cultivate other crops.

The US (the world's largest importer of drugs) and other developed countries have a major obstacle in discouraging countries from supplying the market: an indifference among the the drug-producing countries to US interests or those of other countries. The US population is so fond of drugs that marijuana is now the US's second largest cash crop (after corn) and the peasants could argue that if US citizens are so determined to have drugs, why should they be denied a chance to supply that market? Besides, if a group of peasants were to give up growing drugs, this would only reduce the supply and so force up the price, thereby encouraging others to get into the trade. Additionally, there is the irony that drugs kill fewer Americans (or Britons, etc.) than tobacco and alcohol and yet these remain legal and are a bountiful source of taxation for governments. Peasants cannot understand why their products should attract odium and yet others do not. The solution is not in Latin American jungles and Afghanistan's mountains but on the streets of developed countries like the US and western Europe.

Given the extent of foreign trade, it is difficult for customs officials to locate drug shipments. For example, drugs are often shipped in foodstuffs, such as yams, hollowed-out coconuts and canned oranges. US customs officials can only check about three per cent of the nine million shipping containers that enter US ports annually.

Foreign responses to drug growing and trafficking may clash with other priorities. A good example is Burma (Myanmar), which is one of the world's largest opium producers and a major supplier of the heroin on the US market. The ruling regime does not control the drug-producing areas. The US Drug Enforcement Administration (DEA) has worked with the regime to oppose the drug barons, such as Khun Sa, but this cooperation has been opposed by the US State Department. The ruling regime nullified a general election won by opposition leader Aung San Suu Kyi and killed thousands of protesters. The US (and most western countries) has minimal contact with the ruling regime and DEA claims that this concern with human rights is eroding the campaign against the drug barons.

US drug enforcement policy does not always recognize two basic principles of the Westphalian system: the sovereignty and self-determination of other countries. These two principles mean (in theory) that a country cannot invade the territory of another to capture a fugitive without permission. To address this problem, countries have bilateral extradition treaties with each other, governing the handing over of such fugitives. However, to observe such treaties takes time and may alert the fugitive that they are being pursued. It is easier just to go into a country and smuggle out the fugitive. The US has done this several times in recent years with regard to alleged drug traffickers, such as the well-publicized grabbing of General Noriega (who had also ironically been of assistance to the CIA), which required a full-scale invasion of Panama.

Another dimension is the irony that poor countries sell drugs to developed countries to earn money to repay the banks in those developed countries for foreign loans.

Finally, the leaders of drug cartels are a paramilitary force. National governments are too bureaucratic. Their response times are too slow. They are linked to so many foreign relationships that require consultation and agreement with allies and must cater to many domestic political interest groups that it takes them too long to react to initiatives by drug lords or religious fanatics and terrorists. By contrast, many of the drug barons are skilled, well-armed killers.

Money laundering

One of the biggest bank frauds in world financial history was centred on the Bank of Credit and Commerce International (BCCI), in which about US$9.5 billion was lost or stolen. There was no international mechanism to police the billions of footloose funds, legal and illegal, being shifted around the world by computers. The 1980s gave the world national deregulation, but not the global surveillance that should have gone with it.

BCCI was rooted in the secret tax havens of Luxembourg and the Cayman Islands. Owned by Arab money and run by Pakistanis, it was not only rudderless but stateless as well, with no central bank standing behind it. The Bank of England eventually acted against it but it had got away with a great deal for so long. There is no global system for regulating banking (or checking on auditing arrangements, for that matter). National banking authorities had information about BCCI's potentially criminal activities but they had no way of focusing their concerns.

BCCI was formed in 1972 by Agha Hasan Abedi (born at Lucknow, in India). One major backer was the very wealthy Sheikh Zayed of Abu Dhabi, president of the United Arab Emirates (UAE). It opened its first branch in London, in 1973, although it was incorporated in Luxembourg, with a holding company in the Cayman Islands. It particularly attracted overseas Asians as clients and claimed to be the developing world's banker (especially of the developing world's members living in the developed world). Before its closure, it had operated in 73 countries – that is, in all the major financial centres – and it was one of the world's fastest growing banks.

However, BCCI had three major defects: it always had a shaky financial foundation – most of its equity capital was fake. Equity capital is the foundation of a company. When any company is established, investors contribute money and receive shares of stock in return. If the company becomes profitable, some of the profits may be retained by the company to strengthen the capital base. If the firm loses money, the equity serves as a kind of shock absorber. If a bank loses money, then the equity capital gives it time to reorganize itself. BCCI reassured people that its equity capital came from some of the world's richest men (the oil-rich sheikhs in the Persian Gulf). Some of the initial money had done so but some of the rest had been lent by BCCI to those men, who in turn supplied it to BCCI as equity capital.

Then, BCCI senior staff looted the deposits in their reckless lending and trading and had to use current deposits as the operational capital of the bank. As long as people continued to make fresh deposits, there was a flow of money to cover the losses.

Finally, BCCI had some shady customers. It was a banker for the late Abu Nidal, the Palestinian terrorist. It was a financial intermediary between the US and Iran (the 'Irangate' arms scandal by which the Reagan administration in the 1980s secretly sold weapons to Iran to raise money to fight an illegal war in Central America). BCCI also lent money to both sides to buy weapons during the Iran–Iraq war during the 1980s. It looked after the money of rulers who wished to keep their funds (often stolen from their citizens) offshore – and thus a superannuation scheme in the event of their being overthrown. BCCI was also the bank of drug traffickers – Burma's Khun Sa, for example, who controlled 80 per cent of his region's drug trade, had, in mid-1991, at least US$300 million deposited with BCCI. The CIA's 'pay cheques' to Panama's General Manuel Noriega were deposited with BCCI.

Ironically, BCCI's demise came though the decision of the Manhattan District Attorney, Robert Morgenthau, to investigate alleged BCCI crimes in New York. (This was an interesting example of 'thinking globally and acting locally'.) It was the threat of their tolerance of inappropriate banking behaviour being exposed in a New York court that suddenly forced national authorities to act on the information that they had accumulated over the years – but had done nothing about. The shutdown came swiftly: on 5 July 1991, national authorities (such as the Bank of England) closed down BCCI operations throughout many of the western countries and the Caymans and Hong Kong (British crown colonies).

The shutdown revealed another problem for banking authorities: almost all of BCCI's small customers were honest people, having no connection with its criminal activities, who thereby had their assets frozen (most of which will never be recovered). By allowing the scam to go on for so long, national banking authorities had made the eventual shutdown all the more painful for small customers. At the time of its closure, BCCI owed money to 800,000 depositors with 1.2 million accounts in over 70 countries.

There is, in short, better control over banking at the national level than at the global level.

Mass movement of peoples

Refugees and migrants

There are now probably as many people moving away from their homes and countries as there have ever been in history. There are four categories of international migrant:

- refugee – defined as someone who can prove a well-founded fear of persecution for reasons of race, religion, nationality or being a member of a particular social group or political opinion in his or her country of origin
- temporary or labour migrant – who is admitted to a foreign country to fill a specific job
- permanent migrant or immigrant – who is granted permission to stay in a foreign country indefinitely
- undocumented migrant – who enters a country illegally or who overstays their visa, such as the million or so who enter the US each year from Central and South America.

Most refugees generally would prefer to have remained where they were. However, armed conflicts, environmental degradation and deliberate government policy are forcing people to move elsewhere.

The present pattern of international migration is different from those of earlier ages. Prior to about 1500, the movements of people were motivated by settlement and conquest (such as the Normans taking over England after the Battle of Hastings in 1066). After about 1500, Europeans started moving out to all other parts of the world, such as to the Americas and Australia.

The mass movements in recent decades are due more to people fleeing armed conflict and environmental problems and being forced out by governments (such as ethnic cleansing). The speculation over climate change and the presumed greenhouse effect (mentioned earlier in this chapter) may mean that the world's largest migration has yet to happen. There are concerns that the 1997 Kyoto Protocol on climate change will not be sufficient (even if the US were to accept it). People will need to flee their locations as deserts increase, coastal water levels rise and there are localized famines.

Meanwhile, there is growing resentment against refugees. Why should outside countries that do not produce the human rights abuses and political violence that cause refugees to flee be forced to shoulder the refugee burden? Why, for example, due to the bad luck of their geography, should countries such as Thailand, Turkey and Pakistan have their own stability threatened by the human dislocations caused by their neighbours in Indochina, Iraq and Afghanistan? There is also a fear that asylum seekers or illegal migrants will work for less money and so take local workers jobs.

But it should be noted that refugees are not always a burden. The acceptance of refugees can be a bonus to a country. Three hundred years ago, 250,000 Protestants, known as the Huguenots, fled from France to escape religious persecution. They subsequently made a major contribution to the economic and cultural life of countries that gave them refuge, notably England, Holland and Switzerland. Albert Einstein and the Jews who fled Nazi Germany in the 1930s contributed a great deal to the countries that gave them refuge, such as the UK and the US.

Refugee-populated areas can be centres of rapid economic growth, where new goods and services become available. Richer members of the local population are especially liable to benefit from the new arrivals offering cheap labour and new skills. There may also be the influx of foreign aid and foreign aid workers (who will need to buy local supplies).

In addition there is the national impact on the countries from which the refugees have fled. The people best able to flee are often the best educated people who are confident that they will be able to resume their lives elsewhere. Refugees with marketable skills are more easily accepted for resettlement in an industrialized country. In 1972, Uganda (under the brutal regime of Idi Amin) expelled many citizens of Asian descent whom he accused of running the Ugandan economy; these came to the UK, where they settled in as middle-class people. Countries in the developing world are very short of educated people and so cannot afford to lose talented people as refugees.

No one wants to be a refugee, but anyone can be forced to become one. No one knows for how long they will be a displaced person. People flee from the immediate area of trouble and hope that they will soon go back.

Life in a refugee camp is very different from ordinary life. There is no certainty about how long a person will be in the camp or where they will go if they are moved on. This constant uncertainty underpins all their life in the camp. Should, for example, a child go to school? What type of education would be of use to the child? If their original home is in a rural area, it may not be very useful to learn an urban trade – but the urban trade would be of use if the place where they are currently (and perhaps permanently based) requires such a trade.

There are three long-term solutions to a refugee problem.

Voluntary repatriation

Most refugees want to go home. Voluntary repatriation is always the best solution.

For voluntary repatriation to work, the refugee must be protected from a recurrence of the persecution they fled in the first place. If nothing is done to change the conditions that made people leave their homes, then there is no reason why they will stay in their country if they are forced to return against their will. If there is no guarantee of protection, refugees will not choose to return.

Local integration

Usually, the country of first asylum is just as poor as the country from which the refugee is fleeing and the host government does not have the resources to give much assistance to the new arrivals.

Governments of some host countries have argued that if refugees become self-sufficient while they are in exile, they will have no incentive to go back to their own homeland.

By the same token, those who have managed to accumulate a surplus of cash, food or goods while in exile will be better equipped to go home and become productive members of their own society.

Resettlement

Resettlement is the last option for refugees, when neither repatriation nor local integration is available. It separates refugees from their usual environment and family and it suddenly severs any ties with their country of origin. It is the most difficult solution for the refugees, as radical adjustments are necessary to cope with their new country.

Compassion fatigue

'Compassion fatigue' refers to the way in which people in developed countries have become tired of making donations to help developing world causes, such as refugees. This is partly a by-product of the global television news service. People can, for example, watch 'live' as people die of starvation in an African refugee camp.

The advantage of the global television news service is that viewers feel outraged about a tragedy and demand that something be done. The disadvantage is that viewers become bored with the same tragedy. News has to be 'new'. The same news week after week gets stale and viewers get bored. Compassion fatigue sets in.

Compassion fatigue and the impatience for new news undermines the public's ability to understand many of the complexities of an issue. They want colour, drama and brevity in the news programmes – not a highly sophisticated explanation of the complexity of a crisis.

There is a distinction between responding to a sudden refugee crisis and the daily continuing work of economic and social development, for example. Some emergency work has to be done in response to a natural or human-made disaster, but this technique is often not appropriate as an aid to development. Foreign food aid is a good response to starvation but it is not a good response to development because its free availability deters local farmers from cultivating their own land. Why bother to farm when the customers think that they will get foreign food for free?

Viewers will respond to pleas for emergency aid to help in disasters but there is little interest in encouraging governments to provide long-term commitments of foreign aid. The latter are much more complicated and not so easily made into graphic television coverage. Thus, on refugees, viewers get bored with the same stories and want alternative items. There is little continual reporting of an event therefore and viewers are often poorly informed about how, say, a refugee crisis ends.

Conclusion

No country is an island. No country, no matter how wealthy, powerful and efficient, can solve all its own problems. Each country needs some foreign assistance. This chapter has simply explored four examples: plagues and diseases, pollution, crime and the mass movement of peoples.

Questions

1 How does your country work with others in combating plagues and diseases?

2 What can be done to reduce pollution? If we know what should be done, why don't we do it?

3 How does your national police force work with other police forces to prevent crime?

4 Should there be an international obligation to help refugees?

5 What can be done to reduce the factors that lead to the mass movement of peoples?

05 the United Nations

This chapter will cover:
- the rise of international/ intergovernmental organizations
- the League of Nations
- the composition of the United Nations
- an assessment of the United Nations successes and failures.

Introduction

National governments have found it necessary to create international (or more accurately 'intergovernmental') organizations to facilitate cooperation across national frontiers. While most popular attention has been focused on political and military cooperation (such as UN peacekeeping operations) the real breakthroughs have been in economic and social cooperation ('functional cooperation').

The process has been underway for almost two centuries. Rivers, for example, do not conform neatly to political boundaries. In 1815 the first permanent administrative body was set up by European governments – the Commission for the Navigation of the Rhine. It is still in operation today. The European Commission for the Danube was established in 1856 and is also still in operation.

In the second half of the nineteenth century administrative cooperation between governments began to take on a wider form. The International Telegraphic Union (which is now a UN specialized agency) was established in 1865 with a permanent bureau and some participation by private telegraph companies. In 1874 there followed the Universal Postal Union (also now a UN specialized agency), also with a permanent bureau, and participation by postal administrations regardless of their political status. The mail must get through – despite political differences.

The League of Nations

World War I in 1914 came as a great shock to everyone. No one expected such a large or lengthy conflict. There was widespread agreement that this should be the 'war to end all wars'.

But how was this to be brought about? Much of the debate derived from disagreement over whom or what caused the war. Several unofficial groups and individuals said the fault was due to the system of competing nation-states: the Westphalian system encouraged nationalistic rivalry. The system itself was at fault and so there should be a new international system.

By the same token, most – but not all – politicians believed that the Westphalian system was basically sound, but it had been destabilized by the unification of Germany in the 1870s.

Therefore Germany ought both to be punished for its past deeds and prevented from trying to repeat them.

This basic disagreement was never resolved. A punitive peace settlement was inflicted on Germany and it helped give rise to Adolf Hitler who rose to power in 1933 on the wave of German resentment against being harshly treated. Ironically, the 'appeasement' policy of the UK and France was initiated by people who also believed that Germany had been too harshly treated and so should be 'appeased' (that is, soothed) by being permitted some concessions.

The League of Nations began operations in 1920. It was designed principally as the place where two or more governments would bring their international disputes. It had no automatic right to intervene; governments had to agree to bring their disputes to it. Most governments did not.

US President Woodrow Wilson could not get Congressional approval for US membership of it. Indeed, the US not only rejected league membership but its mood of 'isolationism' also entailed a restrictive immigration policy and the imposition of high tariff barriers to keep out foreign goods. The UK and France, the league's two most important members, were wary of it. They were not accustomed to working together through an international organization.

The league, then, was flawed from the outset. It was able to make some progress in world health, care of refugees, the suppression of slavery and the drug trade, the protection of minority populations and improvements in employment conditions in factories. It settled, particularly in the 1920s, some international disputes. But once militarism built up in Japan, Italy and Germany, the league was powerless to stop the dictators because the member-nations were reluctant, if not downright opposed, to introduce coercive measures to tackle these dictatorships. Consequently, by the early 1930s the league ceased to have much political relevance. World War II began in September 1939.

Composition of the UN

During World War II, the Allied leaders (especially President Roosevelt and Prime Minister Winston Churchill) were concerned that there be another attempt at creating an international organization. It was decided to start afresh, rather than merely reform the discredited league. Winston Churchill said that the war should be called the 'unnecessary war' because it could have been averted had the league been used fully against Germany. Therefore, he wanted the new organization to have a major role in international peace and security in the hope of learning the lessons of the past. The UN overall is by far a more ambitious organization than the league ever was.

The UN contains six 'principal organs': General Assembly, Security Council, International Court of Justice (ICJ), Economic and Social Council (ECOSOC), Trusteeship Council and the Secretariat.

General Assembly

The General Assembly is the world's main political forum. It meets for about the last four months of each year, with all UN member-nations (now 192) present. It adopts resolutions that indicate how the world's governments think on particular issues. General Assembly resolutions are not binding (except in relation to domestic UN affairs). It cannot override national sovereignty.

It is the global debating chamber – but not the global 'parliament' because it does not pass laws. Governments are not obliged to follow any resolution. Indeed, governments may even vote for a resolution and then ignore it (such as the refusal of most developed countries to increase their level of foreign aid to developing countries to the level they have endorsed in General Assembly resolutions, namely 0.7 per cent of GNP).

Security Council

The Security Council is designed to meet at any time, day or night, to handle threats to international peace and security. Its core currently consists of the Permanent 5, which were the Allied leaders in World War II: US, Russia, UK, France and China. The other ten countries serve two-year terms and are elected via the UN's caucus system to maintain a representative balance of the world.

Generals always prepare to fight while diplomatists design methods to avoid having to fight. The ghost of Hitler (who had died only two months before the June 1945 San Francisco conference which finalized the UN Charter) haunts the original vision for the Security Council.

If, the reasoning went, enough countries had worked together in the League of Nations, Hitler would have been deterred from his aggressive foreign policy. Consequently, the league's successor, the UN, was given – on paper at least – wide-ranging power. All UN member-nations agree to be bound by Security Council resolutions (the only part of the UN system with such power) and all member-nations 'shall hold immediately available' defence forces to be deployed as required by the Security Council. A Military Staff Committee, drawn from the representatives of the chiefs of staff of the five permanent members, was created to coordinate military operations.

Because of the Cold War, this elaborate system was never used. Instead, there evolved an ad hoc system of peacekeeping for intervention in disputes. The ending of the Cold War has seen a great increase in the UN's peacekeeping work. The UN is now mounting more peacekeeping operations than at any other time in its history. However, these are still ad hoc ventures, rather than a full implementation of the UN Charter.

International Court of Justice

The International Court of Justice (ICJ) is the world's main legal body. Its roots go back about a century, when it was hoped that wars could be avoided by encouraging governments to use an international court to settle their disputes. The ICJ has been able to settle some disputes and thus avoid what could have become international conflicts.

However, it is not a 'court' in the national sense that is known by the general public. Individuals who are alleged to have committed offences are obliged to attend a court hearing in their own country. If they refuse to attend, that in itself is an offence. But government attendance at the ICJ is not compulsory. Only about one-third of the UN's membership accept its jurisdiction. Due to the Westphalian system of national sovereignty, no government can be forced to accept any international obligation. Thus, governments are within their rights to have nothing to do with the ICJ. The US, for example, has not been a party to the ICJ for about two decades and so boycotts its proceedings.

Another difference between the domestic and the international legal systems arises from the structure of the courts themselves. In the domestic legal system, the lower courts deal with the facts and the higher (appellate) courts deal with matters of interpretation of the law. But the ICJ has to be both a court of trial and of last resort.

The ICJ is hampered on procedural matters by various factors. Judges are often appointed with an appellate court, academic or government background, with an interest in treaty creation (which is useful for appellate work). But they may have limited experience in the work of lower courts and the grubby work of sifting through competing evidence. Only governments may take cases to the ICJ. There is an assumption that governments provide evidence honestly and so the ICJ's task is to weigh up the legal arguments of both sides. There is, of course, a risk that the evidence may be accidentally or deliberately false.

ICJ judges are drawn from all over the world and so there may also be cultural differences in how the evidence is interpreted. Also, there are various national legal systems; the English common law system is not necessarily the standard form for all the world's national legal systems. The world is a long way from having a uniform legal system.

Economic and Social Council (ECOSOC)

ECOSOC initiates reports and makes recommendations to the General Assembly, UN member-nations and specialized agencies on economic, social and cultural matters.

There are 16 autonomous specialized agencies, some of which are well known to the general public and some which are not. They include: the UN Development Programme (UNDP), World Health Organization (WHO), UN Educational, Scientific and Cultural Organization (UNESCO), Food and Agricultural Organization (FAO), International Labor Organization (ILO), International Maritime Organization (IMO), Universal Postal Union UPU) and the International Telecommunications Union (ITU).

There are also the big financial agencies of the World Bank and the International Monetary Fund (IMF). Additionally, there are subsidiary bodies such as UN Fund for Children (UNICEF) and the UN Environment Programme (UNEP).

Until the expansion of the UN's peacekeeping work in the 1990s, at least 80 per cent of the UN's money went into the areas under ECOSOC.

The sums of money involved are minute – in relative terms – but often highly effective. For example, WHO coordinated the international campaign to eradicate smallpox and, as a result, the US alone now saves US$130 million a year by no longer having to vaccinate its population against smallpox. This means that the US saves each year more than its total annual contribution to *all* of the WHO's work. Another UN success story is the eradication of river blindness in Africa. A blind person becomes a burden on the family and is vulnerable to mishaps in a continent that has more immediate worries than looking after people with disabilities. This successful campaign cost a mere US$340 million.

Of course, it is likely that the successful work will not be publicized because the mass media are mainly interested in bad news. Good news stories on the eradication of smallpox and river blindness will remain largely unpublicized and so the general public will remain largely unaware of the progress being made on functional cooperation.

The UN could make even greater progress on economic and social cooperation if only national governments were more willing to work together. The previous chapter highlighted some of the areas in which governments could work together far more to address common problems, such as malaria, threats to the environment, crime and the mass movement of peoples.

Trusteeship Council

Most wars in history have resulted in the winner taking some of the land of the loser – indeed, that may have been one of the purposes of going to war in the first place.

US President Woodrow Wilson encouraged the Allies to agree that World War I would be different. The colonies of the losers would not be absorbed into those of the winners. Instead, they would become 'mandated' territories, with a view to their being put on the road to independence. Japan, which was a victorious Allied country in World War I, lost its colonies after World II. The mandated territories and the Japanese colonies became, 'trust territories' after World War I.

German New Guinea was captured by Australia in World War I. It became a mandate in the 1920s and 1930s. After World War II, it became a trust territory and was merged with the Australian colony of Papua. Papua New Guinea became an independent country in 1975.

The Trusteeship Council has almost worked itself out of a job as the axis colonies have been given independence.

Secretariat

The Secretariat, headed by the secretary-general, supplies the personnel for the main UN bodies. However, the UN is not a large organization (let alone a 'world government'). It has fewer civil servants than either British Rail or Disneyland.

Another limitation on the Secretariat is that the staff should be a truly international civil service. UN staff promise not to take instructions from their national governments but there is a temptation to maintain close links. The USSR and the former eastern European bloc staff were the worst examples of how UN staff were controlled by their governments. There are signs that this has improved with the ending of the Cold War.

The lower levels of the staff work hard and promotion is on merit. Unfortunately, some of the senior positions are used by governments as a dumping ground for retired politicians or active ones whom governments would find more convenient to have out of the country.

Assessment of the UN

The UN and the Westphalian system

The UN is a much more ambitious organization than the League of Nations; whereas the league only hesitatingly paid attention to economic and social cooperation, the UN has made great progress in functional cooperation.

At first sight though, the UN remains locked into the Westphalian system. Governments use the UN not out of any sense of idealistic high-mindedness (however much politicians claim this in their rhetoric), but because the UN is a vehicle for national foreign policy. No country is going to sign any international agreement that will be to its own disadvantage.

An example of the UN's weakness is its perpetual financial crisis. The total amount of money that goes to the UN (with the exception of the loan money that passes through the World Bank) is about US$10 billion per year – which is less than the world spends on defence forces *each week.*

The UN is, however, helping to erode the Westphalian system. This is not as obvious and dramatic as the activities of transnational corporations (to be examined in Chapter 08). But the process is underway.

First, the mere fact that the UN exists is itself proof that governments (albeit reluctantly) acknowledge that they do need to work together on an increasing range of issues, such as health and protecting the environment. A basic example of this is to compare the range of issues being discussed at the annual sessions of the General Assembly. The agenda is far longer this year, covering many more issues than was the case, say, 50 years ago.

Second, the UN Charter is ambivalent towards the Westphalian system. According to Article 2(1): 'The Organization is based on the principle of the sovereign equality of all its Members.' This is the standard Westphalian principle.

But, in Article 2(7) there are two hints of the erosion of that system: 'Nothing contained in the present Charter shall authorize the United Nations to intervene in matters which are *essentially* [emphasis added] within the domestic jurisdiction of any state or shall require the Members to submit such matters to settlement under the present Charter; but this principle shall not prejudice the application of enforcement measures under Chapter VII' [dealing with threats to international peace and security].

The word 'essentially' undermines the absolute prohibition of the UN to intervene in domestic affairs (the League of Nations Covenant was much more strict in this regard). Chapter IX (Articles 55–60) of the UN Charter deals with international economic and social cooperation and foresees a role for the UN in such 'domestic' matters as economic development, health and human rights.

Additionally, as Article 2(7) itself acknowledges, some conflicts that may have domestic origins, can become a threat to international peace and security and so potentially can come within the scope of the Security Council. With the ending of the Cold War and the increase in secessionist movements, there has been far more work for the UN Security Council as nation-states fragment and their disputes spill over into adjoining states (such as the problems caused by the disintegration of former Yugoslavia in the early 1990s and the recent conflicts in Africa). Whether the UN is equipped to cope with the new era of guerrilla warfare and fragmenting nation-states is, of course, another matter.

UN achievements

The UN attracts a fair amount of bad publicity, so here are some of the UN's achievements in an attempt to redress the balance. When viewed in the long term, the UN has been more successful than is commonly recognized. (This only adds to the sense of frustration that if only governments overcame their Westphalian mentality and made greater use of the UN, it would be even more successful.)

Longevity

The UN has lasted three times as long as its ill-fated predecessor the League of Nations. The league was often seen as the 'great experiment', with the implication that it may not be here to stay (which, in fact, it was not). But the UN has outlasted all the predictions of eminent doom. The UK's conservative *Daily Express* first predicted in 1948 that it would soon be wound up but in fact it has lasted the course. Even the current Bush administration (easily one of the most hostile anti-UN administrations in US history) is not seeking to wind it up.

Universal membership

Virtually every country in the world is a member of the UN. The League of Nations never had that benefit. The US never joined and the USSR joined late and was expelled (over its invasion of Finland). Japan, Italy and Germany all resigned because of their aggressive foreign policies. Nowadays, as soon as a territory achieves independence, it seeks UN membership as part of its journey into the international community. If President Bush's 'roadmap for peace' is eventually successful in the Middle East, then an independent Palestine will also join.

The UN survived the Cold War

The UN had a troubled birth, which coincided with the onset of the Cold War. Winston Churchill forged the 'Great Alliance' (US, UK and USSR) against the axis powers (Germany, Japan and Italy). He hoped to keep the Grand Alliance together in what became known as the UN Security Council to maintain international peace and security, but the Cold War broke out and hindered much – but not all – of the UN's work. The Cold War is over and the UN has survived.

Forum for decolonization

Colonization has been a feature of world history for as long as records have been kept, but especially in the last 500 years. In the 1490s Europeans started to move off their rocky outcrop at the western end of the massive Eurasian landmass and travelled to all points of the world.

A century ago, European domination of the world was taken to be the norm. Almost all the world (even including most of Antarctica) was under the control of Europeans or peoples of European descent (such as the US). It seemed that the empires would last for many more years to come. White people, it seemed, were destined to rule the world.

Decolonization was a fixed agenda item for the UN's early decades and almost all the empires have now been wound up. Only a comparatively small number of people are in a colonial situation, for example the British Empire in the Pacific now consists only of Pitcairn Island, with its population of 72 souls and the wreck of the *Bounty*. The struggle for decolonization was waged partly at UN meetings (hence the anger of the *Daily Express*, which wanted to keep the British Empire in one piece).

Functional cooperation

Even during the height of the Cold War, countries were working across national lines to make the world a better place. Technical experts were brought together. The vast network of UN specialized agencies enable the technical cooperation to go ahead, such as sending letters from one country to another, exchanging ideas on educational material and pooling resources on foreign aid. Diseases and pollution do not recognize national boundaries and they need to be combated by international cooperation. Smallpox has been eradicated through the WHO (the first disease in world history to be eradicated) and there are hopes that polio may be eradicated in the very near future.

Forum for small states

The UN has provided a platform for small states. Until 1945, a handful of states ran the world. They still do, of course (although it is now a different collection of states, with other ones emerging, notably China and India), but the UN has enabled other countries to have a say in how the world is run.

Protection of human rights

The twentieth century saw both some of history's worst violations of human rights and also some of the most spectacular international advances in their protection. There is a still long way to go, but there is the recognition that human rights are now a global (and not merely a national) issue. Human rights are still being violated but people know they are and so there is less resigned acceptance that such violations are an inevitable part of life. Additionally, people in other countries have a greater sense of obligation to assist others whose rights are being violated. This is still not the creation of some form of 'international family' but there is a greater sense of 'community' than ever before.

Additionally, respect for human rights is now a criterion in assessing countries. For example, China lost out in the bidding for the 2000 Olympic Games (which went to Sydney) and had to promise to do better, among other things, in the protection of human rights in order to secure them in 2008. The UN has since produced a diverse range of declarations and treaties flowing from the Universal Declaration of Human Rights. There is no precedent at all for this level of intergovernmental action on human rights.

Forum for disarmament

The UN is the global centre for disarmament negotiations. Much remains to be done but at least some progress has been made in reducing nuclear and chemical weapons, and biological warfare has been scrapped.

Protection of the environment

There was little thought given to the environment in 1945 and there is no reference to it in the UN Charter. It is a sign of the UN's flexibility that it has been able to absorb the international protection of the environment into its workload. The first major step was at the 1972 UN Conference on the Human Environment. It has been able to get countries to work together on common environmental issues, such as through the UN Environment Programme (UNEP).

Forum for NGOs

NGOs were involved at the 1945 San Francisco conference that created the UN and they have remained so. Their work shows that governments have no monopoly over information and ideas. For example, NGOs undertake public education work, such as alerting people to the dangers of pollution and generating new ideas for coping with problems. NGOs develop close ties with politicians and (even more importantly) public servants to work on new treaties etc. They are adept at using the mass media for their campaigns and sometimes challenge governments and transnational corporations to do better, such as the current global justice movement.

NGOs provide an alternative route for people who wish to work for a better world. Political parties are not the sole route for working for that objective. Indeed, given the widespread disenchantment with politicians, NGOs are important avenues for peaceful social change. The UN recognizes the importance of NGOs by granting various forms of consultative status to them to enable them to take part in its work. Also, some national government delegations to UN meetings sometimes contain specialist NGO personnel.

Continuing problems: lack of a central vision, money and power

There are two old problems: a lack of a central vision and the way that governments are reluctant to pay their assessed contributions to the UN. Interwoven into the fabric of those two problems is a third one: the Westphalian principle of sovereign independence of countries – they cannot be coerced into accepting international obligations or paying UN membership dues.

These matters are manifested in various recurrent ways at the UN. The UN is a decentralized organization. The General Assembly, Security Council and secretary-general may attract the daily media coverage but much of the UN's work is conducted through specialized agencies, such as UNESCO, WHO and the FAO. Each agency has its own governing board and these are then linked back to different government departments at the national level. Each agency has its own membership. Thus each country may choose which specialized agencies to join. The US, for example, resigned from UNESCO in the early 1980s and took the UK with it. Both have since rejoined. Each agency has its own method of operating and its own objectives. This means that some agencies overlap in the field, with some resulting confusion.

The second problem is money. At any one time, most of the UN members are in arrears in paying their annual subscriptions to the UN. The biggest debtor in recent years has been the US. For most of the period from 1960 to 1980 it was the Soviet Union.

By the standards of government expenditure, the UN runs on small sums of money. If governments regard something as particularly important, they will find the money for it. On this reckoning, the UN is obviously a low-priority item.

There are various discussions each year on how the UN can cut its costs. As Winston Churchill could have said: 'Never before have so many people spoken for so long about so little.'

In sum, the UN is a long way from what its architects could have hoped for in 1945. Various opinion polls show that citizens are far greater supporters of the UN than their respective national governments. The governments remain locked into Westphalian logic.

Westphalian system as a hurdle for UN military operations

The most obvious way – in terms of the media spotlight – in which the Westphalian system obstructs the UN is that the UN has no automatic right either to enter a country or to call for other countries to supply military forces for a UN operation. The UN has been involved in various controversial operations, such as Rwanda in the mid-1990s, when there were urgent pleas in the media for it to stop the mass violation of human rights. But it has no standing army and no standing right to enter any country with any army it might co-opt. Its activities in Rwanda were too little, too late but it was not the fault of the UN secretary-general – the member governments were unwilling to supply the forces to the UN to save the Africans.

The Westphalian principle of 'national sovereignty' can become a shield behind which a dictatorial government can violate the human rights of its citizens. For instance, Robert Mugabe in Zimbabwe is violating the human rights of his citizens but there seems to be little that the international community is doing about him.

Conclusion

The UN is still only a tentative experiment. National governments are often unable to solve their own problems but they are unwilling to surrender more of their authority and resources to the global level for there to be a full response. Governments remain unwilling to use the UN as it was designed to be used in 1945.

Questions

1 Why won't governments make greater use of the UN?
2 What can be done to encourage governments to make greater use of the UN?
3 How could the UN be reformed?
4 What has been the policy of your government towards the UN?
5 Check if there is a UN Association in your country and what the benefits are from your joining it.

06

the European Union and other organizations

This chapter will cover:
- how the European Union was formed
- how the Commonwealth operates
- the Group of 8
- the Association of South East Asian Nations
- the future of national governments.

Introduction

While the UN is the most well-known and most important intergovernmental organization, there is a growing range of such organizations. This chapter provides a sample of them, from the most famous to the hardly known.

There is much that can be said about these but, in the interest of space, this chapter will explore the organizations in the context of globalization. The scorecard (as with the UN) is mixed. On the one hand, there are signs of governments working together but, on the other, there are signs that not enough progress is being made.

Globalization is forcing us to rethink our national system of government – but not enough of a debate is underway. This chapter will show how globalization has both good and bad features.

The European Union (EU)

Uniting Europe

The EU is easily the most important regional intergovernmental organization and is the world's best example of how such an organization is eroding the Westphalian system. The Westphalian system began in western Europe and it is here that it is being transformed.

The EU has had a long process of evolution. For example, during December 1940 (at the bleakest period of World War II) British Prime Minister Winston Churchill was already giving consideration to Europe after Germany's defeat. He said that western Europe should form a 'Council of Europe', which would have a supreme judiciary and a supreme economic council to settle currency questions and so on. He also wanted it to have an international air force drawn from air forces of the council's member-states. Once enrolled, they would be under no one national jurisdiction, but they would never be obliged to cooperate in an attack on their own country. All air forces, military and civil, would be internationalized. As regards armies, every power would be allowed its own militia, because democracy must be based on a people's army and not left to oligarches or secret police.

However, on the vexed question of whether Britain itself should be part of the new European system, Churchill thought that the English-speaking world would be separate from this, but closely connected with it and that it alone would control the high seas. It would be bound by treaty to respect the trading and colonial rights of all peoples and Britain and America would have exactly equal navies. Churchill continued to promote these ambitious ideas, especially for an international air force, throughout the negotiations leading up to the adoption of the UN Charter in June 1945. The EU of today still has a long way to go to match Churchill's vision.

The UK's troubled relationship with the EU (and its earlier bodies) is a continuation of Churchill's own ambivalence towards a 'united Europe'. He wanted a united Europe but he was not sure what the UK's relationship with it ought to be. The UK stayed aloof from the early attempts to unite some of western Europe. Only in the 1960s, when it became clear that some form of united Europe was feasible and gathering momentum, did the UK try to enter it. It was eventually successful in 1973. But it has since remained unclear just how much commitment it should make to a united Europe. The divisions are not on straight political party lines and instead all the main parties have their own differences of opinion.

As an example, the British pound has long been a major international currency. Indeed, it was the world's currency for much of the nineteenth century and the first half of the twentieth century (a role now held by the US dollar). The EU has created the euro from the pooled currencies of participating countries but the UK has remained outside the eurozone. There is a continuing debate within the UK and the EU generally on whether the UK should join the eurozone or not.

Creation of the EU

The EU is a unique intergovernmental organization. It is more than the confederal UN (where the authority resides largely at nation-state level) and yet less than a federal nation-state (such as the USA or Australia).

There was a French proposal in 1950 to pool the coal and steel industries of France and the then West Germany into an organization open to all European democracies. The proposal had great symbolic significance. France and Germany had been at the centre of the two world wars and coal and steel are the basic industries for conventional warfare, the 'sinews of war'. The European Coal and Steel Community was formed in 1951 with the membership of Belgium, France, West Germany, Luxembourg, Italy and the Netherlands. The success of this arrangement encouraged the six countries to apply the same approach to other parts of the economy. This led, in 1957, to the creation of the European Economic Community (EEC).

The EEC's membership and range of activities continued to increase. In 1994 the membership was 12 countries and on 1 May 2004 the Treaty of Accession entered into force, enlarging the European Union to 25 member-states, with eight from eastern Europe. Bulgaria and Romania join in 2007 and there are suggestions that Turkey could be the next to join.

Sheltering behind high tariff walls has benefited EU producers but angered others. The EU continues to support its agriculture sector to the tune of US$150 billion a year. A dairy cow in Europe attracts a subsidy that is higher than the per capita income of more than half the world's human population. European cows have a higher annual income than most Africans.

That said, the EU should be congratulated for restoring societies undermined by decades of communism in eastern Europe and preparing them for joining the EU. Such a successful nation-building project has no recent precedent.

Problems with the EU

The EU has considerable problems. First, there is the issue of creating a sense of unity at the grassroots. Old hatreds (such as between France and Germany) are certainly dying but there is no new pan-European nationalism emerging. There is no new sense of being a 'European' to replace the old national sense of identity. On the contrary, France has done more than most other member-states to push the pace of the EU's evolution but French voters' rejection in May 2005 of the European constitutional treaty suggests that many have lost some of their enthusiasm for their creation.

Then there is a debate over how the EU should evolve. On the one hand, there is a move for a 'deeper' union, which would mean that the current member-nations would pool more functions and cooperate far more, such as with the creation of a single EU foreign policy and a single EU defence force (as per Churchill's vision). On the other hand, there is a move for the current membership to become 'wider' so as to include more of eastern Europe. This dilemma has not been resolved and some member-states (notably the UK) have doubts about both a 'deeper' and a 'wider' union.

Also, there is the problem of creating democracy and accountability within the EU. The real power resides with the European Commission at Brussels (rather than the European Parliament) and citizens feel isolated from the decision making. This alienation has given rise to a new fragmentation within the EU, a return to local sub-national concerns, such as the rise of local loyalties, like Scottish nationalism.

The standard reply to this concentration of power is 'subsidiarity', making all governmental decisions at the lowest possible level. The theory is that the decisions should be made by the people who are going to have to live with the consequences. Subsidiarity is fine in theory but it has a long way to go before being implemented. One argument against it is that local people do not have the 'big picture' and that they will make decisions that benefit themselves but disadvantage the larger society in which they live. Additionally, the prospect of subsidiarity offends the neat thinking of bureaucracies that focus on the uniform creation and implementation of rules. Subsidiarity would permit too many local variations.

Finally, there is the problem of transnational corporations. They like to act as though national boundaries are no more significant than the equator: simply a line on the map. One example of their work is currency speculation. National currency restrictions used to slow down the flow of capital, allowing central banks to control the value of their currency. Western governments (including those in the EU) have scrapped currency regulations. Over one trillion dollars can now flow through foreign exchanges in a day, looking for currencies to bid up or down.

There was an attempt to create a European exchange rate mechanism to standardize the value of currencies. The corporations (some of which, ironically, were based in the EC) disliked that idea. They made a 'run' on the UK pound in September 1992 by selling off the currency. The Bank of England tried to behave as it did in the past to protect the pound's value by buying the pound to boost its value (and it worked with the French and West German central banks). But the corporations were now too big and the bank surrendered after one day's trading (out of which some corporations made large profits).

The new euro common currency has not yet been subjected to the same degree of financial volatility arising out of foreign exchange speculation. But the corporations are still looking for ways of making money out of currency speculation.

In short, the EU is being tugged in contrary directions. On the one hand, the global economy is being knit together through government deregulation (thereby allowing more scope for corporations) and new forms of technology, communications and transport. On the other, there is some nationalist reaction to all these changes, which is slowing the pace of regional integration.

Lessons of the EU

Europe's example of gradual integration on a regional basis is possibly one for other parts of the world to follow. Just as Europe could not be united overnight, so no government is going to accept an immediate leap towards world government. Just as Europe has had to be built gradually, by cooperative power, so, at world level, there must be a major advance in similar cooperative power – a new economic order, worldwide agreements on certain key environmental issues, progress on security and disarmament and so on. Europe's unity can help these processes.

The EU has not been established easily or quickly. It is still not as federated as some would like. If western Europe alone has taken so long, it is not surprising that progress at the global level has been even slower.

The Commonwealth

Three types of 'commonwealth'

There have been three international 'commonwealths' in the twentieth century. The 'old' commonwealth was the group of white-dominated countries within the British Commonwealth, notably Britain, Australia, Canada, New Zealand and (for a while) South Africa.

The 'new' commonwealth was the group of newly independent countries that were formerly British colonies (or mandated or trust territories of the 'old' commonwealth). The 'old' and 'new' commonwealth come to over 50 countries (over one quarter of all the countries in the world).

The more publicized current commonwealth is the Commonwealth of Independent States (CIS) that has emerged from the former USSR. But that title has little lasting significance and its use will fade away faster than the 'new' commonwealth.

The new Commonwealth

The Commonwealth's main significance for globalization has already peaked. It was the transmission system for British people, finance and culture to be imposed on about one quarter of the world's people. Its inclusion in a book on globalization is a matter for historical record, but the Commonwealth continues to linger on. It is an organic and evolving structure; it has no constitution or charter. Its intangible nature helps it to evade a final execution. For example, 32 of the members are republics but this does not prevent them from being members.

The Commonwealth is a voluntary association consisting of 53 member-states. With about 1.8 billion people, it has almost one-third of the world's population and contains both some of the world's largest and richest countries as well as some of the smallest and poorest. Mozambique, a Portuguese colony until 1975, has been allowed to join, despite its lack of a history of British colonialism, because all of its neighbours are in the Commonwealth. An independent Palestine (as foreshadowed by President Bush's 'roadmap for peace') would also be eligible to join (as is Israel) because of the British mandate in the Holy Land after World War I.

The Commonwealth is important both for the work it carries out and the facilitation it provides to enable others to work together. It provides another international forum for diplomacy. It implements student exchanges and the provision of technical aid. Additionally, the Commonwealth contains about 120 associations for co-operation at the professional and technical level. The London-based Commonwealth Partnership for Technology Management (CPTM), for example, is a forum for government and the business sector to meet privately to discuss potential development projects.

Group of 8 (G8)

The G8 is the world's most exclusive political club. It contains the world's seven most powerful economies (the G7) and Russia. The G7 countries are: the UK, Canada, France, Germany, Italy, Japan and the US. These dominate international trade and finance and are also flourishing democracies where there is the rule of law.

Russia has been involved since 1998. It is a poor country (with an economy less than that of the state of California), with a ramshackle democracy. But it has nuclear weapons. The G7 thought that it would be useful to have Russia as a member to keep open international diplomatic dialogue.

The group meets each year to discuss global problems. Its decisions are not binding on any government and they have no international legal significance. Each meeting is well publicized, making it one of the most important diplomatic events of the year.

This is all quite a development after only 30 years, when a group of six men came together to discuss common economic problems. In 1973 the Arab countries suddenly attacked Israel. To deter western countries from supporting Israel, the Arab oil-exporting countries and Iran withheld their supply of oil to the international market. There was speculation that the international economy would collapse.

Israel managed to win the war, but the Arab countries and Iran have kept up the price of oil. They argued that the price of oil (expressed in US dollars) had gone down in the 1960s because the US government had eroded the value of its own currency. They had underwritten the costs of the dramatic expansion of the western economy – and now they wanted more money for their unique commodity. In 1973 the US brought together an informal gathering of senior financial officials from Britain, France, Germany, Italy, Japan and the US to discuss what should be done. The US was already working through the usual diplomatic channels, such as the UN, but it also wanted a smaller, less formal group to get together privately to discuss the international crisis.

The US was also bogged down in the Watergate crisis. This resulted in the resignation of Richard Nixon in August 1974. His successor, Gerry Ford, had very limited foreign affairs experience. He also had problems working on the US recovery because this had been the first time a US president had been driven from office. Therefore, for what became the first meeting, Valéry Giscard d'Estaing, the French president invited the heads of those six governments to meet at Rambouillet in 1975. Right from the outset the presidency of the group has rotated between the group's member countries on an annual basis. The original G6 grew to become the G7 in 1976, when Canada was invited to join. It later became the G8 in 1998 when Russia became involved (after the Cold War).

The president for the year decides what should be on the agenda. The agenda has gradually expanded from energy and trade to include such issues as global security, terrorism, peace in the Middle East, health and Iraqi reconstruction.

The G8 process has attracted many criticisms. It has an élite membership which is seen to be out of touch with the real problems. Each one is held in a luxury holiday or conference resort, well away from the problems they are supposed to be sorting out. They may be talking about ending poverty but they see none of it during the summits.

The annual sessions appear to be more photo opportunities than real working sessions. The early meetings were small, intimate affairs with little publicity. Few officials were invited. However, now each leader attends with a very large delegation. For example, the US delegation to the 2001 summit in Genoa contained over 600 officials. Little of a practical nature could be accomplished in only two days of negotiations.

The question is often asked as to whether the summits really make much difference. It is worrying that the group first met to discuss the spiralling cost of oil and instability in the Middle East – and 30 years later, these are still major concerns. There have been many discussions – but not necessarily much progress.

Perhaps the real power over many global problems resides somewhere else, such as the power of transnational corporations. There is much G8 debate over the need to increase foreign aid but the corporations put far more money into developing countries through their foreign investment than do governments in official foreign aid.

Russia's inclusion in the group remains controversial because it is not a wealthy country and neither is it a democracy: there is growing concern over President Putin's increased centralization of power. If the meeting's membership is now based on power – rather than democracy – perhaps China (which has the world's third largest economy) should now be invited to join.

Finally, the political complexion of the meetings changes and there is little consistency. Some American presidents like to work though international organizations (such as Clinton), while some do not (such as Reagan and the two Bushes). In some years, most of the leaders are from the left of the political agenda, while in other years they are from the right. The 2005 summit had several leaders that had only a short time left in power. German leader Gerhard Schröder lost the September election, while French leader Jacques Chirac had another two years left in office but has just lost a humiliating vote over the European Constitution, Canadian leader Paul Martin lost power in early 2006, while Bush has a very low approval rating. Weak leaders are often unwilling to take strong stands.

Association of South East Asian Nations (ASEAN)

Asia's version of the EU is a very weak copy. ASEAN began in 1967 at the time of the Vietnam War. The small countries to the south of Vietnam were worried about the communist threat moving south and so thought they should work together to resist that threat. But ASEAN has never been sure just how the member-states should work together. Each country is very concerned about its own national sovereignty and so there have been no trans-boundary institutions created. There is no ASEAN common agricultural policy or common foreign policy. There is no ASEAN military organization. ASEAN is simply a meeting place where heads of government and foreign ministers come to talk.

ASEAN is a very diverse region financially. Oil-rich Brunei is one of the richest countries in the world, while Cambodia is one of the poorest. The richest country, Singapore, now has a far higher per capita income than its former colonial master (Britain) and its people have the same life expectancy. Also, all the ASEAN countries are committed to some form of market economics. The former socialist countries (such as Vietnam) were not allowed to join ASEAN until they had started to reform their economies on market lines. All the countries encourage foreign investment.

There are four obstacles to ASEAN becoming a more united organization. First, ASEAN was created out of a sense of fear: the members knew what they feared (communism) – but they did not know how to combat it. Ironically, all the former communist countries are now members of ASEAN. There is, then, no clear vision of how ASEAN ought to evolve into a more ambitious regional intergovernmental organization.

Next, ASEAN countries have histories of rivalry and war. Many of them are arguing over the ownership of the potentially oil-rich Spratly Islands in the South China Sea as well as other arguments over borders. There have been no wars in recent years but as the ASEAN countries get richer so they have been buying more defence equipment. There is no obvious reason why they need the new equipment – after all, the wars in Indochina finished a quarter of a century ago but it seems to be an automatic action that as countries get richer so they buy more equipment. As one country buys equipment, so others follow suit – even if there is no clear strategic reason for doing so. A few years ago for example, Indonesia bought many ships from the then East German navy – but they have been of little use in dealing with Indonesia's major military problems (all of which have domestic roots, such as the rebellions in Aceh and West Papua).

All of the countries are very concerned about the loss of political sovereignty. Economic sovereignty is being eroded because of increased foreign investment but the rulers wish to still retain a high degree of national control over, for example, their own human rights policies. The newer members, such as Vietnam, are particularly opposed to any interference in the internal affairs of ASEAN members.

This policy has created some problems. In the 1990s, for example, as the violence got worse in Indonesian-occupied East Timor, the ASEAN countries were silent on the subject because they did not want to offend one of the member countries, Indonesia. In 1999 Australia filled the vacuum and sent in a military force until the UN could deploy its own force.

An additional problem with ASEAN's reluctance to get involved in the internal affairs of member countries is that this makes ASEAN look out of touch with this new era of increased concern over human rights. For example, Burma (or Myanmar as the current military dictatorship calls it) has had a very poor record on human rights. Some Asian human rights NGOs have been critical of ASEAN for agreeing to have Burma as a member because it makes ASEAN appear to agree with human rights violations. Furthermore, ASEAN members have not actually criticized Burma's human rights record.

Finally, ASEAN does not know how it wishes to expand. There are two options, one is to include still more members. While the other is concerned with 'dialogue partners': countries that are not eligible to become ASEAN members but which are important for the ASEAN member countries. One such group consists of the northeast Asia economic giants: China, Japan and South Korea. Another is to the south: Australia and New Zealand. There are, then, countries that would like closer links with ASEAN, which contains some of the world's fastest growing economies. However, ASEAN does not know how to develop those links because it still does not have agreement among its member-states on how it should evolve into a more unified regional grouping. It is a long way from becoming an Asian version of the EU.

The Bank of International Settlements

The power of money

Standing behind the Bank of England (which is the British banker's bank) is yet another bank: the Bank of International Settlements (BIS). This is the banker's banker's bank and is the least known part of the global banking system. Once a month, the world's 11 most powerful central bankers gather in the Swiss city of Basle to discuss common problems. The meetings are not open to the public and are not publicized. This is not a sinister organization aimed at global financial domination (although some extreme left-wing and right-wing American political groups have argued that it is) but in the cosy world of banking, it is part of the final line of defence when there are 'runs' on national banking systems.

Most national banking systems now have some form of central or reserve bank to coordinate some of their activities (such as the Bank of England). A central bank is a banker to other banks. The final daily cash settlements within the banking system and between the banks and the central authority take place through a number of accounts held by the central bank. This means that the commercial banks involved must keep sufficient funds in the accounts held with the central bank.

A central bank also supervises the national banking system to ensure that banks do not operate fraudulently and that their customers' deposits are secure. The basic concept is 'capital adequacy': the need for enough realizable assets within a bank or other financial institution to enable it to absorb losses and thus avoid the risk of insolvency. Countries used to set their own capital adequacy levels but this has changed and a system was created by the BIS: the 1988 Basle Accord.

The BIS

The BIS was created in January 1930. It is the world's oldest international financial organization. Although based in Switzerland, the BIS is an international entity and Swiss officials have no right to enter the building without permission. It has immunity from Swiss criminal and administrative jurisdiction. The BIS is owned and controlled by the central banks. According to its charter, it is 'to promote the cooperation of central banks and to provide additional facilities for international financial cooperation.'

The BIS was originally created to handle the payment of German war debts. Following Germany's defeat in World War I, the Allies and the US (which regarded itself as separate from the Allies) said that Germany had to pay for the war under a system of 'reparations'. The repayment system never functioned fully. In 1930, with yet another attempt to get the reparations system working, the BIS was created to handle what were supposed to be flows of money from Germany into the Allies and the US. When Hitler came to power in 1933 he stopped the system of repayments entirely.

However, the central bankers liked the BIS idea and kept it going. The need for such a banker's banker's bank had become clear a century ago, with the increased expansion of national economies and the important role of stable banking for those economies. With the similar increase in international trading, there had to be a system for coordinating the role of banks across borders.

Indeed, there had been the October 1929 Wall Street crash and there were fears (accurately as it turned out) that the world was heading for a major financial crisis. The Great Depression began in 1930 and was one of the major economic events of the twentieth century. These events reinforced in the minds of the central bankers the need for an international central bank to stand behind the national central bankers.

The BIS's board of directors is drawn from the Group of 10 (G10), which actually now has 11 members: Belgium, Canada, France, Germany, Italy, Japan, the Netherlands, Sweden, Switzerland, the UK and the US. Another 34 central banks are members of the BIS, which are invited to the annual meetings in June each year. Another 80 central banks use the BIS as their international central bank. Thus almost all the world's central banks now work through the BIS.

The BIS has three main functions. First, it manages about seven per cent of the world's foreign exchange reserves. The bank is more concerned with liquidity than profitability, so that its central bank clients can withdraw funds without publicity at a moment's notice. None the less, the BIS has about US$8.5 billion accumulated through the movement of monies in helping central banks manage their external reserves.

Second, it is a forum for international financial cooperation. The monthly G10 meetings are the élite seminars for central bankers. More generally, the BIS enables central bankers to meet together out of the public eye to discuss matters of common concern. The 1988 Basle Accord on how banks are to maintain adequate capital reserves grew out of these private discussions.

Third, the BIS undertakes research into the international financial system. The research is not geared to find particular investment opportunities or particular investments to avoid, but instead on how best to maintain international financial stability in an era of globalization and great change. Some of the research papers are published.

Above national politics

The BIS is not a government institution as such. It was created in an era when national governments had very little role in running economic policy. The prevailing belief in 1930 was that an economic recession was like an earthquake or flood – an act of god that had to be endured. There was nothing that governments could do to avert them or reduce them. Nature had to take its course.

That world view was to change in the later 1930s, with support for the views of the British economist, John Maynard Keynes. He argued that governments should play a far greater role in shaping national economy policy, such as through tax cuts and employment-creating public works projects in recessions. He argued that government intervention would assist an economic recovery. When the recovery was underway, the additional funds should then be taken out of the economy by increased taxation to avoid inflation.

Some of Keynes's most bitter critics came from the national banking communities. They did not trust politicians with money. They argued that if politicians were to be allowed to print extra money, then they would use that power to bribe voters and so there would be a loss of the financial discipline imposed by adherence to strict banking principles. They predicted (accurately, as we saw in the early 1970s), that there would be inflation of national currencies.

Bankers did not think that politicians would have the courage to increase taxation rates (especially near elections) which would mean that financial problems – particularly inflation – could drag on through lack of political courage. Central bankers saw themselves as above the day-to-day turmoil of politics and so in a much more important position to guide interest rates.

Despite these objections from bankers, after World War II, western governments became more involved in national economic policy. The Great Depression was seen as one of the reasons why Hitler came to power and so it contributed to the onset of war. Voters expected more from their governments – to set national economic policy and to reduce unemployment.

However, the BIS remained outside that ambit. The central bankers have kept it as their institution. This helps explain its lack of publicity. Politicians – much more than central bankers – issue media statements but they have little need to comment on an institution that is not directly under their control. The BIS is happy with the lack of publicity.

Criticisms of the BIS

The BIS is criticized for three main reasons. It is claimed by some people that the BIS is a secret organization. This is not quite accurate because its existence is known to people who comment on banking matters and it has its own website (www.bis.org). However, it is a *secretive* one. Central bankers do not court publicity in the way that politicians do. They do not need to. Indeed, it is a nuisance for their work if they do court publicity. The world now seems to hang on the utterances of the US Federal Reserve chairman (one of the G10). A slip of his tongue can cause problems for financial markets. Central bankers usually do not like the excessive media scrutiny they now occasionally attract.

The BIS is a clubbie European institution. Eight of the 11 of the G10 are European. When central banks are admitted, they do not get admitted to the inner body. For example, in 1996 Brazil, China, Russia and South Korea were admitted but they are not part of that inner circle – even though each of them has a national economy larger than that of, say, Belgium (which is part of that inner circle).

Finally, the BIS conducts research into financial stability but it has to be careful about how that research is used. For example, the BIS was correct in its mid-1997 assessment of the problems of the South Korean banking system. The BIS had detected signs of the Asian financial meltdown before it took place but had to be careful about how it presented its research. If it publicized its warning too much, then it could have been criticized for bringing about an Asian crash. The BIS took a more low-key approach, which has meant that it has been criticized for not doing more to warn about the problems in the South Korean banking system.

The future of the BIS

What is the role of international financial organizations in an era of globalization? The main drivers of change are now transnational corporations rather than national governments. The corporations have created an international consumer market, where national boundaries are no more significant than the equator. Money, ideas and fashions cross from one country to another. A person with access to the media or the internet can see what other people are enjoying and seek to get it for themselves. Oil companies, car companies, CNN, Coca-Cola, McDonald's, Microsoft and IBM are refashioning the global economy.

Meanwhile, a banking era has ended. Credit used to be, in effect, rationed by banks. For example, it was very difficult to get a big bank loan such as a mortgage (and single women need not even think about applying for one). Now banks are awash with funds and go to great lengths to encourage people to borrow. The philosophy of 'saving for a rainy day' is now seen as old fashioned and discredited. People live from one credit card statement to the next. (In the US, a person trying to pay cash for ordinary items, such as a hotel bill, is viewed with suspicion: they are possibly too poor to get a credit card.)

There are problems here for the BIS's traditional role. Central bankers are now more the observers of international finance rather than the controllers of it. In short, the world's international system of finance is heading for a new era – and one with little supervision or control.

The future of national governments

A new role?

National governments will not disappear in the new global era but they will have to adjust to a new role. Governments have traditionally been the main actors in world politics – now they are having to share that power as other entities are gradually setting the running. In short, governments are losing control over the development of their societies.

A post-democratic society?

Electors are voting more and enjoying it less. Whoever becomes a US president usually receives less than 40 per cent of the votes because many electors do not bother to vote: the poorer you are, the less likely you are to vote because voting is seen as irrelevant to many poor Americans. Even in the new democracies in eastern Europe, there is already voter fatigue.

It is fashionable to talk about the 'post-ideological' era of party politics. In other words, it is claimed by political scientists that there are no longer any major differences between the parties. In the UK, for example, Tony Blair could easily be a member of the Conservative Party, while the previous prime minister, John Major, the son of a trapeze artist, could easily have been a member of the Labour Party.

There is a massive split in politics but not on main political party lines. Instead, it is between the political parties, on the one hand, and the alienated masses, on the other, who have contempt for politicians: whoever you vote for, a politician always wins. Recent scandals concerning politicians have contributed to the contempt many people have for them as individuals out for personal gain.

There has not been enough attention to what globalization means for the future of the democratic system. For example, at a time when so many careers now require training and accreditation, politics is one of the few activities where there are no previous requirements for candidates. They are a country's last set of amateurs. What needs to be done to make them more expert?

Indeed, do we need politicians as such? They constitute representative democracy: electors vote for a person to represent them in parliament. Why not have direct democracy, where each person is linked to a networked computer and is asked each day for their views on particular isues? Governments would have a very accurate view of what their citizens thought. We could move from representative democracy to e-democracy.

These are some of the fundamental questions that need to be examined. They are much more significant than the usual issues that get reported on the front pages of newspapers, such as murders and sporting results. Globalization is forcing us to rethink our national system of government – but not enough of a debate is underway.

Conclusion

This chapter has examined some of the other major examples of cooperative power. It has covered regional groupings and the BIS. The overarching theme has been the dispersion of power. No one now seems fully in control. This is very different from the highpoint of the Westphalian system, at which time certain national governments made the key decisions. There may have been disagreements over which governments were in control but no one doubted that governments as such were in control. Now power is much more dispersed.

Questions

1 Should the UK be a more active partner of the EU? If so, how?
2 What do members of the Commonwealth get out of being in it?
3 Why does the G8 not provide more foreign aid?
4 What can be done to publicize the role of the BIS?
5 Is there any point in getting involved in national political parties?

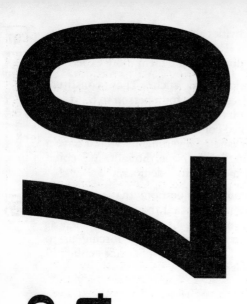

07

transnational corporations

This chapter will cover:
- how the corporations evolved
- the creation of the global economy
- the impact of transnational corporations on the Westphalian system.

Introduction

Corporate power is the second driving force of globalization. The main vehicle is the transnational corporation. A transnational corporation is a company that engages in foreign direct investment and owns (or controls) activities in more than one country.

Transnational corporations are now the main global economic force overshadowing, the basic unit of global politics, the nation-state. They are part of the new global order that is eroding the Westphalian nation-state system. Governments are no longer the masters of their economic and social destiny. Transnational corporations have eroded the notion of a national economy; there is now only a global one.

This chapter looks at the rise and influence of transnational corporations. They have an influence that is not adequately recognized in the mass media (most of which are coincidentally owned in western countries by transnational corporations) and there are few references to such corporations in government debates.

Evolution of the corporation

Corporations are one of the world's greatest economic and social inventions. They enable a financial project to outlast the life of its founder.

The rise and fall of the Fugger family is a well-known example of the danger of operating without a fixed company structure. The Fuggers were German bankers of the sixteenth century. At their height, the Fuggers owned gold and silver mines, trade concessions and even the right to coin their own money. Their credit was as great as the wealth of the kings whose wars (and household debts) they financed. But when old Anton Fugger died, his eldest nephew, Hans Jacob, refused to take over the banking empire because he had other interests; Hans Jacob's brother, George, said he would rather live in peace; and a third nephew, Christopher, was equally uninterested. None of the potential heirs to a kingdom of wealth apparently thought it was worth the bother: they already had enough money.

The legal basis of the corporation enables it to live on after the founder and the rest of the family has died.

Transnational corporations go one stage further. The reach of the nation-state used to be larger than that of business enterprises; a corporation's economic spheres of influence were contained within national political boundaries. There were, of course, some foreign traders, for example, the Phoenicians of 3,000 years ago, the Europeans who bought silk from China and the British East India Company. But these were much smaller versions of today's transnational corporations. The trade involved was minute (all the cargo transported in one year by all the ships of the East India Company could easily be accommodated onboard a single modern container vessel that visits the Port of London). There was no conscious exchange of technology, no systematic attempt to increase local production anywhere by new ideas and new methods.

Now transnational corporations sprawl across national political boundaries. They can also change character to maximize profits. For example, if a government tries to protect its own industry by keeping out imports, they will try to buy local companies in that country and so produce goods within that country.

Transnational corporations have evolved through four stages. From about 1895 to 1945, there was the emergence and consolidation of oligopolies (a small number of large corporations dominating a market) in key sectors in north America, western Europe and Japan. An example was the company founded by Alfred Nobel to manufacture explosives. Nobel invented and patented dynamite, then started producing it in his native Sweden. Demand was great everywhere: miners and roadbuilders could not get enough of it. He had to export much of his plant's production, in spite of the dangers of transport. More than one cargo of dynamite exploded unexpectedly on its way to Germany, Russia or America. Nobel then did something still characteristic of transnational corporations, instead of expanding his original factory and continuing to export from there, he founded a new one in Germany, then another one in Russia, another one in America and then many more. All were using his patents, thus introducing new technologies into the host countries.

In the next stage, from 1946 to the mid-1960s, transnational corporations rose to their position of prominence. They were responsible for roughly 80 per cent of the international trade conducted outside the communist bloc. In some commodities there was a high degree of 'vertical integration', in other words a corporation owned, for example, its own tea plantations, which sold tea to its own blenders, which then sold the tea to retailers. This represented 100 per cent ownership. In other commodities, however, corporations had to buy from independent producers, so that the percentage was lower.

From the mid-1960s to 1990, the corporations consolidated their dominance. There were mergers across national boundaries and a rise in the significance of non-US corporations, such as Japanese and western European ones.

The last stage began in 1991, with the ending of the Cold War and the opening up of the former USSR to transnational corporations. China is also more willing to have corporations invest in it. There is, for example, an oilrush into the former Soviet Islamic republics such as Kazakhstan. From the Arctic Circle to China's Tarim Basin to the waters off Vietnam, the end of the Cold War has opened immense stretches of oil and gas fields to transnational firms as host countries strive to develop their resources and earn hard currency. Additionally, countries that were not part of the communist orbit but kept their oil industries under tight national control are also opening up to the capital, technology and management skills that international oil firms offer. In other words, virtually the entire globe is now within reach of the corporations. Coca-Cola, for instance, is now sold in more countries and territories than there are member-states of the UN.

The global economy

From national to global

If national economies are being merged into a new global economy, what are some of the characteristics of this new economy?

The most obvious characteristic is that it is global. In other words, the economy is not just the US and a few friends getting together. Most countries in the developing world have always been part of that global economy. They have had little choice. They were given independence in the years after World War II but there was then a form of 'neo-colonialism' (new colonialism). The developing world colonies were now politically free but their economies were linked back to the former imperial countries.

The USSR and its satellite countries in eastern Europe tried to remain aloof from the global economy, but their citizens wanted the consumer goods of the western countries. This thirst helped erode communist control. The most isolated part of that bloc was Albania (which was even suspicious of the USSR). It, too, has succumbed to the Coca-Colonization of the globe. In May 1994, the president himself opened the Coca-Cola bottling factory – it took the average Albanian the equivalent of one-and-half hours pay to buy one bottle. Albania became the 197th country where Coca-Cola was made, leaving only a handful of blank spots, most notably, Iraq, Cuba and North Korea.

As to China, the late Chinese leader Deng Xiaoping once said 'to get rich is glorious'. The key moment came with the passing of the communist leadership and the turning away from centralized communist control. After Deng's accession to power in 1977, China's leadership made a conscious decision to embark on far-reaching economic liberalization and to integrate China into the world economy. China is gradually abandoning the idea of self-sufficiency and national control over the economy.

Market reforms have lifted 400 million people out of poverty. This is one of the most dramatic revolutions in world history. The Great Wall of China has been joined by the Great Mall of China. There is now greater attention to exports and entering world markets. One of the initial techniques was to experiment with market reforms and with opening up the economy to foreign investors and to freer trade in geographically contained zones. When those experiments were highly successful, China was progressively opened up, a development hastened by the realization that transnational corporations would be unlikely to bring investment and sophisticated technology to China unless freed from local ownership and other constraints. A sustained series of reforms has gradually reinforced the 'open door' policy and these have continued even in the aftermath of the events of the 1989 Tiananmen Square massacre. If the Chinese economy can keep growing as fast for the next 30 years as it has for the last 15, then it will have the world's largest economy.

Vietnam is also joining the global economy. After the end of the Vietnam War in 1975, an aggrieved US imposed a trade ban on all of the reunited Vietnam (its trade ban on Hanoi began a decade earlier with US increased involvement in the war). The ban kept out American companies but not French or Australian ones. They began trading with Vietnam soon after 1975. However, the communist leadership was hesitant about trading with foreign companies. The leadership gradually changed its mind when it saw that China was doing well with market reforms and the USSR's communist experiment had ended. The leadership was thus more amenable to foreign corporations. US-based ones were still restricted by the US government and so they encouraged President Clinton to lift the ban (which took place in early 1994).

Vietnam has learned another lesson from China: US-based companies make the best ambassadors in the US for a foreign country. The outrage over the Tiananmen massacre led to US human rights organizations calling for trade boycotts etc. US-based companies have successfully argued that the US ought not to use trade as a lever to protect human rights – a view naturally not shared by the human rights NGO community. The US government has accepted the views of the business community. Vietnam has an equally unpleasant human rights history and so is hoping to evade the usual human rights complaints by mobilizing its 'ambassadors' in Washington DC to look after the interests of both Hanoi and the ambassadors.

Finally, India has decided to join the global economy. Mahatma Gandhi was an economic nationalist. He stopped wearing foreign shirts and was a forceful proponent of homespun. This set an example for others and it became the symbol of India's campaign for freedom. In the early twenty-first century, foreign shirts are increasing in popularity and are being made in India under licence from transnational corporations.

Satellite television reaches over 600 million people (out of a total of about one billion). It appeals particularly to the emerging middle class (which is growing at about 20 million a year). Unlike China, India has imposed few restrictions on what advertising is broadcast and so this fuels the demand for consumer goods. The problem is, of course, that expectations are rising at a faster rate than the capacity of the Indian government to satisfy them. It seems hard to believe that the Indian standard of living could ever reach US levels but politicians are obliged to keep assuring voters that living standards are going to get better. If they do not give that promise, other candidates will certainly do so – and get elected. For the emerging middle class, this may be true – but many people will not enter that class. Additionally, there will be environmental limits to India's growth (as with the economic growth of all countries). Thus, there will be great strains imposed on the Indian nation-state.

A new global consumer culture

The most obvious part of the new global culture is consumerism. If you want to do well, sell people what they need; if you want to get rich, sell people what they want.

The global consumer culture contains such everyday items as soft drinks (notably Coca-Cola and Pepsi), McDonald's (there is a new store opening somewhere around the world every 15 hours), television programmes (such as *Dallas* and *Dynasty*), movies and pop music. There are also 'tie-ins', where two or more products run together to reinforce each other, such as the Harry Potter novels, movies, CDs and toys.

Another aspect is the creation of the global middle class. This class often has more in common with members of the middle class in other countries than they do with the working class/peasants within their own country. For example, a US-based corporation will be more concerned with selling to the emerging middle class in India or other parts of Asia than it is to the people who cannot afford to buy its products in New York.

The class therefore crosses national boundaries and has largely a-historical approach to life. They are interested in present pleasures – not past events.

Finally, as people get richer, so they are given more options for their money. Corporations have always to find new ways of extracting money from consumers. We have now reached the level of the 'experience economy'. For example, a humble coffee bean can now go through four stages of existence. In the first stage, the producer sells it in a sack (as 'commodity'). Then a corporation (such as Nestlé) produces a jar of coffee (a 'good'). Then a person may buy a cup of coffee in a cafe (a 'service'). The new fourth stage is the 'experience': buying a cup of coffee in a fancy location with film stars on the walls (Planet Hollywood). In each stage the coffee bean is increasingly expensive because of the value-added component.

The global workforce

Another development is that the corporations are staffed by a form of global civil service, rather than 'national' personnel. Corporations have been far more successful than the UN in encouraging their staff to see themselves as global workers rather than ones with national loyalties. Before national identity comes the commitment to a single, unified global mission. A person does not have to have a particular nationality to work for a particular corporation. The worker's task is to provide customers with exceptional value. Country of origin hardly matters. Products have become denationalized.

Transnational corporations are increasingly organizing themselves into multi-tier networks including parent firms, foreign affiliates, firms linked through subcontracting, licensing and similar contractual arrangements and firms tied together through alliances. These networks include all the major corporate functions – research and development, procurement, manufacturing, marketing, finance, accounting and human resource development – and occur in both developed and developing countries. These developments are therefore fostering worldwide economic integration. For example, many telephone enquiries from customers of corporations in English-speaking countries are taken by Indians, in India.

Global impact

The impact of transnational corporations on the Westphalian system may be seen in four ways:

- Global business has changed the pattern of economic relationships. Before the eighteenth century, most English people were peasant farmers living in villages or hamlets. Their local contacts and village institutions were dominated by the necessity of self-sufficiency. People could and did travel beyond the village in order to trade; they were not necessarily prevented by poverty or lack of transport. However, compared to the later eighteenth century and after, there was relatively little trade and the bulk of it was between people who knew each other and who were defined and linked by a common local social structure. The local market, bringing together local producers and consumers, typified this type of economic relationship. Furthermore, most market towns were orientated towards local rather than specialist trade.

  That pattern of life has now gone. For an American or Briton to drive to the supermarket to buy food for the weekend is in itself an experience in global trade (although the consumer would probably be unaware of it). Very little of the trip would be local – the consumer's wants, clothes, car, petrol, supermarket design and supermarket products all have global dimensions. They think locally and buy globally.

- The corporations not only do not need a host government to open up or guarantee foreign markets, they may do better on their own. National identification can be a burden. If a product is identified with a particular country (such as Coca-Cola and the US) then a government may try to keep it out simply as being part of showing its displeasure with US foreign policy. It is notable that the few countries that do not permit Coke to be sold are all those antagonistic to the US (such as Iran and North Korea). Generally speaking, corporations can enter national economies under the guise of providing goods and services to the consumers – while eluding the complaints about colonialism that would haunt a foreign government enterprise. They do not want politics to get in the way of making money – and neither do the consumers.

- Corporations are simply responding to consumer demand. They make available what people want to buy. They may stimulate consumer demand but they did not create it. Many people with money have opted for a consumption-driven lifestyle. They have been exercising their free will. For example, McDonald's does not march people into its outlets at the point of a gun. Nike does not require people to wear its trainers on pain of imprisonment. If people buy those things, it is because they choose to, not because globalization is forcing them to.

- National governments no longer have full national control over their economies. An example of this problem is the inability of governments to generate full employment. There has been the transfer of jobs from developed to developing countries. Many of the jobs lost in developed countries will never return. The traditional jobs (especially in manufacturing) have gone permanently to low-cost developing countries. Indeed, jobs in the manufacturing industry are going the way of agricultural jobs: few people work on the land but those who do are now more productive than ever before. Much the same could be said for people working in factories in developed countries. Some of the jobs will remain and the workers will be more productive than ever before (thanks to assistance from machines). Transnational corporations are encouraging the intertwining of national economies. They themselves move across national boundaries and so forge links between countries. This intertwining then limits the scope of government action.

There is, therefore, a paradox: as a country becomes more economically developed, so its people (particularly in the middle class) want a greater say in how the country is governed. But as that country becomes more economically developed so, generally speaking, the government has less influence in economic matters because the country is increasingly locked into the global economy and so has less scope to determine its own future. This adds to public cynicism about politics: whoever you vote for, a politician always gets elected. They promise a great deal but deliver very little.

It is therefore necessary to see the impact that corporations are having on national governments.

Conclusion

Transnational corporations are the main driving force of the global economy. They have evolved from the European company structure formed some centuries ago. Now the company structure is itself global in that it is no longer specifically 'European' or even 'North American' and is copied in many other regions. Some of the biggest corporations are now in Asia and they are buying up European and North American corporations.

Questions

1 What are some of the oldest transnational corporations in your country?
2 How reliant are you on transnational corporations for goods and services?
3 What 'national' goods and services in your country are truly nationally produced?
4 Which (if any) of your well-known 'national' brands are now owned by foreign corporations?
5 How good are you in rebutting manipulation by advertisers?

08

transnational corporations' challenge to governmental power

This chapter will cover:
- how Bill Clinton learned the hard way about the power of corporations
- the rise and fall of governments in economic policy
- Adam Smith's impact on economics
- the revolution triggered by John Maynard Keynes
- the rediscovery of the 'market' in economic policy.

Introduction

The increased power of transnational corporations has crept up on national governments. There has been no sinister plot – instead not enough attention was being paid by politicians to the economic transformation of politics. The transformation has been one of the most significant in the last century or so. This chapter traces the rise of corporate power.

Education of a president

In February 1991 President George Bush won the Gulf War and became one of the most popular presidents in US history. There was a general feeling that he would be easily re-elected in the November 1992 election. However, Governor Bill Clinton thought that he could win the election by concentrating on the declining state of the economy. The election campaign slogan was: 'It's the economy stupid.' There are various explanations for the Clinton victory and one of them was his attention to the economy. Thus, he arrived in the White House well informed on the US economy. Or was he?

He was introduced to the real power of corporations – and his own limited power – during an economic briefing by economist Alan Blinder soon after his victory. Clinton had promised to 'grow the economy' and create more and better jobs. Blinder cautioned that this policy could add to the government's deficit. The Reagan and Bush administrations had spent the previous decade adding to that deficit. The Clinton administration could have problems raising still more money from the financial market (the 'bond market') through the sale of government bonds and with the Federal Reserve (headed by Alan Greenspan).

At the president-elect's end of the table, Clinton's face turned red with anger and disbelief: 'You mean to tell me that the success of the programme and my re-election hinges on the Federal Reserve and a bunch of f***ing bond traders?' he responded in a half-whisper. Nods of agreement came from his end of the table. Clinton, it seemed to Blinder, perceived at this moment how much his fate was passing into the hands of the unelected Alan Greenspan and the bond market.

President Clinton did not know as much about economics as he thought. In particular, while governments may come to office, they may not necessarily come to *power*. On the contrary, transnational corporations are now the main global economic force. They have a great deal of influence on governments.

They – rather than national governments – set the pace of economic change. The anti-globalization demonstrators are right to identify the problems that some corporations create, such as the exploitation of labour (including child labour), manipulating national taxation regimes to avoid paying tax and environmental destruction.

They can also play havoc with foreign currency transactions. For example, American banker, Andy Krieger, was one of the legends of the foreign currency speculators in the late 1980s when he speculated on the New Zealand dollar ('Kiwi'). On one occasion he sold the equivalent of the entire money supply of New Zealand. There was nothing personal in this; he had nothing against New Zealand (about whom he knew little). It was simply his job to make money.

Ironically, New Zealand finance officials privately told him later that they did not mind his driving down the price of the Kiwi because it would make exports cheaper and spur economic growth. This 25-year-old could do in minutes what the government had not been able to do – drive down the Kiwi's value and force economic change on a lethargic business community. For a few years, New Zealand then had a booming economy.

In 1995, for the first time, the majority of the world's 100 largest economies were not states but transnational corporations. The annual income of Microsoft's Bill Gates is greater than the gross national product of many poor states.

The rise and fall of governments in economic policy

In economic terms alone, the twentieth century saw the rise and fall of national governments. A century ago, a British citizen, for example, would not have expected much from the British government by way of economic assistance. There was no welfare state or government assistance for higher or technical education. But also, of course, tax rates were low and taxes came mainly from charges on imports. Half a century later, the government was steering the economy. Now the government has again withdrawn from that primary role – and the vacuum has been filled by transnational corporations.

Merchant power

Around the fifteenth century, local rulers started to rebel against the Church's influence. This was more a matter of creating a sense of national identity rather than seeking greater wealth. Rulers wanted to run their own affairs.

Under the 1648 Westphalian system, national governments may have shrugged off much of the Church's influence but they liked the Church's power. Thus they took the power for themselves. But the monarchs also had to share their power and they formed alliances with the growing merchant class. The name for this trend was 'mercantilism'.

The merchants supplied the monarchs with financial support. From the monarchs, the merchants got an end to feudal wars and there was the consolidation of the state to provide law and order. The monarch also provided special trading privileges (via royal charters) and the monarchs used their defence forces to defend the economic activities of the merchants.

The theory of mercantilism was that the wealth of the country depended on its possession of precious metals and so the government had to maximize domestic trade, obtain a foreign trade surplus, foster national commercial interests and create a merchant marine fleet. Mercantilism partly initiated the Europeanization of the globe as explorers went to other continents in search of precious metals.

However, mercantilism was also very restrictive for both merchants and ordinary people. It relied on a close relationship between monarchs and merchants – and merchants were often impatient with the speed at which monarchs were willing to change policy. It also represented a form of monopoly power that may not have been in the interests of the ordinary person.

The creation of 'limited corporations' facilitated the growth of merchant power. People had been getting together for centuries to work jointly on projects but the partnership lasted only as long as those particular people lived or for how long it took to bring the project to fruition. The profit (if any) was split and the organization disappeared.

The limited corporation gave a corporation an unlimited life. The liabilities of the members of the corporation were limited only to the amount of money contributed by the partners (notably through shares). The shares could be handed on to a person's descendants or they could be sold (stock exchanges began in the eighteenth century). The corporation itself outlived the death of its original founders. It was recognized in law as having its own personality and standing and it was able to undertake a wide range of economic activities.

Adam Smith and the role of the market

Markets over merchants

The rise of modern capitalism began in 1776, with the publication of Adam Smith's *The Wealth of Nations*. The market – rather than government involvement – should set the pace for economic activities. Adam Smith's book has been in print for over two centuries. Few other non-fiction books can claim such a record.

Smith was critical of merchant power. He wrote in reaction to the era of government control over the British economy. Medieval society had a complex system of rules defining the rights and duties of individuals in their overall social existence and particularly in the economic sphere. The mercantile system was heavily regulated – by either the state directly or through the delegated authority of guilds and privileged companies. This system was breaking down when Smith wrote his book. There were new forms of production, such as the steam engine, the power loom and spinning Jenny, which required a more flexible social and economic (and eventually political) framework for their success.

Smith was an opponent of mercantilism. He was an advocate of the policy of *laissez faire*, both nationally and internationally. He advocated the free market, competition (which would always assert itself provided monopolistic positions were not supported by the state) and unimpeded international commerce. The British government eventually reduced its involvement in economic activities.

Smith was an advocate of free trade and did not support ideas of national self-sufficiency. He argued that countries should specialize in what they were best at doing. International free trade would not only benefit consumers but also reduce the risk of war because trade would bring countries together. A contemporary example of Smith's idea about the international division of labour is that Australia should specialize in such activities as mining, tourism and farming, while Japan (which has no minerals and little agricultural area) should specialize in, say, car manufacturing and computers.

Smith placed emphasis on leaving individuals free to pursue their own interests. Self-interest (or selfishness) guides people, as though by the influence of an 'invisible hand', so that they – and society – get richer. The private vice of selfishness became a public virtue.

Smith's views on economics gradually merged with the prevailing liberal political views so the UK and the US acquired a new political ideology. The government had no role in regulating the economy. Its role was to provide conditions that permitted maximum economic and political freedom, such as maintaining law and order at home and maintaining free trade overseas.

Economic depressions (such as that of the 1890s) were not seen as a government responsibility. Like bad weather, they were something to be tolerated in the expectation that they would pass eventually.

With the acceptance of Adam Smith's ideas by western governments and the reliance on the market, a new era emerged. Governments – unlike the thinking of the thousand years of Church influence – now accepted that they had little role to play in economic activities.

Adam Smith and transnational corporations

Adam Smith was the great champion of the market system and free trade but he would probably have been a critic of transnational corporations. Smith could not foresee the rise of corporations or what they could do to the market system. Had he known, given his criticism of monopolies, he would probably have warned us of the consequences.

An example of how corporations can erode the market system is the decline of 'consumer sovereignty'. The theory is that the consumer is supreme and can dictate what the market should produce: demand determines supply. However, as the next chapter will show, corporations now spend a great deal of money in manipulating consumer taste. Thus, supply often determines demand. A corporation, having spent a great deal of money in developing a new product, cannot afford not to have consumers buy it.

The role of marketing is to make sure that consumers know about all the new products and services. The Sony Walkman, for example, was not created by consumer demand; consumers did not know they needed one. It was invented first and then demand was generated to ensure that people bought them. The iPod is another such example.

John Maynard Keynes and the role of government

The Keynesian revolution

The Great Depression of the 1930s was worse than its predecessors of the 1840s and 1890s. The essence of the Keynesian revolution was to draw governments further back into economic activities.

The British economist John Maynard Keynes (1883–1946) transformed economics. He argued that the market system could not be left to solve all economic problems and so the government had to assume some responsibility for economic management. The idea that the economy should be managed to secure objectives like full employment, stable prices, a healthy balance of payments, a satisfactory growth rate and so on would have struck the Victorians as incomprehensible. Under Smith's advice, goods and capital were left free to flow where they would. The government raised taxes to pay for its own upkeep, including defence and law and order, but not to influence the volume of economic activity. Governments made no attempt to prevent unemployment – that was not their job.

Keynes challenged the thinking of economists such as Adam Smith. The latter saw full employment of those who want to work as an automatic fact of life. If a trader brought cabbages to market, he was bound to sell the whole batch – provided he was prepared to lower his price sufficiently. And what was true of cabbages was also true of labour. All workers who wanted jobs would find one – so long as wages were flexible. It was only when unions or governments tried to keep wages artificially high that employers could not afford to employ everyone looking for work. Governments should confine themselves to good housekeeping – balancing their budgets – and leave the economy alone to run smoothly along its own path.

'Supply creates its own demand.' This was the claim of Jean Baptiste Say (a nineteenth-century French economist and popularizer of Adam Smith). Say's law said that there could be no long-term unemployment because workers would spend their wages on purchasing goods being made by other workers. Indeed, the only limit was the amount of resources and number of employable workers available. The Great Depression disproved Say's law.

Keynes saw things very differently. For him, the number of workers employed depended on the ability of companies to sell the goods they produced. The key factor was the level of spending. In other words, Say got the order wrong: demand will create its own supply. Expenditure creates its own income.

Cut wages and government expenditure (as his contemporaries in the Great Depression in the 1930s advocated) and still more people would be put out of work as goods remained unsold through a lack of purchasing power. Keynes claimed that full employment, far from being the norm, was an extremely unlikely result of unregulated capitalism. There was no guarantee that total spending would add up to just the amount needed to buy all that could be produced with full employment. If it were insufficient, producers would find that they had unsold stocks and would lay off workers who, in turn, would have less to spend on other goods.

Unemployment could only be avoided if the government stepped in to make good any shortfall in spending. It could try to increase private spending by measures like tax cuts or lower interest rates. Or it could put more money into circulation by public works programmes, such as building houses or roads (even though this would mean that the government ran a budget deficit).

Keynes argued, then, the economy was not self-regulating. This was a different perception of the economy from that of Smith and Say. Left to itself, as the 1930s showed, the economy could not be guaranteed to flourish.

The Keynesian revolution's main message was that full employment could only be achieved when the government was prepared to intervene – perhaps drastically and continuously – in the free working of the economy. To many people in the 1930s, observing the situation in Stalin's Russia and Hitler's Germany, this proposition was alarming. Keynes himself believed in a capitalist rather than a socialist society. Nevertheless, Keynesian theory did demand a revolutionary change in the relationship between the government and the economy.

Adam Smith himself was not opposed to public works programmes (such as building roads). Moreover, such programmes had been carried out in medieval Europe. The difference with the Keynesian revolution was the extent of the public works programmes (and other government involvement in the economy) and the encouragement to governments to have temporary budget deficits as a by-product of these stimulation measures.

Keynes offered hope. Depressions were not like plagues and famines, after all. They were not meant simply to be endured. Governments were able to stop them and should acknowledge that they had the responsibility to do so.

The revolution winds down

The Keynesian revolution worked. That seemed to be the good news of the immediate post-1945 decades, when western governments put Keynes's ideas into operation. The period from 1945 to the late 1960s saw the virtual elimination of large-scale unemployment in the western economies. Governments accepted responsibility for achieving full employment and used their budgetary weapons to top up demand to the necessary level. The fears of another great depression evaporated. The world's greatest consumer binge took place. Never before had so many people had so much wealth to buy so many goods.

Some people still argued that the Keynesian revolution was doomed to fail. The increased state intervention required by Keynesian policies would destroy the efficient patterns of resource allocation and eventually undermine incentives to private enterprise. The warnings were ignored at the time. Life seemed too good to pay attention to such warnings.

However, high unemployment rates returned to the western world in the mid-1970s. The 1973 Middle East War and the Arab decision to increase the price of oil contributed to the recession. The new way of western economic life, which was born in 1945, died queuing for petrol at a service station in October 1973.

The Keynesian revolution had apparently run out of steam. A new phrase was coined to describe the economic malaise: 'stagflation', a combination of stagnation and inflation. In the

1950s and 1960s, many countries were willing to go into debt because they accepted the Keynesian argument that the debt would be financed automatically by economic growth. But this argument assumed that interest rates would remain lower than economic growth rates. In the 1970s, continuous deficit financing meant an increase in interest rates above economic growth rates.

Additionally, the nature of unemployment itself changed. While Keynesian theory provided the basis for a policy of removing unemployment, it did not explain why unemployment should be present in the first place. For Keynes, the challenge was to resolve the problem of both workers and machines being unemployed. He saw that the missing element needed to get them back into production was spending. But today's unemployment increasingly affects just the workers. Increased government spending does not necessarily create more jobs. On the contrary, computerized technology means that production can be expanded with far fewer workers. Pumping more purchasing power into the economy no longer automatically creates more employment for humans.

Technology does not necessarily just kill employment: it also rearranges some employment opportunities. Workers are needed to look after the new technology (such as the computer industry technicians and the computer shopping outlets). Also, because there is more output for less work, increased productivity could mean that workers have more time for leisure (such as greater holiday time) and so create new service industry jobs. Also, the manufacturing jobs lost in developed countries are transferred to developing countries. All these variables make it difficult for a national government to devise national employment strategies.

Keynes and transnational corporations

The Keynesian revolution was eroded partly because national governments no longer have full national control over their economies. Keynes died just before the birth of the modern era of transnational corporations. It is not possible to assess how he would have factored that corporate power into his economic thinking. His admirers believe that had he lived he would have been equally talented in coping with the problems of transnational corporations.

Governments in developed countries cannot now generate full employment due to global labour competition. There has been a transfer of jobs from developed to developing countries, where labour costs are low and environmental protection legislation is weak. Many of the jobs lost in developed countries will never return. Traditional jobs (especially in manufacturing) have gone permanently to low-cost developing countries.

This creates a race to the bottom. Different countries compete for foreign investment, thereby forcing down labour conditions and standards. This 'downward harmonization' is the pressure to reduce wages to the levels of those in low-wage countries because of the greater capacity of both companies and investments to move around the world. This is creating a new economic grouping in developed countries: the 'working poor'. These are people with jobs but very low-paid ones.

Reluctance to pay tax

Keynes wrote on the assumption that governments would be able to raise enough money to pay for their programmes. Governments are finding it harder to raise money. They could not afford the Keynesian programmes even if they had the political will to implement them.

Corporate taxes have dropped dramatically in recent decades. This change was based on the justification that corporate taxes are inevitably passed through to customers, workers or employees. The percentage of total taxes paid by corporations is far lower than in the Keynesian era. This helps explain the gap between the rich and poor in a developed country. Dividends from shares go overwhelmingly to the already rich to make them even richer.

At the international level, the taxation system becomes even more complicated because of 'transfer pricing'. Every international transaction involves at least two tax jurisdictions. Transfer pricing refers to the accounting within a corporation of charging different costs for the supply of goods or services to another part of the corporation based in another country. Therefore, the tax jurisdictions are played off against each other. Ideally, from a corporation's point of view, the figures will show a 'loss' in a country with a high rate of tax and a 'profit' in one with a low rate. As with the downward harmonization of wage levels, so there is a downward harmonization of taxation: any government promising to dramatically increase company taxation would be threatened by an exodus of corporations.

Tax havens

Transnational corporations have to be registered somewhere – but they do not need to be registered in the countries where they make most of their money. Business has become global yet the law has remained to a large extent confined to national boundaries.

Tax havens are very important for the movement of money, both for illegal reasons (such as hiding the proceeds of drug selling) and for tax minimization purposes.

National governments do not have much influence, though. The corporations can afford to pay higher salaries and so attract smarter lawyers and accountants than the government regulatory bodies. It is a very unequal struggle.

The market returns

New right 'economic rationalism'

The Keynesian revolution did not convert everyone. Right from the outset, in the 1930s, Keynes had his critics. For example, Friedrich von Hayek (1899–1992) saw a largely unregulated market economy as a safeguard of personal liberty. Thus, Hayek opposed Keynesian governmental interventionism. Nature had to take its course. Depressions were a natural part of economic life and had to be prepared for, tolerated and survived.

The new right – 'economic rationalism' – waited in the wings for the Keynesian theory to run into problems. The swing from Keynesian to new right/economic rationalism began in the late 1970s and was evident by the early 1980s in the policies of the western governments. As if to emphasize the irrelevance of party labels, new right policies were introduced by conservative governments in the US and UK and by Labour governments in Australia and New Zealand. This makes national elections merely a form of ritual. There were different party labels but the scriptwriters were the same.

New right/economic rationalism gained that prominence because there was a policy vacuum. The oil shocks, stagflation and the return to unemployment of the 1970s created a genuine crisis within the old social welfare–Keynesian consensus that had dominated post-war politics.

Corporations fill the vacuum

Ironically, if economic rationalism filled the vacuum of the failure of the Keynesian revolution by reducing the role of government, so transnational corporations have filled the vacuum caused by the reduction of government intervention in the economy. This reduction is a result of privatization and deregulation.

Privatization is the selling of government assets, enterprises and services to private entrepreneurs, in the expectation that they can run them more efficiently. The theory is that government ownership encourages relative inefficiency in two main ways. First, public enterprises are immune from the threat of takeover and so can avoid the discipline of the financial markets. Second, they are more vulnerable than their private counterparts to political and industrial pressure. Privatization may lead to increased efficiency but it also can mean less national government control over its industry if the shares are bought by foreigners.

Deregulation in popular language is abolishing 'red tape'. The assumption is that individuals and corporations could be more enterprising and productive if only they were freer to do so.

The more deregulation there is, the more a country is exposed to influences from outside that country. Thus, governments throughout the 1980s did not so much have national sovereignty stolen from them (such as by transnational corporations) as they gave that national sovereignty away through deregulation. Having discarded it, they will not be able to get it back.

Popular capitalism

The Cold War is over – and capitalism won it. But, ironically, capitalism has had a poor image in most capitalist countries, with traditional memories of greedy old bosses exploiting the poor and downtrodden workers. Therefore, while NATO was busy combating the Soviet Union overseas, its leaders such as Margaret Thatcher were also busy with their own domestic charm offensive to win over their citizens to the joys of capitalism.

In the early 1950s, the New York Stock Exchange started a 'people's capitalism' programme, with the then very ambitious aim of making the great majority of American wage earners become the owners of companies via shares. This was – hard as it may seem now to imagine – a major task because most Americans did not trust the wealthy élite on Wall Street with their own money. Older Americans remembered losing money in the Wall Street crash and the Great Depression in the 1930s. They had had their fingers burnt once. Keeping money in the bank may be boring but it was seen as a safer option.

However, through their pension funds, the workers soon became the largest holders of corporate stocks in the US. The popular capitalism movement wanted to take that pension fund development a step further by encouraging direct shareholder participation by the workers. Popular capitalism has had four purposes.

- It provided the moral basis for waging the Cold War against communism. It showed that capitalism was on the moral high ground because it had so much popular support. This was not an ideology that was forced on the masses (as, for example, Lenin, Chairman Mao and Castro had done with their revolutions in Russia, China and Cuba).

- It has given the workers a stake in their economy. It is no longer 'us versus them'. They now have a direct investment in the economy via their shares and personal superannuation schemes. They had become shareholders and capitalists.

- It has been the mechanism by which governments have found some of the customers for their privatization of government assets. Instead of relying solely on institutional investors for funds, governments have used popular capitalism to gain access to the pockets of their citizens. (A Keynesian would point out that the citizens were buying what they had already owned via government control!)

- Finally, it was designed to break the back of trade unionism. Conservative western leaders have argued that trade unions are a relic of the past, an obstacle in the current era and an irrelevancy for the future. Whether such a damning assessment is accurate is another matter. But Mrs Thatcher was certainly successful: there are now more shareholders in the UK than there are members of trade unions.

Popular capitalism has created a social and economic revolution. Share ownership used to be seen as simply an élite activity. The rich invested in shares, while the poor gambled on dogs and horses. Both could end up losing money, of course, but shares are usually a safer way of making money. Poorer people thought that share ownership was socially not for them – and their union friends would oppose such an activity because of its perceived siding with the bosses. That psychological barrier has been broken and a social revolution is underway. Younger people are joining in share ownership with none of the reservations of their parents. They are also far less likely to join a union.

This is also an economic revolution because it means that more money is going directly into shares and other forms of investment. This helps to explain the expansion in the stock exchange. More employees are also becoming shareholders in their own companies: they now have a financial incentive not to go on strike.

To conclude, the 'workers' are now 'capitalists'. They have been reinvented via their consuming passion.

Conclusion

This chapter has traced the evolution of the power of corporations. Few could have guessed a century ago that corporations would become as powerful as they are today, but there is overall widespread support for corporations because they produce what people want to buy.

Questions

1 How have you become aware of the power of transnational corporations?
2 Do you think that corporations having so much power is a good thing or a bad one?
3 Could you imagine what the world would be like without them?
4 Do you think that national governments should go back to controlling economic activities?

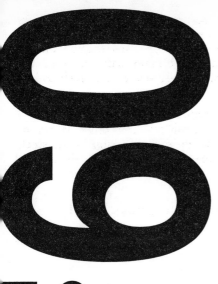

09

consuming passions

This chapter will cover:
- the evolution of humans from subjects to citizens and now consumers
- consumerism as a new idea
- the situation in developing countries
- the rise of free trade
- health implications of consumerism.

Introduction

Transnational corporations are on the leading edge of economic change and the consumer revolution. The corporation is one of the greatest forces for change in our time.

The modern corporation's capacity to influence governments is different from that of a century and a half ago, when the Industrial Revolution was charging ahead in the UK. The government was often reluctant about helping new industrial companies because it wanted to retain the support of conservative rural interests. The engineering genius Isambard Kingdom Brunel (after whom a British university was later named) was one of the main figures in developing the British railway system. Each major railway project required an act of parliament and each was only achieved after a long struggle. Now governments are far more accommodating to the interests of the corporations. And the consumers are grateful.

Consumerism as a new idea

People were not 'born to shop'

There is no evidence that consumerism is a part of human nature. Much of the west had no genuine tradition of heavy consumption before the beginning of the twentieth century, probably not until the 1940s. People in developed countries (and increasingly in developing countries) now live in a world dominated by the paradigm of personal gain and consumerism. But it has not always been like this.

To get a sense of context, it is important to note that consumerism is contrary to most (if not all) of the world's major religions. These emphasize in various ways a life that is inwardly rich and outwardly simple.

An early modern economist of the seventeenth century, Sir William Petty, warned that the promise of gain may not be enough to tempt people to work. The Industrial Revolution's factory system was getting underway in the UK. But a raw working force, unused to wage work, uncomfortable in factory life, unschooled to the idea of an ever rising standard of living, will not work harder if wages rise; it will simply take more time off. People will work simply to get enough for the basic necessities that week and then spend the rest of the time relaxing, meeting relatives or attending religious activities.

Stanley Jevons was another early economist and author of one of the first economics textbooks, *The Theory of Political Economy*. In 1857 he was watching a cricket match between Sydney and Melbourne, which had attracted a large crowd of people and so disrupted the business life of Sydney. He noted that people were willing to go without money in the interests of watching sport.

For people coming from a pre-industrial culture, there was more to life than just working for money. For example, family obligations, entertainment and religious ceremonies may have been far more important to them. This problem dogged the European imperialists as they set sail to conquer indigenous peoples in other lands. The indigenous peoples did not have the same high regard for personal wealth. Indeed, they may not even have had much interest in money as such. A Dutch trading ship crashed against the Western Australian coast in the seventeenth century. Its treasure of gold and silver coins stayed on the beach for three centuries because the local indigenous peoples had no use for them.

Rise of consumerism

Consumerism has provided a modern reason for living. The rise of industrial society has meant that, with the consequent decline of religious life and traditional ways of living, industrial societies have had little to offer by way of a purpose in life other than to be materially successful. Consumption has become the new idol and money is the measure of all things: 'I am rich because I work hard; I deserve to be admired by society.' To give purpose to living, people need some retail therapy by visiting their local cathedral of consumerism.

The basic message of consumerism is the importance of spending money as a way of solving your problems. The corporations, especially those in media and advertising, exploit the very appetites (lust, greed, pride, jealousy, anger, loafing and indulgence) that Christians in an earlier age called 'deadly sins'. They are now regarded as 'virtues'.

In the middle of the twentieth century John Maynard Keynes encouraged economists to apply psychology to their profession. Factors such as envy and self-esteem were as important in determining consumer spending habits as income and inflation. Keynes was writing in reaction to the previous economists who urged people to save. They had adopted a Victorian puritanism based on self-denial and hard work. Thrift (or saving) – and not consumption – was the engine of the Victorian economy. It established the moral virtue of capitalism and provided the upper level of the working class with its main hope of improvement. These economists were imbued with the worldview of people like the Methodist John Wesley who recommended to his followers: 'Gain as much as you can, give [to charity] as much as you can, and save as much as you can.'

But for Keynes it was spending ('demand') that would drive economic growth much faster. Therefore there should be more encouragement to spend, such as by governments providing public works programmes to put money into circulation so that people could kick-start economic growth by having some money to spend. Keynes wanted the government to end unemployment (which his predecessors regarded as something inevitable and about which governments could do little) and this could only be achieved through increased expenditure, by government, companies and individuals.

Spending became a national duty.

Sophisticated marketing

If you want to do well sell people what they need; if you want to get rich sell people what they want. People may have limited needs but they have unlimited wants. A person actually needs very little to survive – as most of human history has shown – but there is an unlimited number of wants to be cultivated. Having acquired the new product or service they then wonder how they managed to exist without it previously. Fax machines at home, the internet and mobile phones are all current examples.

'Sell the sizzle and not the sausage.' In other words, the marketing is based on what the product or service can do for the consumer and not the actual product or service itself. If a company is marketing drilling bits, it is not selling a tool but holes in the wood or wall.

Cigarette advertisements do not sell cigarettes but a lifestyle. 'Marlboro Country' symbolizes an escape to freedom where nobody can tell you what to do. The horse-rider projects an image of maturity, toughness and independence – seen as aspirations of the young and restless. 'Peter Stuyvesant' offered an 'international passport to smoking pleasure' in sophisticated exotic locations. A person could not afford the air ticket and so the next best thing was to buy the cigarettes.

By the same token, an advertising campaign could also kill a brand. In the 1960s, there was a British advertising campaign for 'Strand' cigarettes. This showed a man walking alone down London's empty rainy, wind-swept Strand and then he lit up a 'Strand' cigarette: 'You're never alone with a Strand.' Unfortunately, nobody wanted to display their empty life to their tobacconist by buying a brand that suggested that they had no friends. The brand was withdrawn very quickly.

However, a current success story in eastern Europe is the 'Go West' brand. For east Europeans who cannot afford to go to western Europe or the US, the next best thing is evidently to buy a packet of cigarettes.

Corporations conduct sophisticated surveys of consumer behaviour. For example, stores may have good marketing strategies but they do not give enough attention to tactics, such as junk food on high shelves out of the reach of children, hearing-aid batteries on bottom shelves where older people cannot bend over to get at them. Stores should provide plenty of baskets because people will buy more goods on impulse when they have a convenient way to carry them. Aisles should be wide enough to avoid shoppers who fear getting jostled from behind. Chairs should be provided for menfolk to sit around and talk while their wives go off shopping in the store.

Music makes the retail world go around and affects shop behaviour. Music that fits a shop's demographics may well tempt the listener to linger longer and so make more purchases. Classical music implies 'up market' (although contemporary jazz is also acceptable for that demographic). Increasing the tempo of music in restaurants speeds up the turnover of diners in busy periods, while during quiet times (where restaurateurs want some people in the place – customers do not like to enter an empty place), slower paced, quieter music can encourage diners to stay longer and order another coffee.

'Product placement' is where a producer has an arrangement for its product to be used in a television programme or movie in such a subtle way that a viewer may not consciously grasp the advertisement. The 2002 James Bond movie, *Die Another Day*, was the biggest ever in terms of advertising and movie tie-ins (estimated at about US$120 million). As examples, Ford provided several Aston Martins for Bond and he drank Bollinger champagne.

The internet is opening up many new marketing opportunities. Thousands of corporations have developed websites on the internet where 'visitors' can register to get more information. In return, visitors often provide information about themselves (name, address, demographic profile). Improved software means that corporations can write directly to the person ('Dear Mary') on an individual basis, rather than on a general one ('Dear customer'). 'Customer relationship marketing' means that a customer's purchasing record can be tracked so that a message can be sent to a customer noting that they bought, say, one book by a particular author and so would they like to buy the new one? This avoids accusations of unsolicited bulk e-mailings. Email, like the telephone, works best on a one-to-one basis.

A constant concern of television stations is to produce programmes that will attract viewers. Higher rating programmes will attract advertisers who will pay more for their commercials to be broadcast. Programmes that do not rate well will not attract much advertising revenue and so they will not last long on television. This helps explain why television companies – especially commercial ones – have to produce superficial and entertaining news programmes: they have to attract viewers or else they will not get the advertising revenue.

Advertising is the vehicle by which a television company (or radio station or newspaper) sells an audience to a manufacturer. The manufacturer only wants to advertise its products when it knows there that there will be people watching or listening. Thus the so-called 'soapie' television series, such as *The Days of Our Lives*, are screened when manufacturers assume that homemakers (mainly women) are at home and watching television, and so that is good time to advertise detergents. Products for children get advertised during the television programmes directed at children. Children in advertising terms are 'skippies': school-aged kids with purchasing power.

Even news programmes are advertised like detergents: they need to get the viewers to get the advertising revenue. Each of the networks presents its newsreaders as the 'brand image' of its news service in two ways: on each channel, the introduction to its major evening news programme is built around the newsreaders, not the news; and each channel's promotions for its news service concerns the (alleged) personalities of its newsreaders, not the content or quality of its news.

However, advertisements can be a health hazard. Advertising is designed to make people feel dissatisfied. No matter how attractive your wife may be, she will become even more attractive by purchasing new cosmetics. No matter how handsome your husband is, he will become even more handsome by purchasing a different aftershave or a new car.

To conclude, there is now even a medical term for the extreme spender-benders: 'compulsive shopping disorder' (CSD). Naturally, there is a pill for CSD: Luvox. It is a selective serotonin reuptake inhibitor (SSRI) that acts on a compulsive shopper's underlying depression by ensuring sustained levels in the brain of the feel-good agent serotonin. It is a sister of Prozac. Luvox was launched in 1996 and is used in 80 countries by 28 million people to restrain their spending habits.

The situation in developing countries

Thanks to the power of transnational corporations, the process is global. For example, there is the impact of television on village life. Most people in a village may not have visited the major cities of their own country but are now transported each day to such locations as Britain's *Coronation Street*, US *Dallas* or Australia's *Sylvania Waters*.

They congregate together in the communal hut that contains a television. The village may have no water or sewerage system but it does have a television set. Now the children want Swiss chocolate, New Zealand milk and beverages such as Coca-Cola and Pepsi. Adults are not immune either. The women crave 'energy-saving, wonderful and marvellous' Japanese electric rice cookers, fashionable clothes and makeup. The men hanker after stereos, expensive trousers and a car. The irony is that most villagers cannot afford to have one square a meal a day and lack the basic facilities taken for granted in the towns. The children may spend more time in front of the village television than with their schoolbooks.

This is an example of the 'revolution of rising expectations'. Not too long ago, people in developing countries – including western Europe prior to the second-wave Industrial Revolution – spent almost all their lives in one location. There were few opportunities for long-distance travel. They were poor and assumed that others (except for the rulers in their castles and manor houses) were equally poor. Nowadays the poor know they are poor because the television tells them so. They expect their governments to do something about it.

Governments in developing countries have a tougher time handling development than did the first world governments. The creation of a developed country does not occur overnight, nor is it a pleasant process because it may entail the dislocation of people (such as the movement of people from small rural holdings into urban factories). This also happened during the UK's Industrial Revolution.

However, the UK had two advantages over a developing world country today: it had a much longer time to make the turbulent transition and its citizens were not demanding consumer goods (so that money went into factories, shipping, roads, railways and canals, rather than television sets). Countries in the developing world are having to leap into the Industrial Revolution, propelled by an impatient population.

This is one of the reasons for the rapid expansion of transnational corporations in the developing world: the corporations are seen as the best way to modernize a country. They did not have to force their way in; they have been invited in by anxious governments who think that they create rapid economic growth better than the government can.

The rise of free trade

World trade is growing

The rise of transnational corporations has been facilitated by the policy of free trade. This is now the dominant economic policy of most governments. World trade is growing more quickly than national economies. In other words, countries are doing more trade with each other as the years go by – and are doing so at a faster rate than their own national economy is growing. Free trade has been hailed as one of the reasons for this era's greatest amount of economic growth in world history. Never before have so many people made so much money in so little time.

But other people are not so sure. The riots in Seattle in December 1999 and more recently in other locations across the globe are a sign that many politicians and NGOs in the global justice movement have doubts about the development of free trade.

The current world trade system goes back to the end of World War II in 1945. The diplomats who designed the UN wanted to avoid another depression (which they argued had given rise to Hitler). This meant the encouragement of free trade. The argument was that protectionism in the 1930s had made the depression worse. The diplomats proposed the creation of an International Trade Organization (ITO) to regulate trade. The United States Congress opposed the ITO because it thought that the ITO would hinder its own global economic expansion and so the idea lapsed.

As a temporary measure, the General Agreement on Tariffs and Trade (GATT) was negotiated in 1947. By this time, the Cold War was underway and all the Soviet bloc countries were boycotting the UN's economic activities. (Only with the end of the Cold War, did Russia and the eastern European countries become involved in these activities.) GATT therefore consisted of the rich western developed countries and pro-western developing world countries. GATT members were responsible for about 90 per cent of world trade.

Membership of GATT was not automatic. Countries had to negotiate to join. They had to agree to the principles of non-discrimination and reciprocity: there should be no special favourites or victims in the trading policies of member-countries. GATT member-countries should not give favours or harsh treatment to any other GATT member-country. If two GATT countries negotiated a special trading arrangement, then that had to be offered to all the other GATT member-countries.

GATT progressed by a series of 'rounds' of negotiations, with each round resulting in some tariffs being reduced. The Uruguay round began in 1986 involving 111 countries and taking seven years to complete. The Uruguay round was the most ambitious round because it included items not previously addressed, such as banking and computer software. It also arranged that GATT should be replaced by the World Trade Organization (WTO). This has overseen the Uruguay treaty's implementation and the continued expansion of world trade.

The 1999 Seattle conference was supposed to initiate yet another 'round' of negotiations but it got disrupted by demonstrations and opposition from governments in developing countries. There has been little progress since then because the negotiations are stalemated. For example, some countries want the EU to reduce its agricultural subsidies. The largest single item in the EU's budget is the subsidy paid to farmers. The farmers are very efficient and they are growing a large amount of food. There are now too many farmers meeting the EU's food requirements, especially since cheaper food could be imported from developing countries. But what would the farmers do if they left the land? Where else could they work?

How 'free' is free trade?

Free trade is not necessarily 'free'. One of the most controversial examples of free trade in developed countries is the importation of cheap goods that undercut the price of domestically made goods. Critics of free trade are concerned that, first, about 250 million children across the world go to work each day – rather than to school. They work in appalling conditions and get only meagre payment. For example, a child in Indonesia will receive only a few cents for making sports shoes that sell for about US$100 in developed countries.

Second, other people work in slave labour or prison labour camps, particularly in China. The authorities have an incentive to exploit prison labour because they know that they can make money overseas from what is produced in prison.

Third, many cheap goods flood into the shops in the developed countries and their price undercuts locally made goods and so the local factories are being forced to close up. This means that there is a 'race to the bottom' as the labour costs of each developed country get reduced so as to compete with the costs of developing countries.

Finally, the collapse of the working class labour market means that angry unemployed workers turn to extremist, nationalist politicians who promise a break with the international trading system and have a return to the era of high tariffs. Blue collar workers lack confidence in the established political parties, which are seen as being too close to big business.

No smooth way to have a revolution

No country has yet found a smooth way to move into the industrial era. Charles Dickens wrote about the brutality of that nineteenth-century British era in his novels. If he were alive today, 'Oliver Twist' would be living in China or South Korea. According to developing countries, the developed countries have no right to lecture others on how they ought to develop because the industrialization process of the developed countries was itself so violent.

Furthermore, developing countries have few natural advantages where developed ones have many. As an example, most of the world's scientific research and development is carried out in developed countries. Therefore, the vast majority of humankind cannot compete on technological grounds. Cheap labour costs constitute one of the few advantages developing countries do possess. Inserting human rights conditions in contracts is a 'non-tariff barrier to trade'. In other words, the developed countries cannot – under WTO – use tariffs to keep out cheap goods from the developing nations and so they invent human rights conditions as another form of barrier to do just this.

Added to this, cheap goods are popular with consumers in developed countries. While there is some concern about loss of jobs (such as in the textile industries) most people in developed countries now enjoy being able to buy a larger range of goods than they could four decades ago. Poor people in Britain in the 1960s often had to buy second-hand clothes but now they can get cheap new ones made in China.

Finally, cheap labour costs do not last forever. As a country develops, so its labour costs also increase as the country develops a middle class. Forty years ago, western developed countries were worried about the import of cheap Japanese goods. As foreign money poured into Japan, so a middle class developed that did not want to work in factories. Salaries had to be increased to entice Japanese workers to work in factories. Eventually, costs became too high and so the Japanese factories were transferred to the (currently) cheap labour factories in southeast Asia, Pakistan and India. Eventually, labour costs will become too high there also and so factories will have to move on again.

Meanwhile, developing countries that do become richer also become a market for the goods and services from developed countries. As countries become richer, so they are able to afford more goods and services – and this is good news for the developed countries. Britain now benefits from Asian affluence because students from Asia come to Britain to study.

To sum up, there are no easy answers to this matter and there are competing viewpoints. What is commonly agreed, however, is that the pace of change, for good or ill, is being driven by transnational corporations.

Is the 'good life' killing us?

Challenge to public health

There is an irony in public health. On the one hand, there is considerable scope – thanks to medical technology breakthroughs – for people to live longer. And yet, on the other hand, the same society that has created the modern science is also eroding the physical and psychological capacity of people to survive.

Silent revolution

One of the twentieth century's great achievements was the dramatic increase in life expectancy in the developed western countries. Indeed, increased life expectancy is one of the indicators of a 'developed' country. During the last century, the average person received as much increased life expectancy as a person in the previous 5,000 years. Around 5,100 years ago people had a life expectancy of about 25 years; in 1900 it was around 50 and by 2000 it was 75 years. This helps explain the concern over old-age pensions. When the Germans invented the idea of an automatic government pension for a person reaching 65 just over a century ago, very few Germans lived that long and so this was actually rather a hollow promise. Now reaching 65 is common and this has created concern over the adequacy of pensions.

This progress has come about through advances in clean water and sanitation, medical science, building technology (very few people in a developed country will now die in a burning building where that used to be a relatively common cause of death) and the creation of safer workplaces. Additionally government departments took on these measures as a standard item of work. For example, a century ago (with the exception of reticulation of water and working conditions) very little was being done about these issues by government legislation. At the same time, these have become lucrative areas of practice for domestic law firms.

Underpinning this progress has been functional cooperation by international organizations, such as WHO and the International Labour Organization (ILO), which facilitated the creation of common government standards and the sharing of experiences across national boundaries.

Is the pace of life too fast?

Hurry sickness is encouraged by employers, promoted by advertisers and inculcated by television and the internet. Thus, people now 'multitask': children do homework and listen to music, adults drive and listen to educational audio tapes, they cook and watch television, they exercise and watch television and they drive and have telephone conversations at the same time. But are humans really up to this 'multi skilling'?

Tomorrow often arrives first in California. The 'road rage' trend was first noted there. Some impatient drivers on the Californian freeways shoot at cars ahead of them to speed them up. There is now a common bumper sticker: 'Don't shoot – I'll move over.' There have even been reports of helicopter shootings, as passengers become impatient with other helicopters getting to the heliports first.

There are various other forms of 'rage' initiated by people impatient with delays. Examples include 'telephone rage', as customers are kept waiting listening to music 'while your call is important to us' or are led through a complex telephone menu. There is 'aircraft rage' as customers are told their flights are delayed or they are 'caught between the moon and New York City' in a holding pattern waiting for the plane to land.

Meanwhile, the pace of change in business presses ahead. This is now a 24-hour world. The old agricultural idea of work in daylight and sleep at night is now redundant. A declining number of workers function Monday to Friday, nine to five. Service providers (such as big law firms) operate around the clock as do the global stock exchanges, with one coming onstream as another closes. Sydney is a favourite location for foreign businesses because computer upgrades and repairs can be done in the European 'downtime'. Mobile phones mean that staff can be accessed at all time.

The workplace as a health hazard

The US Department of Labor has reported that murder has become the number one cause of death for women in the workplace and for men it is the third (after machine-related mishaps and driving accidents). The obvious reason for this are the ones often invoked to explain the problems of violence in American society as a whole – more guns. Taxi drivers, police officers, hotel clerks, security guards and shop assistants are most at risk, with robbery the most common motive for murder.

But there are also the increasingly harsh work environments and a contining wave of layoffs, which have made workers feel dispensable. People, understandably, get upset when there are no raises and then there are layoffs but the Chief Executive Officer (CEO) still gets a $50,000 bonus. This growing disparity plays into this atmosphere of violence. Making workers even more desperate is the prospect of finding positions with lower pay, fewer benefits and little job satisfaction.

Traditionally, it has been assumed that the victims were the blue-collar workers in the manufacturing industry. But it could be argued that the new victims of the hazardous workplace are white-collar workers, who are working harder in a 'sweatshop' situation in order to achieve greater corporate profits. These people are working longer hours than ever before (such as being vulnerable to being contacted via pagers and mobile telephones). The rise of the flexible workplace, with companies seeking to have jobs done 'just in time' has meant that people have to work flexible hours to meet these changing demands.

To sum up so far, there has been progress in combating contagious diseases and making buildings and workplaces safer, but new health problems have emerged.

Obesity as an international issue

One of WHO's main concerns is now to do with overeating. Some of the developing countries – which are normally seen as the ones with a lack of food – may also contain citizens who are overeating. While a whole group of causes of death has been reduced, a new group has emerged: 'lifestyle diseases'. Obesity is now a major problem underpinning such causes of death as heart attacks and strokes. Obesity cost the US 12 per cent of the national healthcare budget in the late 1990s (US$118 billion), more than double the US$47 billion attributable to smoking. About 3,000 people were killed on 11 September 2001 – 100 times that number (about 288,000) died in 2003 in the US from overeating. It is possible that obesity will be the most important reason why we cannot push the silent revolution even further.

The world has come a long way since 1954, when Ray Kroc, who made his living selling milkshake machines, began hearing stories about a very successful hamburger stand in San Bernardino, California. This popular restaurant had eight milkshake machines in operation (making 40 milkshakes simultaneously). He travelled to the place and met the owners Mac and Dick McDonald. He noted the quality of their food. He devised a scheme whereby the lessons of the manufacturing world in factories could be applied to the restaurant business. His methods included standard food production, uniform systems for food preparation and the creation of clean locations for consumers.

Perhaps the fast food industry has become too successful, too much part of the western way of life. In much the same way as lawyers have done well out of suing the tobacco industry for its unhealthy products, so they are now turning their attention to fast food. In the US, where there's smoke, there's a lawyer. Now they are examining the litigation opportunities in fast food. This coincides with various official reports on the risks of obesity, especially in children. Burger overload may become yet another symbol of how consumerism is killing us.

Causes of obesity

A major cause of obesity has been the progress made in the increased cultivation of food. More food is being grown than ever before and in all developed countries by fewer people. Thanks to improvements in technology (such as the chemical industry and fertilizers) food is now being grown on previously marginal or unproductive land. The 'green revolution' has done the same thing for rice in developing countries. Meanwhile, the increasing numbers of democracies is a good sign because there has never been a famine in a society with free media. At the prospect of a looming food shortage, food can be transferred across the country or across national boundaries.

Progress in free trade has also increased the supply of food. While much remains to be done to increase foreign access to the American and EU food markets, more food is now crossing national boundaries than ever before.

Another area of progress is in the overall quality of life. Thanks again to improvements in technology most people in developed countries no longer have to do the harsh physically intensive work that their forebears did. White-collar workers now outnumber blue collar in all developed countries. Very few young people will ever work on a farm, inside a factory or down a coalmine. This progress also applies to life at home, where so many gadgets have improved life – and now economic globalization and free trade are taking these improvements into the former developing countries.

Downsides to this progress

The disadvantage to all this progress is that it is contrary to what the human body is used to. Humans have evolved over the millennia to be able to cope with both feast and famine. Humans are designed to gain weight during the good times to tide them over the bad times of food shortages. This survival factor is built into the genes. Millennia ago, people who did not fatten up during a good harvest died out in the subsequent famines and so the present humans are the descendants of those survivors who could store fat. The problem is that we are now living in perpetual good times. There are few food shortages. Any looming shortage can be solved by importing food because of the improvements in free trade and international transportation. Meanwhile, some of the other forms of technological progress have created other problems. Modern technology is labour saving and so humans are not burning off the calories they used to when walking to school or work, working on farms, factories and down the coalmines and doing household chores. Harsh, labour-intensive daily work used to make people fit and lean (but also wore them out to an early death).

Passive overeating comes about through eating food that is too rich in fat and sugar. It may be that people are not necessarily eating more food in terms of absolute weight of food but what they are eating is overloaded with too much fat and sugar, particularly the case with 'fast food'. It is too energy dense for the type of work and lifestyle that they now have. Fast food would have made more sense a century ago when there were greater opportunities to burn off the extra calories.

Battle over obesity

WHO now has obesity on its agenda. This controversy is the opening salvo in what will be a long battle. The obesity issue is hardwired through to a number of staple items that will prolong its life on the agenda. On the one hand, for people who are concerned about globalization, obesity is a manifestation of the power of transnational corporations to influence public taste. For example, there are already calls for banning advertisements for fast food during children's television programmes. There will be attempts to ban sugary soft drinks from schools and to put health warnings on fast food and sugary soft drink containers. The currently (unsuccessful) American attempts at litigation against fast food companies will continue (and will be inspired by the eventually successful litigation against tobacco companies).

On the other hand, others will argue that transnational corporations are not to blame. No one is ever forced to eat fast food. People have freedom of choice. They should live more active lifestyles, watch less television and play fewer internet games. They should take more responsibility for their lives. They should have more self-control.

Meanwhile, others will complain that overeating distorts the planet's health priorities. Only about ten per cent of the world's health research goes into diseases that account for 90 per cent of the global disease burden (such as malaria and sleeping sickness). Most of the victims are too poor to buy medicines and so the pharmaceutical corporations do not bother to do the research. Meanwhile, the diseases of the wealthy attract the research because they are rich enough to pay for the medications and treatment.

Finally, the number of overweight people on the planet – more than one billion – now exceeds the number of malnourished people. Perhaps 'make poverty history' needs to be matched with 'making overeating history'.

Tobacco control

The campaign against one of today's biggest killers has taken a further step forward with the adoption of the 2005 UN treaty on tobacco control. About 13,500 people worldwide die from smoking-related diseases each day. Proof of international recognition of its importance has come from the speed with which the treaty has entered into force. It has become one of the most rapidly embraced UN treaties of all time. The treaty also says something generally about the progress made in international cooperation on a matter of common concern. Beneath all the bad news of conflict and brutality, there is some good news that countries are willing to work together on a common problem.

The WHO's Framework Convention on Tobacco Control (FCTC) was proposed in May 1995, it was adopted by the World Health Assembly in May 2003 and it entered into force on 27 February 2005. Its speedy ratification is partly a symbol of the growing concern about the impact of tobacco.

Tobacco consumption is the world's single leading preventable cause of death. It will prematurely end the lives of ten million people a year by 2020 if current trends are not reversed. Tobacco is the only legal product that causes the death of half of its regular users. This means that of the current 1.3 billion smokers, 650 million will die prematurely due to tobacco.

The irony is that the death is self-induced. This is a personal lifestyle decision; no one is forced to take up smoking. This is in stark contrast with the state of health elsewhere. As noted earlier, progress has been made in eradicating some other causes of death. Therefore, WHO is now adding to its list of campaigns the problems that people are bringing on themselves via tobacco. This is the first time that WHO has used international law to tackle tobacco. It is a signal, given the treaty's success, that WHO may eventually use this route for other measures to encourage greater international cooperation on promoting health.

The framework convention

The treaty is a 'framework convention'. It is not so much a detailed, comprehensive finished product in itself, as the basis for additional international measures. The technical term is the 'progressive development of international law' – the gradual expansion of international law to cover more and more issues that were previously only covered (if at all) by national laws. It therefore establishes the basis of a continuing diplomatic process gradually to restrict the consumption of tobacco. States that agree to be bound by this treaty will adopt other treaties ('additional protocols') covering specific issues, such as tobacco advertising, tobacco sponsorship of public activities, tobacco product regulation and the illicit trade in tobacco.

The treaty sees itself as part of the UN's human rights work in that each person has a right to health. It is therefore part of the UN's broadening of what constitutes human rights. The creators of the original 1948 formulation, in the Universal Declaration of Human Rights, would probably not have thought of opposing tobacco as a part of the human rights regime they were creating. Indeed, the declaration was probably drafted in a smoke-filled room as was common in those days. The international human rights regime is being both broadened and deepened. The regime is now being accepted by more and more countries and is also covering more aspects of human life.

The treaty does not prevent countries that have accepted it from adopting tobacco control measures stricter than those laid down in the treaty. It therefore aims to create the international harmonization of tobacco control measures that can be supplemented not only by later protocols to this treaty but also by stricter unilateral national standards. Parties to the treaty agree to educate their citizens about the dangers of tobacco. They also agree to adopt measures to reduce the demand for tobacco. This means, among other things, the use of taxation as a disincentive to buy tobacco, placing warnings on tobacco products and banning tobacco advertising promotion and sponsorship. There are also limitations on the sale of tobacco to children. Where possible, the ban on advertising, sponsorship and promotion is to be done within five years. Tobacco packaging must include health warnings covering at least 30 per cent of the packet.

The treaty also provides for international cooperation and information sharing on restricting the sale of tobacco. Parties agree to submit periodic reports to a conference of the parties on what they are doing. The treaty also creates a new international forum to handle the periodic reports: a conference of the parties (with WHO providing the secretariat). Periodic reports are a standard form of UN implementation (such as in many human rights treaties). Governments are now accustomed to this additional paperwork and its scrutiny by international organizations and NGOs.

Periodic reports are in themselves a small sign of how there is growing international cooperation and greater acceptance of international scrutiny of national policies. It is difficult to imagine governments as recently as the 1950s agreeing to submit reports to an international organization on what they were doing about a domestic matter. They would have seen it as an infringement of their national sovereignty.

They would have been even less enthusiastic about their reports being read by NGOs (indeed there would have been few such NGOs in existence at that time). Now governments are accustomed to submitting such reports, there are international organizations to receive them and there is a growing range of NGOs to analyse them. These are all beneficial signs of globalization.

Politics of tobacco control

Tobacco control is a controversial issue. It has been a battleground between some of the world's most powerful corporations and a growing band of health NGOs. There has been only gradual realization that tobacco is harmful. It has been part and parcel of global lifestyle for about four centuries and the anti-tobacco campaign has, at times, struggled to make any headway.

The politics of tobacco control has four points worth noting. First, there is the importance of research. The medical profession has made great progress generally in the development of research tools, sharing of information and implementation of best practice in all fields of health. The profession prides itself in attracting some of a country's most intelligent undergraduates and likes to think that it is intellectually more rigorous than many other disciplines. The research on the harmful impact of tobacco has gradually won acceptance that smoking is a danger to health. One of the earliest studies in the UK, for example, was done in 1951 – on the smoking habits of doctors themselves.

The fact that health professionals are among the smokers has been one of the tobacco industry's defences: if health professionals smoke, surely tobacco cannot be that much of a health hazard? Similarly, tobacco was often part of a military person's rations – if governments saw tobacco as part of the everyday life for a service person why was it seen as a health hazard? The industry also pointed out that there was no advertising at all in the former USSR and yet people still smoked and so bans on advertising in the west would have little effect. These arguments went back and forth. There is now general agreement that smoking is, indeed, a health hazard. But it has been a long campaign.

Second, NGOs have driven the campaign against tobacco. They have had a better record for consistency than politicians. They have kept on keeping on. They also work across national boundaries to pool information, such as the Network for Accountability of Tobacco Transnationals (NATT), which consists of 75 consumer, human rights, environmental, faith-based and corporate accountability NGOs in 50 countries. It was formed in 1999 to ensure a strong, unified voice for an effective tobacco control treaty.

In the US, NGOs decided some years ago that the tobacco corporations were too big to beat politically in Congress because the corporations are big donors to all the major political parties. The NGOs then started to work through the legal system. Other litigation was initiated by state governments with day-to-day responsibility for financing their health systems. They are concerned about the health costs of smoking. The lawsuits have often gone against the corporations with huge payouts. (Their success has prompted litigation on other matters, such as guns and, as we have seen, fast food.)

Third, tobacco corporations have had to look outside the west for new customers. The western markets are more difficult to penetrate because of the success of campaigns against smoking. The growth areas are particularly in the developing countries, especially Asia. These are also growing in the sense that 90 per cent of the babies born today are born in the developing countries. Western markets are largely stagnant but developing countries have accepted the treaty. They are willing to learn from the western debate over the health hazards of smoking and seek to curb it in their own jurisdictions. Even China, whose government is effectively the largest tobacco company in the world, has signed the treaty.

Finally, underpinning this struggle is the fact that the international community (national governments, international organizations and NGOs) are seeking to regulate transnational corporations. This may be a harbinger of other initiatives. One of NATT's founding members is the Infant Formula Action Coalition (INFACT). This began in 1977 with a campaign to restrict the marketing of infant formula milk. That campaign was eventually successful in devising regulations on how the milk could be marketed to mothers. Now there will be even greater attention to the international social responsibility of corporations.

To conclude, the campaigns against fast food and smoking have been partly driven by NGOs. It is now time to see the impact of NGOs on the Westphalian system.

Conclusion

The creation of the global consumer culture has been a surprising development. It has evolved suddenly, overriding many religious systems and the basic philosophy of communism. Indeed, some critics claim that it is a form of religion in its own right. It has captured the public imagination – and people apparently cannot get enough of it. Transnational corporations have been the main vehicle for this transformation.

Questions

1 Why do you think consumerism has caught on so quickly?
2 Should governments advise their citizens on healthy/ unhealthy products – or should they leave purchasing decisions to the private judgment of their citizens?
3 How has your own life been affected (if at all) by the global consumer culture?
4 Do you think that the pace of life is now too fast?
5 Is the EU correct to be so generous to its farmers? Or should the EU allow in cheaper food from developing countries?

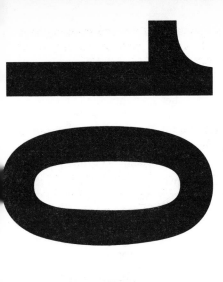

10

people power: nongovernmental organizations

This chapter will cover:
- the definition of an NGO
- the size of NGOs
- NGOs and the decline of national party politics
- the characteristics of NGOs
- four case studies of NGOs.

Introduction

A nongovernmental organization (NGO) is any organization outside the government (such as the public service and the defence forces) and business. The expression 'nongovernmental' is in itself Westphalian: organizations are either governmental or they are not. This book uses the term nongovernmental organization simply because it is the standard term used in UN circles – but a new, more positive (and less Westphalian) term is required.

In the US, another name for NGOs is the third sector. The term is used to make the distinction between the first sector, which is government, and the second sector which is profit-making industry (such as agriculture, manufacturing and tourism). The third sector is more easily defined in terms of what it is not (rather than what it is): it is not part of the government and it is not primarily motivated by the need to be profitable. The third sector has a different philosophy and worldview from the other two sectors. It is the community non-profit sector. Yet another term for NGO is new social movement. Another is civil society organization.

The size of NGOs

It is impossible to calculate the number of NGOs as they keep springing up in response to some need. There is no doubt that NGOs are increasing both in number and in membership. The NGO sector is perhaps the biggest unknown success story in US history. It employs more civilians than the federal and state governments combined, with a budget that exceeds all but seven countries in the world. The US non-profit arena may be divided into a number of areas, such as religion, private education and research, healthcare, arts and culture, social sciences, advocacy and legal services, international assistance, and charitable foundations. The US has well over one million NGOs spread across these categories and is obviously the world leader – but studies in other countries would produce a similar pattern.

Practically all adults and many young people in developed countries belong to at least one NGO. NGOs go beyond the high-profile advocacy or fundraising/relief ones, such as Amnesty International, Greenpeace, Friends of the Earth, World Vision, Oxfam and the national Red Cross Society. NGOs also include churches, trade unions, cooperative societies and service clubs (such as Boy Scouts, Girl Guides, Rotary and Zonta), and community groups (such as Meals on Wheels, Lifeline/ Samaritan telephone counselling services, Alcoholics Anonymous and gardening and chess clubs). There is, then, a great deal of work done through NGOs.

NGOs and the decline of national party politics

Most NGOs were created in the twentieth century. Indeed, many have been created since World War II and are to be found in all aspects of life. Local and national political activities are increasingly concerned with competing pressures from NGOs. A parallel development to the decline in the significance of national governments is that of political parties. Activists prefer to join single-issue groups (NGOs). For example, there are probably as many members of a national environment movement, as there are members of all the national political parties combined. People are still active in political change – it is simply that they no longer see political parties as the best vehicle for that change.

People are disenchanted that when their political party does get into power, it is often unable to introduce the policies they would like. As this book is arguing, this disappointment is due to the fact that increasingly – thanks to globalization – national governments are no longer masters of their own destiny.

Additionally, party politics polarizes every issue. Opposition parties are virtually automatically obliged to oppose government policies in order to maintain their credibility as an 'opposition'. The mass media – always on the watch for clash and conflict – go to the opposition precisely to get a critical opinion of the government. By contrast, NGOs can bring people together across party lines to work for a greater goal, with fewer personal agendas and conflicting egos.

Characteristics of NGOs

An expanding role

NGOs have moved a long way from the image they had in the nineteenth century, when the few that existed were seen mainly as dealing with people in crisis. For example, people who were made homeless or destitute went to these organizations (usually a Christian-based one) for assistance. They provided the forerunner of the welfare state.

However, governments in the twentieth century accepted that they must carry out much of this crisis intervention work. Owing to last century's changes in taxation, governments now have far greater resources to do this work. NGOs now share crisis intervention work with governments, thereby permitting them to take on other complementary roles, such as research and advocacy.

In the field of foreign aid, NGOs were formed to deal with an immediate crisis, such as a famine. An extension to the work was long-term development. This may be illustrated in the difference between supplying food in a famine and helping people plant their own crops. The next extension was to ask why people were poor when others in that society were rich. This then brought NGOs into the debate over the best way for a country to develop – a still unresolved question! Another extension was to bring the development issue back home via 'development education', whereby people in developed countries were challenged to reflect on what contribution they may (unintentionally) be making to the plight of the developing world.

Thus, an involvement in one issue leads onto others, so that NGOs can get a more holistic view of problems.

In short, NGOs can see the linkages between issues because they are less compartmentalized than governments. The evolution of peace research is an example. The 85 years of the League of Nations and the UN have shown that negative-based peace strategies (namely, stopping violence) have had a very limited success. Peace research NGOs have therefore argued that such work needs to be complemented by positive peace strategies, which include economic well-being, self-determination, human rights, non-violence and creative conflict resolution and the protection of the environment. Thus, the work of NGOs is now more sophisticated than it used to be.

People helping people

NGOs mobilize the community. They enable individuals to take an active role in working for a better society. One way in which this is done is through voluntary service as NGOs are a vehicle whereby people can volunteer their services. People will offer their time, money and gifts-in-kind to NGOs – but they will tend not to volunteer to do the same for official government bodies. Volunteers play a very important role in NGOs. They provide supplementary services to the staff – and, indeed, in some they are the closest thing to 'staff'.

NGOs are now more professional. The 'Lady Bountiful' image of the nineteenth century has gone. The staff are paid (albeit not necessarily very well) and are often well qualified. NGOs now provide careers for people who wish to help their fellow human beings. Some tertiary educational institutions have taken this concern for professionalization a step further by creating a specific diploma course for managing NGOs.

NGOs mobilize the community spirit. They can get people together to deal with natural disasters such as floods or they provide voluntary counselling such as Good Samaritans or medical personnel working in African disaster zones.

Community involvement

NGOs can themselves be important to the volunteers. They provide them with an opportunity to take an active role in community welfare. They also help the self-image of volunteers who through, say, unemployment or retirement from the paid workforce may feel marginalized and even unwanted.

NGOs, therefore, provide a vehicle out of the self-absorption and self-obsession that characterize so much of contemporary life. Since money is often the measure of all things, consumerism is important. The mass media (especially television) encourage this infatuation with self-absorption, greed and consumerism. To paraphrase the French philosopher Descartes, 'I consume, therefore I live.'

However, not everyone worships the idols of consumerism. Not everyone is self-absorbed. Some are more concerned about other people. In service they grow and there is plenty of time to grow. Assuming that a person has a 75-year lifespan, with entry into the paid work force at 21 and retirement at 55, with a 35-hour week – only eight per cent of life is spent in the paid workforce. NGOs can provide plenty of opportunities to use the other 60 per cent of waking life. Indeed, a paid worker stops working at, say, 65 – but there is no age limit on how long a person can be active within an NGO.

The warning voice

NGOs do not try to foretell the future – but they may warn people that if they persist in their current actions, dire consequences will ensue. For example, environmental NGOs, which pride themselves on research, have been warning about environmental problems. This is important because universities in many countries are going through various financial crises and so there is not so much scope for practical research to be conducted. Additionally, much of the research that is conducted and written up is too detached from the general public. Academics talk too often to one another and too little to the general public. NGOs conduct their own research and can popularize esoteric university research. They are also good at using the mass media to publicize their findings.

The leading edge

NGOs show that a good way to bring about change is to establish a model of how they would like things to be. In other words, providing warnings is not enough: it is also necessary to provide an alternative. Thus, NGOs are often on the leading edge of change. Through their advocacy work, they provide innovations, fresh thinking and new visions so they, rather than government, often set the pace of change.

An example is the London-based Intermediate Technology Development Group (as it was then called), founded by Dr E. F. Schumacher. ITDG has popularized Schumacher's 'small is beautiful' ideas. ITDG is not advocating some romanticized return to nature and primitive living but wants a change in economic policies, with technology based on four principles:

- Workplaces should be located where people live (thereby avoiding the need for migration into the overcrowded cities);
- They should be cheap to organize (thereby avoiding the problems of borrowing a great deal of capital to get started);
- Manufacturing systems should be uncomplicated (so that the demand for high skill levels is avoided);
- The production should be based on local materials for local use (thereby avoiding high transportation costs).

Many NGO projects in the developing world are now based on these principles (without necessarily explicitly acknowledging Schumacher and the ITDG for the insights).

Continuity

NGOs survive the fads and fashions of governments and outlive the terms of elected governments. They provide a continuity of care and a continued focus on social justice issues when governments might prefer to ignore those issues. One example is the consumer boycott against the makers of infant formula powdered milk. The argument over infant formula in the developing world rests on three points.

- The use of it detracts from breast milk, which provides initial near-perfect nutrition, protects against disease, and is virtually costless.
- Lactating mothers are less likely to conceive than mothers who are not breast feeding and also, because powdered milk is often mixed with unclean water and served in unclean bottles, its unnecessary use can lead to malnutrition, disease and even death.
- Powdered milk, which is often supplied free in hospital, has to be paid for when mother and child return home and so breast feeding, which is free, represents a financial burden for the family – especially when the alternative is not a financial burden.

There are, however, some circumstances where infant formula is justified. Consequently the critics have not campaigned against it in principle, but about the aggressive marketing techniques of the companies, for example, offering inducements to hospital employees to recommend infant formula.

In the late 1970s, groups began to call for boycotts of other products made by the infant formula companies, such as Nestlés, which makes Nescafé coffee. In the US, the boycott was coordinated by the INFACT. Two major supporters were the National Council of Churches (NCC) and the NCC-sponsored Interfaith Center on Corporate Responsibility, which acts for Protestant denominations and Catholic orders in trying to persuade corporations in which they invest to adopt voluntarily more 'socially responsible' business practices. Other churches took up the campaign.

The WHO responded to the campaign by drawing up a voluntary set of marketing guidelines. The international code states, among other things, that there should be no free samples, promotion of products in health facilities or gifts to health workers. An International Baby Food Action Network (IBFAN) was established to stop the unethical promotion of bottle-feeding products. It has also been encouraging governments to adopt binding legislation to assist the observance of the voluntary code.

The infant formula campaign has become the classic case study of the effectiveness of consumer boycotts. It has greatly influenced international organizations, changed the practices of transnational corporations and has been a good medium by which to inform people in developed countries about economic and social development. Although the campaign has still not achieved all that was hoped for, it showed that the boycott technique could be effective. It was an example of 'thinking globally and acting locally' since it gave the individual or family a specific task to do that would contribute to a better world. Every time people buy a product, they cast a 'vote' in favour of that product and yet they seldom think of the ethical consequences of casting that vote. The campaign called on people to think about the social responsibility of their consumer patterns.

A key factor in this campaign was the NGO continuity. Influencing intergovernmental organizations is hard and often boring work. It requires continuous public support, local organizing, lobbying at home and the building of expertise on a specific issue. To focus on single issues and set ambitious but, at the same time, achievable goals is the right recipe for success. Staying power to follow through on favourable intergovernmental decisions is necessary to ensure continued commitment by the organization and by individual governments. Few governments will act without public pressure.

Another case study of continuity is the environment movement Greenpeace, which has a trademark that is now almost as famous as Coca-Cola's. Greenpeace started in Canada in 1971 when the environment debate was then dominated by conservationists, who were concerned about trying to preserve parts of Canadian wildlife. Greenpeace argued that this was too simplistic and that, as the entire global eco system was under threat, there had to be a more sophisticated approach to saving the earth. This coincided with the preparations for the 1972 UN Conference on the Human Environment, where the UN was also taking a broader view of the environmental crisis.

Greenpeace has grown in strength. It has a larger budget than the UN Environment Programme (which was created a year later by the 1972 UN conference). It is one of the world's most famous – if not *the* most famous – environmental NGO. What was dismissed as a 'trendy' NGO, with a flair for publicity (such as its activities against French nuclear testing in the South Pacific), is now recognized as a major factor in shaping the environment debate. Incidentally, most national departments of the environment were created around the time of the 1972 UN conference (in order for governments to be represented by ministers of the environment). Therefore, Greenpeace is older than many national ministries for the environment and the UN Environment Programme.

People work in NGOs to make a difference. They are not there simply to make money (which is unlikely anyway, given the salary scales). Volunteers donate their time and skills and there is, then, a degree of commitment here that may be lacking in politicians and public servants who are simply doing their job. Politicians and public servants may be fine individuals, with a dedication to the task then occupying their time, but they are unlikely to be focused on that task for long; they will be transferred or promoted elsewhere and new staff will arrive. NGOs keep on keeping on.

Four case studies

Humanity in war

The Red Cross has become one of the world's most famous symbols. Red Cross organizations are as busy now as at any time since World War II. The Red Cross founder Henri Dunant (1828–1910) was born in Geneva and was a banker and a businessperson. His involvement in the Red Cross's creation came in a roundabout way. He had no interest in war and (as a Swiss person) had no direct experience of it. During the 1850s, he was interested in developing North Africa via an irrigation system. This required France's permission since it was the governing power. In 1859 he sought a meeting with Napoleon III. His pursuit of the ruler took him to Solferino on 24 June 1859, where Europe's largest battle since Waterloo in 1815 was being fought.

Dunant was appalled at the suffering he witnessed there. He forgot his desire to discuss finance and instead he created a makeshift hospital. Most people who died in wars at that time were not killed during the battle, but died afterwards due to lack of medical care. Florence Nightingale (1820–1910) had campaigned during the Crimean War a few years earlier to raise the status and quality of the nursing profession.

Dunant wrote a *A Memory of Solferino*, in which he called for the creation of 'relief societies for the purpose of having care given to the wounded in wartime by zealous, devoted and thoroughly qualified volunteers.' He also suggested the adoption of an international agreement recognizing the inviolability of medical services and of the wounded. The book became a bestseller and generated considerable debate across Europe.

His home city of Geneva responded to the challenge. The Geneva Society of Public Welfare appointed a committee (including Dunant) to examine his suggestions. This 'Committee of Five', which later became the International Committee of the Red Cross, convened an international conference on a private basis, at which 16 governments were represented. This created the first Geneva Convention in 1863.

In an era with so many international organizations and conferences, it is necessary to take stock of that paragraph. It is too easy to take for granted the immense achievement of 1863. A group of private individuals – not governments – decided to convene a meeting of governments, to fill the vacuum created by a lack of government leadership. The meeting led to the creation of both one of the world's most famous organizations (the Red Cross) and a new strand in international law (the Geneva conventions). In this current era, when there are claims that the individual cannot do anything worthwhile, it is worth reflecting on what one person and that one book brought into being.

However, all this achievement was at great personal cost to Dunant. While he was so active on Red Cross affairs, he neglected his business which failed and he was declared bankrupt in 1867. For a citizen of Geneva, this was one of the worst events that could ever happen, for Geneva citizens who went bankrupt had no civil rights and he had to leave Geneva. For the remainder of the century, the Red Cross forgot Dunant and he disappeared from its official history. The rapidly expanding Red Cross could not afford to have its good reputation linked to that of a failed banker.

Dunant himself was unsure just how he spent his life as a tramp. In 1887 he arrived, prematurely aged, at the Swiss village of Heiden. He spent most of the remaining 23 years of his life as a charity case in the village's hospital.

In 1895, a foreign journalist passed through the village on holiday. He got to hear the stories the villagers told about the old man in the hospital bed. The journalist interviewed Dunant and the story swept around the world. Once again, Dunant's life took another turn. Although he never moved from his hospital room, honours flowed into his room and his ideas out of it.

Meanwhile, at the other end of Europe, in Sweden, Alfred Nobel was troubled by his conscience by how he would be remembered in history as the inventor of dynamite. It was causing a great deal of suffering – and he was one of the world's richest men because of it. Baroness von Suttner had been reading the press reports of the Red Cross's founder and suggested that Nobel create a peace prize – and she knew of just the right man for it. Henri Dunant was awarded the first Nobel Peace Prize in 1901.

Rotary International

WHO has predicted that polio will be eradicated globally in the very near future. This will be only the second disease (after smallpox) to be totally eliminated from the planet.

Some of that success is due to the world's first service club, Rotary. Rotary has had a far greater impact on the lives of people than is commonly thought. A person does not need to be a member of Rotary to share its benefits. For example, in 1985 the Rotary PolioPlus programme set out to work with organizations like WHO, United Nations Children Fund (UNICEF) and national governments to eradicate polio. It has raised about US$500 million for this cause.

Rotary was created by Paul Harris. He had been raised in a small town in Vermont, in the rural northeast quarter of the US. He became a lawyer in the big city of Chicago in the mid-west but yearned for the fellowship of the small town in the big city. He thought of some form of club for professionals that would give them the type of friendliness he had enjoyed while growing up. He had no idea that he would create one of the world's most famous international NGOs.

On the evening of 23 February 1905 Harris invited three friends to a meeting in downtown Chicago. They discussed Harris's suggestion that business people should meet periodically to enjoy fellowship and to enlarge their circle of business and professional contacts. The club met weekly and membership was limited to one representative from each business and profession. As they continued to meet, the members rotated their place of meetings – hence the name 'Rotary'. After obtaining their fifth member the group was formally called the Rotary Club of Chicago.

By the end of 1905 the club had 30 members. There were now so many members that it was no longer possible to meet at the offices of the members and so they started meeting in hotels and restaurants. Most Rotary meetings today are now held at such locations.

Rotary was formed at a particular time in US history. The US was moving ahead with its industrialization and rapid economic development and was soon to become an economic superpower. But people like Harris could remember an earlier era of small towns: with greater friendliness, less crime and less hurry. This is what Harris hoped to be able to recreate in the big city. However, success in the big city also required what is now called 'networking' – making the right contacts. Although Rotary is not a business organization as such, it is a place where business and professional people can make the right contacts.

Being concerned about business was not enough, though. A century ago American businesspeople were aware that they had to put something back into society. Making a profit was not enough – they had an obligation to help the less fortunate members of their society. The Rotary commitment to putting something back into the community began in 1907, when the Rotary Club of Chicago donated a horse to a preacher. The man's own horse had died and because he was too poor to buy another one, he was unable to make the rounds of his churches and parishioners.

Later on, Rotarians used the motto of 'Service, Not Self', and 'He Profits Most Who Serves Best'. 'Service Above Self' is now the primary motto. Rotary youth exchanges began in 1929. Over 7,000 high school students from around the world have travelled to other countries. Two other programmes for young people are Interact (youths aged 14–18) and Rotaract (young adults 18–30). Service to youth is an important facet of Rotary's work.

Rotary sponsored an international conference of ministers of education in London in 1943 that helped form the UN Educational, Scientific and Cultural Organization (UNESCO). Rotary was represented at the founding of the UN in San Francisco in 1945 and it remains an active NGO within the UN. It also organizes 'Model UN General Assemblies' whereby students learn more about international affairs.

It encourages good business ethics and its members have introduced the fourway test. When considering all possible lines of actions and statements, they are to ask themselves: Is it the truth? Is it fair to all concerned? Will it build goodwill and better friendships? Will it be beneficial to all concerned?

By 1912 Rotary clubs were established in Europe and Asia and 'Rotary International' was created in 1922. The total membership of Rotary is now about 1.2 million, belonging to over 29,000 clubs in over 160 countries. Membership is by invitation only and reflects a wide cross-section of the community. Rotary started as an all-male club but in the late 1980s women were admitted as full members of which there are now about 145,000. Following the collapse of communism in eastern Europe, Rotary clubs have been allowed to re-form after half a century of abolition by the communist authorities. The first Russian Club was chartered in 1990 and there are now a total of over 200 clubs in the former communist bloc. There are also Rotary clubs in China.

Banking on the poor

The mass media focus on the rich and famous. The financial pages of the newspapers give priority to the large companies and entrepreneurs. However, the world's economic recovery will not come merely from big corporate or government employer, it will come from millions of small one-, two- or five-person businesses. The world's 500 largest corporations control 25 per cent of the world's economic output but they employ less than one per cent of the world's population.

In other words, it is with the small enterprises that most people worldwide make their livelihoods: 'micro-enterprises'. The real backbone of world commerce and global employment is made up of the millions of small enterprises that farm small plots of land, cook food, provide daycare, do piecework for clothing manufacturers and carry out countless other tasks that larger businesses do not do. Many of these businesses are so small that even their own governments pay little attention to them.

Commercial banks are often worse: they ignore micro-enterprises. Poor people may want to borrow a few dollars – what we may consider to be a paltry sum – but, the comparatively large cost of paperwork for such loans for micro-enterprises often reduces any incentive to arrange a loan. Yet village moneylenders may charge up to 3,000 per cent interest a year for a loan.

Now there is a revolution in banking: micro-credit. The most inspiring example is the Grameen Bank in Bangladesh (one of the world's poorest countries), founded by a professor of economics, Muhammad Yunus, who won the 2006 Nobel Peace Prize. In 1979 Professor Yunus began an experiment aimed at helping impoverished villagers. Defying the usual rules, he lent them unsecured money to start up small enterprises such as rice processing, rickshaw driving and weaving.

Instead of collateral, the borrowers form small groups and agree to a pact of mutual liability – if one defaults, the others have to pay from their own profits. The participants in a pact often know each other, which creates peer pressure for successful repayment. Along with the compelling need for an income source in a place with few other opportunities, this system has produced a surprising result: a loan repayment rate of 99 per cent.

This is a rate from customers too small for conventional banks to handle – and one much larger than that achieved by the conventional banks for their much richer customers.

The Grameen ('Rural') Bank is now a legend in the area of development economics. It has 35,000 branches, with a new branch opening somewhere around the world each day. The lesson is a simple one: give people the resources and opportunity to do what they want and development will take place. As a deliberate policy, 94 per cent of the Grameen Bank's customers are women: the poorest people in one of the world's poorest countries. But a Bangladeshi female peasant is often a better credit risk than many businessmen in developed countries (as the investors in Enron now know).

Giving a hand up, not a handout

Many of the world's problems seem to be too large for any one individual or organization to tackle, but building a simple house for one family is possible. The NGO Habitat for Humanity was founded by Millard and Linda Fuller in the US in the late 1960s. Habitat for Humanity was created to eliminate poverty housing. Volunteers work with chosen families to build simple, decent homes of solid, quality construction. The houses are then sold with no profit added and no interest charged. Small monthly payments are made to repay the cost of the houses, usually over a period of ten to 20 years. There is a very good record of home repayments.

Neither race nor religion is used as a criterion in choosing the families. The work done by the Habitat families is called 'sweat equity', a concept that requires that they must work several hundred hours to help build their own houses and those for others. Habitat for Humanity is now one of the largest homebuilders in the US and is well on the way to becoming the number one homebuilder in the US – in terms of the number of houses built that would also make it the largest homebuilder *in the world.*

Habitat for Humanity argues that a healthy community comes from people living in their own safe, decent housing, with a sense of pride that comes from owning the property and in having a vested interest in ensuring that the community is highly regarded. Therefore Habitat for Humanity has reclaimed neighbourhoods from drug dealers and squalor and built homes that have withstood hurricanes, earthquakes and floods.

Habitat for Humanity is successful for three reasons. First, it is tangible. No one person or organization can solve all the world's problems but anyone can be a volunteer to help build a home. Among some of the Habitat volunteers have been Paul Newman, the late Bob Hope and former president, Jimmy Carter. Indeed, Jimmy Carter has commented that whenever members of the public talk to him, they are far less interested in what he did to end the arms race or bring peace to the Middle East and are more interested to learn what is happening in Habitat for Humanity.

Second, Habitat for Humanity is a hand up – and not a handout. It is empowerment on the most basic level. Each homeowner family is expected to help build their own house and others.

Third, it is common sense. For example, the self-image of children improves overnight and they do better at school because they have a decent place to study.

Given that NGOs are so significant, it is now necessary to look at ways in which they are challenging the power of national governments, the subject of the next chapter.

Conclusion

NGOs enable people to participate directly in working for a better world and so make a difference. The more politically oriented NGOs enable people to take part in politics without having to belong to a political party. NGOs are working to put themselves out of business, for instance, when everyone is wealthy there will be no need for a Grameen Bank. In the meantime, they are often more effective in carrying out certain projects than governments – the national Red Cross/Red Crescent societies often run the bloodbank. It is more appropriate for charities to do this type of humanitarian work than a government department. They are also often closer to the needs of people – they are the nerve endings of humanity. They also generate ideas and so are on the leading edge of change.

Questions

1 Do you belong to any NGOs? If so, why? What have you gained from your membership?
2 What are recent examples of NGOs eroding the Westphalian system?
3 What limits (if any) should be imposed on NGOs to stop their intervention in the internal affairs of other countries?
4 Should NGOs have increased international status? How could this be achieved?
5 Are NGOs a threat to democracy because they represent only their members and yet they can intimidate democratically elected governments?

11

how NGOs challenge governmental power

This chapter will cover:
- NGO pressure on national governments
- four case studies showing NGOs at work
  - the Club of Rome and the environment
  - the campaign for Antarctica
  - the rise of democracy
  - the hunt for war criminals.

Introduction

There are several global struggles for power underway. This book's earlier chapters examined the way in which national governments are struggling to maintain control over their own affairs. Some of their power has reluctantly been handed over to inter-governmental organizations such as the UN and the EU. We have also examined the struggle between national governments and transnational corporations, particularly on economic matters.

However, just to make things even more complicated, NGOs also challenge the power of national governments and some also take on transnational corporations (see Chapter 12).

NGO pressure on national governments

Governments reluctant to admit to giving in to NGOs

Nation-states, according to the theory behind the Westphalian system, are the masters of their own destiny. This means that governments rarely admit that they have given in to NGO pressure. If they were to do so, then it would mean that governments were not really masters of their own destiny and they would have to admit this to the general public. Such an admission would also encourage other NGOs to be equally active in the expectation of changing government policy.

It is also very difficult to follow a governmental decision-making process to find out how any decision was made and what influenced whom. For example, Amnesty International, whose members write letters to governments asking for the release of political prisoners, is careful not to claim that when its adopted prisoners are, in fact, released this was due to Amnesty pressure. Amnesty International cannot establish a clear chain of causation between its campaign and the release of the political prisoner.

Similarly, an NGO may advocate a policy change and a government may later change its policy – but it is usually very difficult (if not impossible) to state that one caused the other. It is not so easy to assess a chain of causation that links the NGO campaign with the governmental backdown.

The refusal of governments to acknowledge the role of NGOs in changing particular policies is also part of Westphalian logic: governments have to pretend that they are masters of their country's destiny. It may be seen as a sign of weakness to admit that they are being influenced by NGOs. The case studies in this chapter provide examples of where, coincidentally, governments have changed their policies around the time of NGO campaigns.

NGO impact

NGOs erode the Westphalian system in five main ways:

- They can provide an alternative focal point for loyalty, such as the peace movements in many countries that opposed the arms race in the 1980s. Citizens do not always think that their own governments know best. Indeed, some NGOs provide an alternative 'foreign' policy that transcends national boundaries, such as NGOs working together in many countries to defeat the proposed treaty to regulate mining in Antarctica. National governments may not necessarily represent the views of their citizens on all issues – hence the importance of NGOs.

- They show that governments have no monopoly over information and ideas. For example, NGOs undertake public education work, such as alerting people to the dangers of pollution and generating new ideas for coping with problems. They develop close ties with politicians and (even more importantly) public servants to work on new treaties, etc.

- They are adept at using the mass media for their campaigns. They sometimes challenge governments (and transnational corporations) to do better and they are skilled at public relations. They often have a high level of professionalism (such as the quality of their websites, often done by volunteers or IT professionals at a reduced rate because they support the NGO's aims).

- They provide an alternative route for people who wish to work for a better world. Political parties are not the sole route for working towards that objective. Indeed, given the widespread disenchantment with politicians, NGOs are important avenues for peaceful social change.

- Their importance is being recognized in the intergovernmental organizations that grant various forms of consultative status to NGOs to enable them to take part in the work of the organizations. Also, national government delegations sometimes contain specialist NGO personnel as advisers. Politicians and public servants may lack the institutional memory of an NGO campaigner who has spent years working on a particular issue.

Four case studies

The best way to see politically active NGOs at work is via their campaigns.

Saving the global environment

The Limits to Growth (1972 edition) is the biggest selling environment book in world history and helped trigger the environment movement. It was commissioned by an NGO, later called the Club of Rome.

The club began in an informal way. Aurelio Peccei was an Italian businessperson. He had helped build up the Fiat motor car company before World War II and, during the war, was a member of the resistance against the fascists. The Americans appointed him back to the company after the war. He went on to oversee Fiat's activities in Latin America. As a successful businessperson in Fiat and later Olivetti, he believed that business had a social responsibility to help the community.

In 1967, Peccei gave a speech in Latin America on the dramatic changes taking place in the world, especially relating to science and technology. The speech attracted considerable attention and was widely distributed.

Alexander King, who previously had not known Peccei, received a copy of the speech. King was a British scientist, who had been a scientific adviser to the British government, and who was then at the Paris-based Organization for Economic Cooperation and Development (originally created in the late 1940s to distribute US Marshall Aid money to help rebuild Europe). King had arrived at similar concerns and so was anxious to meet Peccei to see how these ideas could be followed up.

The Club of Rome has contributed so much to the change in thinking that has taken place in the last quarter of a century that it is worth recalling the atmosphere in which the club started. This was a period of overwhelming optimism. The 1950s and 1960s were a period of immense economic growth. There was a very low rate of unemployment and a general belief in the western world that another depression of the 1930s type could be avoided thanks to Keynesian government intervention in the economy. Additionally, it was assumed that there was a standard formula for economic growth that could apply throughout the developing world.

Very little attention was given to the environmental consequences of economic growth. Indeed, both capitalists and communists were convinced that there could not be much of an environmental crisis. For capitalists, the market could solve any environmental problem (for example, if resources were used too rapidly, prices would go up and usage would go down). The communists meanwhile had been assured by Marx that technology could solve all problems.

Peccei and King were not so confident about either the market or technology. The club was established as a way of looking at the larger questions confronting global society. The club's worldview was based on three characteristics:

- To *adopt a global perspective* in examining issues and situations, with the awareness that the increasing interdependence of countries, the emergence of worldwide problems and the future needs of all people posed predicaments beyond the capacity of individual countries to solve.
- To *think holistically* and to seek a deeper understanding of interactions within the tangle of contemporary problems – political, social, economic, technological, environmental, psychological and cultural – for which the club coined the phrase 'the world problematique'.
- To focus studies on issues, whether of promise or difficulty, in a *longer term perspective* than is possible for politicians preoccupied with a desire to stay in power.

The club is a club. It is informal – indeed, the first 'president' (Peccei) was never elected as such to that position; he just evolved into it. The membership is kept small (no more than 100 people from about 50 countries) and is by invitation only. It is broadly based, so as to provide a variety of perspectives. Members include scientists, economists, businesspeople, international civil servants, heads of state/government and Nobel laureates. Its finances come from contributions from members, charitable foundations, sponsorship and government grants. It has only a very small secretariat.

How, then, has such a small group of people been able to generate so much publicity? The most obvious answer is that the club tapped into a latent concern. Life in the late 1960s seemed, at one level, to be going so well but, deep in their bones, many people had doubts about whether such an extravagant lifestyle could continue indefinitely. The club spoke openly about what was in the hearts of many people. Its first major project was the commissioning of a group of computer experts in the US to examine what would happen if the earth continued to consume such a high amount of resources.

Limits to Growth (1972) has been described as one of the twentieth century's most influential books. It sold nine million copies in 29 languages. The book was a warning. It did not predict what would happen – it simply warned that if the consumption patterns and population growth continued at their same high rate, the earth would strike its limits within a century. This was not inevitable. People could change their policies – and the sooner the better. The book tapped into the latent concerns of many people but it also ran foul of the prevailing dominant optimistic capitalist and communist views, with their respective faiths in the market and technology. The club was branded as pessimistic and a threat to capitalism (or communism). All this criticism helped the book's sales.

The essence of the warning from the Club of Rome remains valid. There is concern over the price of oil and there are already situations where resources have been reduced. For example, some of the world's fish stocks have gone. There are too many fishermen chasing too few fish: the world's fishing fleet could be reduced by 50 per cent and yet the same amount of fish could be caught. Additionally, there have been years of record weather-related disasters. While there is still some speculation among scientists about the extent of the climate change, insurance companies have already decided that there is a change underway. Some insurance companies have suggested that in the years ahead large areas of the world, including the southeastern US and Indonesia, may become virtually uninsurable.

Saving Antarctica

There is now an agreement banning mining in Antarctica. The Antarctic Treaty Environment Protocol declares the continent to be a 'nature reserve dedicated to peace and science.' The protocol provides for a ban on all mining and drilling activity for at least 50 years. It outlines updated and strengthened rules for environmental regulation covering environmental impact assessment, waste disposal, protected areas, protection of flora and fauna, and tourist activity.

This new agreement is another success for the basic 1959 Antarctic Treaty. The 1959 Treaty has been one of the most successful ever negotiated. It grew out of an international scientific programme created under the auspices of the International Geophysical Year (IGY). IGY ran for 18 months from July 1957 in the Antarctic, during which 12 countries worked together on research ('cooperative power'). The success of IGY encouraged hopes of making the spirit of scientific cooperation more permanent. This was achieved through the 1959 Antarctic Treaty, which does not get nearly as much publicity as it deserves. The Treaty has five main strengths:

- The Treaty has frozen all quarrels over claims. Various countries have made claims to parts of the Antarctic. From about the 1820s, explorers from several countries made various landings but none established a permanent presence there. By the 1930s, seven countries had staked out claims: the UK, France, Australia, New Zealand and Norway (which recognized each other's claims) and Argentina and Chile (whose claims overlapped both with each other and with that of the UK). The largest single claimant is Australia, which claims about 41 per cent of the continent.

  Under the 1959 Treaty, no new claims may be made and none of the present claimants can be forced to surrender their claims. This is important given the nationalist fervour generated by the claims made by Argentina and Chile, which have always taken their competing claims very seriously. They are fortunate in having access (via their claims) to the only rock that is ice free all year round. Both countries have taken pregnant women to their claims to have their babies born there. Despite all this political pantomime, the Treaty process has managed to keep the lid on excitable passions and there have been no conflicts. Similarly, the UK and Argentina during the 1982 Falklands/Malvinas conflict maintained tranquil relations over Antarctic affairs, despite the conflict to the north.

- The Treaty created the world's first nuclear weapon-free zone. Although perhaps only a minor breakthrough in itself, in terms of limiting the arms race, it has been a helpful precedent for more ambitious nuclear-free zones, notably

Latin America, the moon, the seabed, the South Pacific and, most recently, Africa. It also helped the momentum for international arms control negotiations.

- The Treaty was unusual for its time in that it created some form of international machinery. Many countries are willing to accept international obligations (via treaties), yet they want to keep the responsibility of checking that they are actually carrying out their international obligations (rather than create an international authority to monitor their behaviour). This concern is derived from a reluctance by all countries to have any international interference in their domestic affairs. The Antarctic Treaty, by its consultative arrangements and mutual obligations, has created a limited international system of enforcement. The Treaty's success has encouraged later treaties on other matters gradually to be more ambitious.

- The test of any international agreement is whether it is fulfilling its aims. The Treaty certainly is. Memoirs of scientists who have worked in the Antarctic during the past four decades all attest to international cooperation. During the dark days of the Cold War, the level of cooperation in the Antarctic was almost unequalled anywhere else around the world. In the Antarctic, people learn to work together or else they will perish separately. There was no Cold War at the South Pole.

- The Antarctic Treaty is a showpiece of international law in operation. The Treaty is self-enforcing: it is in each country's interest not to violate it because the gains from respecting the Treaty's provisions far outweigh the gains that might result from breaking them. The Treaty is also capable of flexible growth.

The Antarctic Treaty has provided a good basis for others. The 1972 Convention for the Conservation of Antarctic Seals protects some seal species and puts controls on the catches of others. No commercial sealing has, in fact, been undertaken since the convention came into force.

The 1980 Convention on the Conservation of Antarctic Marine Living Resources (CCAMLR) was negotiated in response to large-scale trawling for finfish and krill (shrimp-like creatures) during the 1960s and 1970s, particularly by the USSR. CCAMLR represented a major breakthrough in marine conservation at the time because, instead of considering each species separately, it provides for an 'eco-system as a whole' approach to conservation and marine resources. As an example, whaling in Antarctic waters was banned by a separate body (the International Whaling Commission) but it would be pointless to save the whales from hunting when they could (in theory) starve to death by not having any krill to eat because the krill had been caught by trawlers.

With CCAMLR completed, the Antarctic Treaty consultative parties turned their attention to the need to regulate mining and oil drilling (the draft was known as the Wellington Treaty, with much of the work being done at meetings in New Zealand). This coincided with speculation that the continent could be the scene of an oil, natural gas and mineral rush because some transnational corporations had hopes of exploiting the wealth.

Environmental NGOs, loosely coordinated by the Antarctic and South Oceans Coalition (ASOC), fought that proposal throughout the 1980s. ASOC was told by governments that resistance was futile and that the Wellington Treaty would go ahead – but ASOC kept keeping on.

The turning point came in the late 1980s. The onset of hot weather triggered initial speculation about global warming. *Time* magazine, instead of a 'person of the year', nominated earth as the endangered 'planet of the year'. There was also an oil tanker disaster in Alaska, with the *Exxon Valdez* creating an oil slick the size of the state of Vermont. The captain had been banned from driving a car in his home state due to drunkenness – but not banned from running a ship. ASOC argued that such an oil slick could also be created by an oil tanker disaster in Antarctica.

Suddenly, governments were scrambling to show their 'green' credentials. Mrs Thatcher thought of herself as the 'green goddess of Number 10'. The Australian and French governments were the first two to disown the Wellington Treaty. Eventually public opinion swung round to their point of view. All the Antarctic governments then disowned the Treaty.

ASOC therefore achieved one of the greatest environmental victories of the decade. It forced the Antarctic Treaty consultative parties – and transnational corporations – to stop all dreams of mineral prospecting and oil drilling and instead create a treaty to ban all such prospecting and drilling.

The Environmental Protocol was signed in 1991. By establishing high standards for all human activities on the continent, the Environmental Protocol goes a long way towards safeguarding Antarctica before it suffers from the human impacts felt over most of the rest of the earth. The Environmental Protocol helps solidify Antarctica's location as one of the most significant areas for international scientific cooperation. For a continent with competing claimants, Antarctica has brought out the best of human qualities rather than the worst.

The rise of democracy

When the belly is full, the brain starts to think. In the Philippines (1986), South Korea (1989) and now Indonesia, people power is making itself felt. Dictatorial leaders have a dilemma: if they wish to have rapid economic development, they run the risk of being deposed by the beneficiaries of their policies.

Indeed, by the year 2000 the Asian human rights landscape had changed substantially from that of the mid-1970s. Significant advances towards democracy and the protection of human rights had been made in South Korea, Thailand, Taiwan, the Philippines and Indonesia and, to some extent, in the communist regimes in Vietnam and China. Indeed, some of the countries are now even being run by people who were nominated by Amnesty International as 'political prisoners' in past years. For example, the Taiwanese vice-president, Annette Lu, was a former Amnesty 'political prisoner' and she is now the first woman in 5,000 years of Chinese history to be elected to a senior position.

There are some general trends in the rise in democracy:

- A military-backed regime cannot run a modern industrial state. It can control peasants and it can run a largely agricultural society but a government cannot design computers with bayonets. There has to be a free flow of information in a modern industrial state. This process enables people to discuss not only technical matters, such as computer design, but also the wider issues of how society is governed.
- Eonomic development creates a middle class. This class is urban based, well educated and able to learn (via the mass media, internet and overseas travel) how other societies are governed. Middle-class people then create NGOs to further their political aspirations.
- A peasant society anxious about where the next meal is going to come from is more focused on the immediate issues of survival rather than how society is governed. By contrast, a middle class has time to think of issues other than its

immediate survival and has opportunities to discuss issues with other people (including people overseas), not least NGOs.

- A peasant society has a poverty consciousness: it is poor and it expects to remain that way. It does not like the poverty but it can see little opportunity to escape. However, as a society becomes richer, so expectations rise: people expect to do even better in the future.
- A middle class feels empowered about its destiny. It is less deferential to the ruling élite. It will be less willing to accept that certain people are born to rule or that they should have special privileges.

People power is enshrined in NGOs. There are thousands of such organizations in each developed western country, such as the women's, students', human rights, peace, and environment movements. NGOs provide an alternative opportunity for involvement in public affairs in democratic societies and they are the main vehicle for opposition to dictatorial regimes in the developing countries.

Meanwhile, there seems to be a descending scale of repression in many countries. Not every leader today has the stomach of Pol Pot for the mass murder of their perceived opponents. The USSR is the best example. Stalin was last century's largest mass murderer, but his successors were less violent towards their own critics. For example, in the 1956 Hungarian uprising, Imre Nagy was killed and his body was thrown into a mass grave. But in 1968's 'Prague Spring' Dubcek was moved sideways into a minor public service job, so he was still alive for Czechoslovakia's 'Velvet Revolution' and then had a senior parliamentary position.

Additionally, the international mass media have made controlling an unruly country with student and middle class activists more difficult than in the old days. Suharto came to power in Indonesia in the mid-1960s amid a civil war in which at least 500,000 people were killed. He could not use the same tactics in 1998, when he was under threat (and he had to resign). The whole world was watching the NGO-led rebellion.

Finally, a modern industrial state is interconnected to the global economy. Harsh repression is bad for the country's business image and can scare off foreign investment. Business leaders may have some loyalty to their own country and their government, but they also have to think about the bottom line: violence is bad for business. Leaders can come and go: business goes on.

Hunting down war criminals

Governments have short memories. Thus, it has been necessary for individuals and NGOs to keep the issue of war crimes alive. Sometimes they have been successful and sometimes not. For example, allegations of war crimes committed in World War II continue to linger. Governments may have short-term memories but the victims of war crimes or next of kin and NGOs do not. Additionally, old documents eventually come to light and can cause embarrassment for later administrations. Thus, there is a tension between governments and individuals and NGOs that have maintained the memory of particular war crimes.

The politics of the emerging Cold War distorted the list of potential World War II criminals. Various war criminals who fled Europe at the end of the war were accepted into other western countries. Nazi scientists were not put on trial; they were recruited. Operation 'Paperclip' was a US project to employ German scientists in sensitive military and space programmes. Between 1945 and 1955, 765 scientists, engineers and other specialists were hired by the US, motivated by both the desire to recruit these people for its own projects and to prevent the USSR from doing so.

There were no Italian war crimes trials. The US decided that any potential war criminal might, in fact, be useful in the post-war political reconstruction of Italy and in building Italy up against communism. Similarly, in the Far East, the International Military Tribunal also missed out on its potential prime war criminal – the Emperor of Japan – because the Allied Commander, General MacArthur, decided that he would be more useful alive as a figurehead for the new Japanese democracy.

There are the various war criminals who fled Europe at the end World World II and were accepted into western countries, who have been the cause of the recent national war crimes trials. Intelligence services were looking for communists, not Nazis, and so these people were able to start new lives in allied countries. But their victims or the next of kin of their victims have a long memory. Thus, many countries have recently been obliged to recall World War II war crimes and to create special legislation to try these people. The key factor in this revived interest is the flow of information.

A good example of NGO persistence was the late Simon Wiesenthal and his Vienna-based Documentation Centre, which have maintained their efforts in tracking Nazi war criminals.

Many fled to Latin America, especially Argentina, whose leader in the 1940s, Juan Peron, was sympathetic to the Nazi cause. Adolf Eichmann fled there, but Wiesenthal tracked him down and tipped off the Israeli Government, which sent in a team to capture him and put him on trial; he was hanged on 31 May 1962. President Carlos Menem, in an effort to clean up his country's poor reputation on harbouring war criminals, started to make public his country's files on Nazi war criminals in 1992. Due to the persistence of people like Wiesenthal, Nazi war criminals have never entirely disappeared as a political issue – even though many would like them to do so.

Wiesenthal just managed to survive the Nazi death camps but most of his relatives did not. He emerged from the camps in 1945 with a mental list of every SS man he had encountered and a fanatical determination to see them all brought to justice. The Americans were so impressed with his knowledge that they employed him to help them in the de-Nazification of Germany. Of the 91 names on his list, he went on to track down more than 70 of them. In all, Wiesenthal was believed to have helped bring 1,100 war criminals to trial. There is no precedent in legal history for this achievement.

Simon Wiesenthal was born in southern Poland in 1908. He trained as an architect and was practising in Lwow when the Russians occupied eastern Poland as part of the 1939 secret deal with Germany that divided the country. He survived the Russian occupation but the advancing Germans caught him when they invaded eastern Poland in 1941 on their way through to Moscow. He spent the war in several German camps.

Bringing the Nazi killers to justice became his life's work. It was often a controversial task. Some Jews and others just wanted to get on with the rest of their lives. There were also risks that some ex-Nazis or their sympathizers would try to kill Wiesenthal or destroy his collection of documents. Meanwhile, with the onset of the Cold War, most western politicians wanted to focus on defeating the Soviet threat rather than carry on dealing with the defeated Nazi one. West Germany was part of the frontline of the defence against the Soviet Union and so western governments wanted to involve West Germans in the defence of the west rather than keep reminding them of their Nazi heritage.

The Allies established the International Military Tribunal at Nuremberg and elsewhere to try the Nazis they had captured. All the international war crimes work finished by the late 1940s.

The Allied governments wanted to move on. They were not seeking other additional criminals to put on trial.

In 1947 Wiesenthal helped establish a centre in Linz in Austria to collect information on the Nazis still on the run, but the office closed in 1954 because of the lack of support from governments. The official quest to find war criminals would now fade away through apathy.

It seemed to the Nazis on the run that they had got away with their crimes. However, Wiesenthal had made the search for justice his life's work. Despite the lack of official support he battled on. His thirst for justice kept him going, enabling him to triumph in the end.

Conclusion

NGOs enable individuals to work on specific campaigns and to concentrate their efforts. Although NGOs are careful not to boast about their victories (because it is so difficult to tell why a government changes its policy), there have been some significant cases where, coincidentally, NGO actions have occurred just prior to a change in government policy. Certainly for many people involved in NGO campaigns, there is an inner sense of satisfaction that they are changing government policy – so they are willing to continue campaigning. NGOs can also take on the transnational corporations, as we see in the next chapter.

Questions

1 Examine the role of the National Rifle Association in the US to assess its effectiveness in campaigning against 'gun control' measures.
2 What is the most active NGO you know about?
3 Could you imagine yourself having a full-time career in an NGO? If so, which one would you join?
4 What global problems now need some NGO action?
5 Identify a small local NGO doing good work in your community.

12

how NGOs challenge the power of transnational corporations

This chapter will cover:
- how NGOs tackle transnational corporations
- boycotts
- ethical purchasing
- shareholder activism.

Introduction

The popular image of globalization is that of economic exploitation and activists demonstrating for economic justice, such as an end to child labour and 'sweatshops'. As this book argues, there is much more to globalization than just this dimension (important though it is). Globalization is far more wide ranging than just certain goods and services.

The demonstrators are themselves part of the globalization process. NGOs, such as those in the global justice movement, are one form of globalization taking on another form (transnational corporations). NGOs can also call on the other form of globalization – intergovernmental 'cooperative power' – to lift its game and do more (such as the WHO responding to NGO pressure on the infant formula scandal). NGOs also use the tools of globalization (such as television and the internet) to spread their anti-exploitation message. There are many forms of globalization – and they are having a major effect on world affairs.

NGOs are proof that individuals are not powerless. Individuals can challenge governments and transnational corporations. Indeed, in taking on the corporations, they have an even broader range of options. This chapter will examine those options for change and provide some case studies.

Putting justice into business

Making each 'vote' count

A person may vote for a politician about every three or four years, but they can 'vote' for a better society every time they spend their money. Transnational corporations are sometimes challenged by people power and some NGO campaigns, therefore, call on people to think about the social responsibility of their consumer patterns.

'We are not boycotting to put anyone out of business,' said Martin Luther King during the US civil rights campaign in the 1960s. 'We are boycotting to put justice into business.'

Doing well by doing good

It is possible to do well by doing good: to use a person's wealth in the interests of social justice. Tackling transnational corporations is not just a matter of governmental or global action. It can be done in the supermarket.

This is not entirely new thinking. Some aspects of personal consumption (especially tobacco, alcohol and gambling) have long attracted criticism from people wishing to lead a more wholesome life. Given the present governmental campaigns in many countries to encourage citizens not to drink or smoke, this prophetic NGO work is now being vindicated.

It is possible to go one step further: to use money in such a way as to change commercial practices. Money has traditionally been a tool of exchange. Some consumers are already discovering that it is now possible to make money a tool for their campaigns for economic and social change.

Boycotts

From the personal to the political

Boycotts are the most well-known form of guerrilla consumer activism. Some people already boycott alcohol, tobacco and gambling. This was started out of religious conviction (for example, Methodists have traditionally opposed these activities). Such people had a policy of not wanting to be associated with a particular activity and so abstained from it.

As a tool for social change, the boycott approach has become more proactive: a person does not merely refuse to buy a product out of personal conviction but does so for the wider purpose of promoting social change.

From baby milk to nuclear weapons and tobacco

In June 1986, with the Cold War hotting up, the US-based INFACT turned its attention to opposing nuclear weapons. It focused on General Electric (GE), the second largest manufacturer of nuclear weapons in the US. GE was chosen because of its vulnerability to a consumer boycott: over 30 per cent of its sales comes from ordinary consumer items such as washing machines, dryers, home video machines and light bulbs. GE grossed over US$60 billion annually. Its nuclear weapons work, while lucrative, was only about ten per cent of those overall sales.

The campaign encouraged people to question their behaviour: if you oppose nuclear weapons, why support the corporations that build them? People may have felt uncomfortable about joining in peace rallies but buying a 'nuclear-free' washing machine – rather than a GE one – created no discomfort.

GE was a leader in the global market for high-technology medical scanners and diagnostic imaging equipment. Medical NGOs, such as the International Physicians for the Prevention of Nuclear War, recommended to their members that they not buy GE medical equipment – but buy 'non-nuclear' medical equipment instead.

In November 1992, after the INFACT campaign had run for almost seven years, GE announced that it was getting out of the nuclear weapons industry.

In 1993, the INFACT newsletter announced its third campaign for corporate accountability: taking on the tobacco industry in order to stop the marketing of tobacco to children and young people around the world. Tobacco and weapons are the only products that kill or injure when used as intended. The death toll will climb as the tobacco industry's aggressive marketing spreads throughout the world.

The anti-tobacco campaign continues. The problem for tobacco companies is that their products can kill their customers and so they always have to be looking for fresh ones. China is the new field (China has 30 per cent of the world's smokers). It is notable how a campaign begun by a series of small western NGOs has encouraged governments to become more proactive on this issue.

McLibel

McDonald's spends $1.8 billion a year on advertising. The movie *McLibel: Two Worlds Collide*, shows how the corporation also tries to suppress any other information about its operations reaching the public. In 1989 Helen Morris and Dave Steel, two environmental and social activists, handed out leaflets outside McDonald's stores in London on 'What's wrong with McDonald's'. McDonald's sued and demanded an apology. This was the longest and one of the most publicized trials in

British history. The corporation effectively lost, especially in terms of the damage to its image. The trial helped trigger a large amount of soul searching within the corporation about how to salvage its image.

More recently, the *Supersize Me* movie has examined the health consequences of the moviemaker, who ate nothing but fast food for one month, until it almost ruined his health. The movie generated much controversy, not least because it occurred around the time of growing concern over obesity and some attempts to sue McDonald's for allegedly ruining the health of the plaintiffs. Most of the litigation has failed but, like the anti-smoking litigation campaign, some lawyers expect eventually to succeed on health grounds.

In the meantime, the providers of fast food have had to rethink their strategies. McDonald's still sells French fries and hamburgers but it also sells salads. It is trying to convey an image of providing healthy food.

Buy nothing day

The Buy Nothing Day is an international awareness-raising campaign against needless levels of overconsumption and advertising. For some, the consumer culture is out of control. People used to shop to buy what they needed. Now many shop for other reasons: to impress each other, to fill a void or simply to kill time. The Buy Nothing Day movement was a simple idea with deep implications. It forced people to think about the 'shop-till-you-drop' mentality and what this mentality does to the rest of the world, not least the environment.

It encouraged citizens to ask the following questions when buying items: Is it made from renewable resources? Is it locally made? Is it an environmentally sustainable industry? Does the production process produce toxins or pollutants? Are the workers treated well? Is there too much packaging? Do I really need it? How long will it last? Where will it go when I throw it away?

The tyranny of brands

Yet another sign of the strength of the anti-consumerism movement is the popularity of Naomi Klein's book *No Logo*. This has been a publishing sensation in that it started its rise to popularity by word of mouth, rather than by a glossy advertising campaign. The book examines the impact of brands and marketing on consumers and it is critical of sweatshops in Asia that produce goods (such as sports shoes) at a low cost that are then sold at a high price in developed countries. The global justice movement NGO is itself a good example of this new era. Just when it seemed that western student activism was a thing of the past and students were concentrating more on careers than causes, so the global justice movement has risen spontaneously to challenge the disadvantages of economic globalization.

Ethical purchasing

Driving the dollar further

Ethical purchasing complements boycotts. As in the GE example, an ethical purchaser would deliberately buy a product or service (in this case, a washing machine) from a corporation that was not also making nuclear weapons.

For the individual, this means buying things for their usefulness and necessity, rather than for their status (a point made by Klein's concern with 'logo' products). It means rejecting anything that produces an addiction in the consumer and refusing to be influenced by the advertising industry into acquiring new models, rather than just making do with the current model for longer. It also means enjoying things without owning them, such as public libraries.

There are also implications for the organizations that purchase in bulk and so handle large sums of money. For example, using local government purchasing contracts to 'reward' companies that are not also producing weapons.

Fair trade

A variation of the boycotts and ethical purchasing is to buy goods that are made by workers who are not being exploited. This takes at least three forms.

First, some alternative trading operations have been created to import goods from developing companies that are not exploiting the workers, such as Trade Winds Tea and the Oxfam shops. Thus people can buy items with a clear conscience. Coffee, after petroleum, is the most heavily traded commodity in the world and yet many of the world's farmers make a very poor living from it. While the coffee industry is booming, it comes at great cost to the small-scale farmers of Latin America, Africa and Asia who grow more than half of the world's coffee. Most of these peasant farmers lack reliable market information, direct access to buyers and credit and so they are forced to sell their harvests to middlemen for a small sum of money. There is now a Coffee Fair Trade movement developing in the US. The Fair Trade model offers four fundamental criteria: direct trade with disadvantaged farmers, a fair price, timely credit and support for sustainable agriculture. There are now more than 120 different coffee companies across the US that sell Free Trade-Certified coffees.

Second, there is the Clean Clothes Campaign (CCC). The CCC began in 1990 in the Netherlands and has spread to many other developed countries. The CCC informs consumers about the conditions in which their garments and sportswear are produced and pressurize retailers to take responsibility for these conditions. The main demand is that they should accept a code of good conduct which includes the following: employment is freely chosen; there is no discrimination in employment; child labour is not used; freedom of association and the right to collective bargaining are respected; living wages are paid; hours of work are not excessive; working conditions are decent; and there is a system of independent monitoring.

Finally, the most well known example of this work is the Body Shop chain, whose founder was Anita Roddick. She tried to raise the ethics of the cosmetic business. Ironically, she was removed in the late 1990s by financiers, who were concerned that the chain was not making enough money. She received a large payout as compensation. Her fate is a warning that the ethical consumers have to be in for the long haul and not just be creatures of fashion.

Shareholder activism

Vigilante investor

Moving from goods to finance, there has been the rise of the 'vigilante investor', the person who uses investments for social purposes, as well as to make money for themselves.

Many people in developed countries are contributing to pension/superannuation funds. These funds own the bulk of the shares on stock exchanges. In due course, some consumers will pay more attention to how their money is being used. Of course, as with ethical purchasing and Fair Trade, this requires people to take an interest in their finances.

But not everyone is as vigilant as they should be. Seventy per cent of British bank account holders earn a very small rate of interest, even though by shopping around they could do much better. Thus, the ideas in this chapter require a degree of activism – not least taking an interest in what your money is doing and whom it is doing it with. If people are going to earn good interest in the interest of others, they first have to have an interest in their own interest.

Buying shares in corporations of which one disapproves

There are four forms of action. One is to buy shares in corporations of which the person is critical. Buying shares in a corporation enables the shareholder (who is thereby one of the 'owners') to raise at annual general meetings issues of concern about corporation policies. They can, for example, have resolutions adopted instructing the management not to invest in, say, certain countries or products or to produce a report on what the corporation's impact is on, say, developing countries.

Socially responsible investments (SRI)

Interest in social investment funds began in the US in the late 1960s with people wanting to make sure that they did not invest in the military-industrial complex. Because of the Vietnam War, the complex was booming and some people were troubled that they may be opposing the war publicly and yet benefiting from it financially. The first ethical investment fund with social responsibility was created in 1971: the Pax World Fund.

This form of investment is now firmly established – and doing well for its clients. The largest US fund is Christian Brothers Investment Services Inc (CBIS), with about $2.8 billion in assets under its management. The Catholic Church is big business in the US – and in Australia it is now the country's largest employer with the downsizing of the big corporations. There is a lot of denominational money (let alone money from other sources) to go into Catholic investment funds.

The biggest limitation to SRI is the lack of demand for them. Personal investors are often unaware of them and financial advisers are reluctant to recommend them. It is incorrect to think that profits can only come from investments in companies whose produce may trouble a person's social conscience. Individuals no longer have to be torn between investments in the planet's future and their own. Their principal can be reconciled to their principles. But more education is required here.

Investment guidelines

The third approach is to draw up investment guidelines. For example, in November 1972 the American Baptist Home Mission Society and the Women's American Baptist Home Mission Society adopted guidelines governing the use of their money. There was to be no investment in major defence contractors, or corporations that injure the environment, discriminate against women or minorities, or are involved in repressive regimes like South Africa.

The implementation of a set of guidelines may require the sale of investments ('divestment'). In late 1989, for example, the Evangelical Lutheran Church of America became the first mainline US Protestant denomination to establish a schedule for total divestment of its pension funds from corporations investing in South Africa. The New York-based Catholic Coalition for Responsible Investment operated with a similar set of guidelines in advising its 160 orders. Divestment should be a last resort. It recommended that there should be the opportunity for conversion by first having several discussions with the corporation concerned.

The most famous case of divestment was the withdrawal of funds from South Africa. In 1971 the (US Anglican) Episcopal Church made business history when it called (as a shareholder) for 'its' General Motors company to withdraw from South Africa. This began the long process of both informing Americans about the evils of apartheid and using investment as a lever on the minority white government. The anti-apartheid movement is often cited as a compelling example of the growing impact of NGOs and the increased role of state and local actors in influencing US foreign policy. The movement engaged thousands of Americans in concrete efforts to put pressure on the South African apartheid regime and to reverse the Reagan administration's policy of 'constructive engagement'. Even for

Americans who did urge divestment or stage a protest in front of a South African consulate, the movement contributed to a broad-based US fascination with South Africa. Many Americans may not know much about Africa, but the events and activities that surrounded and emanated from the anti-apartheid movement forged a special connection between US and South African societies.

The World Council of Churches was also involved in this campaign, paying particular attention to encouraging Shell to stop its investment in South Africa.

Going where the banks will not

The final approach is for NGOs to go where the banks will not. These projects may occur where the amount required to be borrowed is so small that the banks lack the financial incentive to provide the money – the cost of the paperwork would exceed any eventual return. These people lose out not because they have unprofitable proposals but ones that are too small. Groups concerned with the advancement in the developing world can be helpful here.

The great growth of the micro-credit movement (such as the Grameen Bank in Bangladesh) is a good example of where a small sum of money can go a long way. A group of women obtain a small sum of money to set up, say, their own sewing business. There is a very high rate of the debt being repaid. It also adds to the self-esteem of the women. It is an irony that people who need money most often have to pay the highest rate of interest because they lack collateral.

Alternatively, the proposals may be large but appear to be unprofitable. The standard example of success is from one of the worst of Chicago's slum areas: the South Shore Bank. This is the first neighbourhood bank in the US. In 1973 the bank, equipped with money from outside the area (including to date several millions in Church deposits), started providing loans to local borrowers to renew the neighbourhood, such as for housing, energy conservation and training programmes. The bank could not afford to consider loan defaults as part of the cost of doing business the way bigger institutions did, so it devoted extra time and care to each customer. Whether the budding entrepreneur was a man or a woman, South Side provided training to ensure that its loan recipients had a clear business plan and a good chance of success. It has been a very profitable venture. From the beginning, the community bank's mission was not defined in terms of profit for shareholders but, rather, the redevelopment of the derelict South Shore slum. In almost three decades, the bank has both redeveloped the South Shore and been a successful financial venture. It has done well by doing good.

The implication of this type of banking is that it is good for depositors. Depositors in the 1990s were paying for the banking excesses of the 1980s, when irresponsible loans were made to people who could not – or would not – repay the money. Ordinary depositors were paying for the scandals of the 1980s. But at Chicago's South Side, there is no scope for such irresponsibility in loans – and therefore it is a safe place to make deposits. South Side is setting an example in integrity for banking corporations.

Conclusion

This chapter has argued that money, which has traditionally been a tool of exchange, may also be used as a tool for positive economic and social change. It can enable the NGO opponents of some forms of economic globalization to push for economic and social change. Individuals need not be powerless when confronting corporations.

Many people in developed countries are contributing to pension/superannuation funds. These quiet giants own the bulk of the shares on stock exchanges. Consequently, these people are capitalists (whether they like the label or not) and ought to pay attention to how their money is being used. Does their retirement money go to places they never dreamed of?

The socially responsible use of money is an opportunity to introduce a new competitive factor into the marketplace. It is a way of encouraging corporations to compete to have the best record for, among other things, production for a peacetime economy, good pollution control, fair employment practices and for providing a safe workplace for their workers.

Finally, for global justice movement NGO activists who are concerned about peace and justice, using their money responsibly is one way of putting their money where their beliefs are. Globalization can be made fairer for everyone.

Questions

1 Are human beings motivated solely by consumerism?

2 What other NGO campaigns against transnational corporations are you aware of?

3 Are you willing to change your lifestyle in the interests of helping poorer people (for example, buying goods from developing countries)?

4 What are the implications for the global environment of global consumerism?

5 What are the implications for a global 'under class' arising from the creation of the global middle class?

13

the reaction against globalization

This chapter will cover:
- religious fundamentalism
- white male rage
- the global justice movement
- globalization in the novels of Robert Ludlum.

Introduction

There is considerable reaction against globalization and it is coming from a variety of sources. The views range all the way across the political spectrum, from the extreme right across to the extreme left.

This reaction is to be expected given that it is such a wide-ranging phenomenon. Globalization is a modernizing and destabilizing force that is slicing through many aspects of life. Some conservative people feel threatened by all the change and the influx of foreign ideas, people, goods and services. There is a nostalgia for the past, when life seemed less hurried, more ordered and less threatening. That golden era appears all the more golden the further people move from it, as time and change whisk them along.

Meanwhile, social justice NGOs and individuals in the global justice movement are concerned about the victims of globalization, such as the people in the sweatshops in developing countries and the increasing corporate wealth.

This chapter contains examples of the reaction against globalization. It examines both the conservative reaction and the global justice movement reaction. It ends with a note about the rise of anti-globalization in novels.

Religious fundamentalism

It was common among western sociologists in the 1950s to argue that religion was dying out. It may linger on as a private matter for some people but essentially people were far more interested in consumerism than going to places of worship. Ironically, religion is now a front page issue. It seems that some people who feel threatened by globalization have looked to religion to provide a response. There has been a dramatic rise in religious fundamentalism.

Religious fundamentalism defines people by what divides them. It focuses on the differences in humankind, rather than what unites them. It is often partly motivated by a form of xenophobia (against either strangers of another country or of another religion) and a loss of members to other causes (perhaps more secular ones).

Hinduism

There is the campaign against 'foreign influences' in India. The Hindu fundamentalist party, Rashtriya Swayamsevak Sangh (RSS) has had a campaign against Coke and Pepsi, as part of a larger movement to boycott the sale of foreign goods in India. RSS officials claimed that Coke and Pepsi were the most visible symbols of the transnational corporation invasion of India. The RSS campaign was called 'Swadeshi', which is a term borrowed from the movement launched by Mahatma Gandhi against British-made goods during India's freedom struggle in the 1930s and 1940s. The use of this term was political opportunism because RSS had otherwise little love for him – it was an RSS member who assassinated Gandhi in 1947 because RSS said that he was too close to the Muslim minority. But for RSS this was a useful slogan since it tapped into a tribal memory of Hindus and enabled the RSS to exploit Hindu fears about Indian Muslims (there are more Muslims in India than in neighbouring Pakistan).

The RSS tapped into the concerns that Indians had about the globalization of their country. India is, for example, the largest maker of movies – much larger, even, than Hollywood. But filmmakers have had to operate under strict censorship rules. Explicit scenes are forbidden; the camera moves off the lovers and looks at moving bushes. Pirated western videos, however, are gaining in popularity and Indian parents feel that they are losing control over the viewing habits of their children.

The history of Coke in India is an example of the country's changing attitudes towards globalization. Until 1992 outside firms were not allowed to control more than 40 per cent of a domestic enterprise; now they may acquire as much as 51 per cent and, with special government permission, even 100 per cent. Coca-Cola has now bought Parle, India's leading soft drink company.

Ironically, encouraged by Parle chairman, Ramesh Chauhan, the government expelled Coca-Cola in 1977 for refusing to reveal its secret formula and to decrease ownership from 100 per cent to 40 per cent. Chauhan followed up with a five-year crusade in the press and in parliament against Pepsi-Cola, trying to block its entry into India. Now realizing that he could not fight two giant transnational corporations, Chauhan sold Parle to Coca-Cola for an estimated US$60 million.

This is a facet of the anxiety about the pace of change. Indian political cohesion is a delicate balancing act between the different religious and ethnic groups, powerful trade unions and employers and the underlying tensions of a majority Hindu society in which the ancient system of caste – which ascribes one's social rank at birth – is being challenged by the poorest and least powerful. Supporters of India's economic reforms can already point to a string of successful joint ventures with foreign companies and a corresponding increase in productivity and quality in local industry. But just as new modern industries are thriving, so outdated industries are dying, killing off millions of jobs in a country with no welfare safety net. Increased economic activity is already making worse serious environmental problems as more cars pour onto the roads, more coal is burnt to produce electricity and new factories put pollutants into the air and waterways. Satellite television has reached over half of the total population of about one billion, fuelling demand for consumer goods more rapidly than economic growth can line people's pockets.

Islam

The world of Islam has also had some examples of anti-globalization. For example, in 1989 British writer Salman Rushdie, author of *The Satanic Verses*, was issued with a death sentence by the late Ayatollah Khomeini in a *fatwa*. In 1994, Bangladeshi author Taslima Nasrin fled her country to western Europe to escape legal charges and a *fatwa* in respect of her own writing. In early 2006 there was anger at cartoons published originally in Denmark ridiculing the Prophet Mohammad. The three episodes have globalization implications.

First, in none of the cases would the mobs calling for the deaths of the writers or Danish cartoonist nessarily be familiar with the actual writings or cartoons. In particular, *The Satanic Verses* is an extremely allusive and opaque novel but religious leaders have been able to arouse the mobs into great frenzies – and they have used modern communications technology to do so.

Second, all three cases are examples of where people can think globally and act locally. *The Satanic Verses* death toll reached about 60: more than 20 Pakistanis and Bangladeshis were killed in riots in 1989; in July 1991 the Japanese translator of the book was stabbed to death in Tokyo; in July 1993, 36 people were killed in a Turkish hotel blaze when Islamic radicals tried to kill the person who had made a translation of parts of the book. Many other people have been wounded, such as the Italian translator of the book, who was stabbed in July 1991 but survived. About a dozen people were killed in early 2006 over the Danish cartoons.

Third, the Rushdie case contains several ironies. He is a British subject living in London, who has been sentenced to death by an Iranian leader (who has since died and so apparently the *fatwa* cannot be revoked). He is being protected by British police, while the British government is anxious to expand trade with Iran and so plays down the *fatwa* issue. Meanwhile, Rushdie has been helped by some NGOs that have been keeping his fate in the public eye, notably the International Committee for the Defence of Salman Rushdie, which is housed at the Article 19 (freedom of information) NGO in London.

Finally, on a slightly frivolous note, Americans who were outraged by the lack of French support for their 2003 invasion of Iraq, renamed French fries as 'Liberty fries'. In February 2006, Iranians decided to stop eating 'Danish pastries' and instead renamed the cakes 'roses of the Prophet Mohammed'. Here is an example of thinking globally and acting locally – and borrowing an activist technique from overseas.

Another controversy concerns Islamic clothing. Islam provides its believers with a detailed code of conduct covering all aspects of their lives. Muslims are expected to be constantly aware of their faith. It is not just an event that takes place in a place of worship on a particular day. Clothing, like all other aspects of daily life, gets some attention. The problem is that the religious ruling is not clear.

The clothing controversy in France has gone on for well over a decade. France has a strict division between religion and the state which goes back to the French Revolution of 1789, when the Catholic Church was seen as corrupt and siding with the royal family. Aristocrats were executed, the Church was reduced in power, priests had to swear allegiance to the state (and not to Rome) and the country eventually became a republic. French intellectuals of that era regarded religion as divisive, intolerant and backward. Government schools were banned from being used for religious purposes.

The influx of Muslims from the former French colonies in North Africa, beginning in the 1950s, has created all sorts of tensions. The first migrants did not want to have in France the type of dictatorial mullahs they had left behind in Africa. They liked the French principle that religious belief is a private matter and not regulated (let alone imposed) by the state. But now a younger generation (much to the surprise of their parents and grandparents) has sought to rediscover their conservative traditional Islamic roots. They want to wear particular forms of clothing. France is the most well known European battleground because it has the largest Islamic population in western Europe (as many as five million out of the continent's 13 million). But there are similar disputes in most western European countries.

Trying to make sense of the particular controversy over clothing is hindered by some of the basic facts of Islam. There is often a lack of agreement over the detailed regulations of the faith. For example, there is general agreement that Muslim women are required to dress modestly but how is this basic instruction to be interpreted? There is no one standard method of 'Islamic dress' found around the world.

There is no central Islamic authority to rule on controversial issues. Just as Christian denominations vary in authority systems (the pope, the archbishop of Canterbury etc.), so there are similar variations in Islam. In some branches of Islam, a man establishes his own place of worship and has to attract followers. This is a free market system of religion – mullahs who do not attract followers do not flourish. This free market means that there are many Islamic opinions and spokespeople. It is often confusing to outsiders trying to work out the one standard Islamic line on an issue.

Islam began about 1,400 years ago in present day Saudi Arabia. Some of its rules reflect the particular conditions of its time and may not necessarily be applicable to the modern era. Islam now has about one billion followers (almost one-fifth of the world's population) but only about ten per cent of them are Arab. Many non-Arab Muslims have sought to blend their faith with their local circumstances. There is therefore a lot of variety and many Muslims want a more modern faith, not a traditional Arab one.

Finally, some Muslims regard the making of pictures of living creatures as forbidden by religious law. (This helps explain the stunningly attractive Islamic buildings with bright colours – the skills of the artists went into bright geometrical patterns, rather than portraits and animal landscapes.) Therefore, there are not many illustrations from the early Islamic era to see how people actually dressed at that time. The standard illustrations are from the handful of European tourists, who may well (like tourists throughout history) have only painted and sketched the more eye-catching clothes.

For example, it has been claimed that the *hijab* was reinvented in the 1970s as a symbol of Islamic militancy. It became part of the new way of advertising disapproval of modern dress standards and drawing attention to the traditional purity of the faith. But, it is claimed, the *hijab* is not required as a standard item of the faith.

A similar controversy exists over men and beards. There is nothing in the Koran itself that orders Muslims to wear beards. The Prophet Mohammed wanted Muslims to be separate from the pagans and beards were a way of showing easily that they were separate. They also were a way of identifying fellow Muslims in a hostile location when a Muslim under threat wanted assistance. Therefore, the prophet may have had in mind that growing beards could be encouraged – but was not mandatory. Many Muslims throughout history have regarded themselves as true believers – but they did not wear beards.

Yet another area of confusion arises from the way that the specific issue of clothing gets caught up in the wider issues of government policy over religion and citizenship. On religion in schools, France and the US have a strict separation between religion and the state (traditionally called the 'Church–state split'). In the latter, it is even illegal to have prayers before a school sporting match.

However, Australia and Britain have a less firm split between the Church and state. It is not so absolute. For instance, governments give funding to religious schools and religious social welfare organizations. Therefore the controversy over Islamic dress has been slower to emerge in Britain and Australia than in France.

Christianity

Christianity also has some instances of reaction against globalization. Two of last century's most well known American Christian evangelists, Jim and Tammy Bakker, pioneered the use of television for evangelism purposes; people could stay at home and so avoid the inconvenience of going to a local church. They used a form of modern technology, ironically, to criticize modern developments. The Bakkers evoked a mythical earlier

American era, away from the present era of change and confusion and just gave the folks 'old time Christian religion' blended with commemorating key American events. They tapped into the tribal memory of – or at least the nostalgia for – the pioneering days. The fourth of July (rather than Christmas or Easter) was traditionally the target date for the completion of new buildings at Heritage USA, the Christian Disneyland they created in North Carolina. Unfortunately, Jim Bakker was a crook and so went to gaol for the misuse of money donated to Heritage USA.

Bakker avoided political controversy, although he had an underlying sympathy for conservative candidates, such as Ronald Reagan. Jerry Falwell of the Moral Majority and Pat Robertson, however, were overtly far more political (with Robertson – a son of a US senator from Virginia – displaying vice-presidential aspirations in 1980). Both saw the US as God's chosen country, surrounded by enemies (especially in the USSR and the UN), and the importance of the US having its own set of priorities in international affairs, irrespective of the views of other countries. The Moral Majority was one form of globalization (an NGO) opposed to the 'cooperative power' form of globalization (notably the UN) and was highly suspicious of the values of the other form (transnational corporations).

The end of the Cold War robbed the religious extremists of an 'anti-Christ' to oppose (in the USSR). However, they still resent the fact that the US is losing its pre-eminence in the world and a continue to have hostile feelings towards the UN. American Christian groups (and their supporters overseas) are particularly concerned about 'world government'. This is called 'armageddon theology'.

There is much speculation about the end of the world and the return of Jesus. However, the armageddon theology is a fringe Christian activity and is not part of mainstream Christian thinking. The core of the theology is the claim to be able to predict the date of the Second Coming of Jesus and the end of the present world. This is done via interpretations of certain Biblical passages. There will be the Rapture, when true believers will be whisked off the face of the earth. Those remaining will go through the Great Tribulation for seven years. This will be a period of great suffering for all the other people remaining on the planet.

Armageddon theology appeals to pessimistic people. Their taste for theology is derived from their perception of secular trends. This explains its popularity among some Australian, British and American Christians – they see declining church numbers, feel overwhelmed by all the secular changes taking place and are fearful of the future. Fear and suspicion are key characteristics among adherents to this theology. There is a fear of globalization, a suspicion of large international organizations and a worry about giant computers, bankcards and barcodes.

White male rage

The politics of anger

'White male rage' refers to the way that some poor, blue-collar (or unemployed), white American males are angry that they are being pushed (as they see it) to society's margins. Women, people of Asian and African origin all seem to be getting preference over them. White male rage is being blamed for the upsurge of politically motivated violence in the US, such as the Oklahoma bombing (in which 167 people were killed) and the bombing of abortion clinics. Intolerance has always existed. It is not due solely to the present pace of change but the pace of change has certainly added to some political extremism. There are signs of white male rage in other developed western countries. These groups have some similarities.

- They are white supremacist, anti-Jewish and anti-Asian. This is partly a reaction to the end of the Europeanization of the globe. For the past 500 years, starting in the 1490s, Europeans have gradually extended their control around the world, with the USA taking over much of that role later last century. That era has ended and Asian countries are growing rapidly. Some people are having difficulty psychologically coping with the ending of white dominance of the globe, the winding up of European empires, and the rise of many independent states in those former colonies.

- There has been a revolution in the protection of human rights. This began in the late 1940s as a reaction to Hitler's persecution of the Jews. A leader who violates human rights at home will eventually start to violate them overseas. Therefore, it is in the international community's interest that there should be international protection of human rights. However, some conservative people are having difficulty coping with equal treatment for women and people of different races.

- There is hostility towards the government (be it local, state or national). There has been an expansion of the role of government in the twentieth century, as citizens have expected governments to provide more services, such as the welfare state, and combat unemployment. But for some people government is more 'big brother' than 'big mother'. There is resentment at paying taxes and filling in forms.

- Transnational corporations now dominate the global economy. Whatever your problem, you can solve it by spending money – 'retail therapy' – at a 'cathedral of consumerism' (a shopping mall). Children are now less likely to listen to their parents because they now have other role models. Indeed, they will have less contact with their parents because they will spend more time watching television or playing with their computer games. Some parents fear that they are losing control over their children.

- Politics is increasingly one NGO competing against another. Most voters do not count for much – unless they live in marginal constituencies. Therefore, the political landscape includes some of the extreme right-wing activist NGOs, part of whose campaigns are directed at left-wing environmental or human rights NGOs.

- Extreme right-wing NGOs are based on the cult of the 'rugged individual': society consists of individuals competing against all other individuals. There is no sense of community. It is a case of 'survival of the fittest': 'Do unto others before they get a chance to do it unto you.' These groups are opposed to co-operative power and organizations such as the UN or EU and foreign aid NGOs.

Sources of anger

The politics of anger has three sources. The first is the process of globalization. Governments (as noted earlier) are no longer the masters of their economic destiny. Transnational corporations are now the main global economic force. Transnational corporations have eroded the notion of a national economy; there is now only a global one. About half of what is called 'international trade' is actually trade conducted within different components of the same corporations. The pace of global economic change is increasing. World trade is growing faster than national economies. In other words, countries are doing more trade with each other as the years go by – and are doing so at a faster rate than their own national economic growth.

The idea of a 'job for life' has gone in developed countries; some unemployed middle-aged people (usually men) fear that they will never have a full-time job again; some young people fear that they will never get a full-time job at all. Those that have jobs, are working longer hours. Most young people in developed countries accept that they will not enjoy the same high standard of living as their parents. Meanwhile, the heads of corporations are being paid very large salaries, irrespective of how well the corporations actually perform. The rich are getting richer.

Another source of anger is that people feel taken by surprise by all that is going on. The mass media give people what they want, rather than what they need. For example, television news programmes are brisk, brief, colourful, laden with emotion, short on facts and with no analysis of underlying trends. The process of globalization has been underway for some decades. There has been no grand conspiracy and it has not been done in secrecy. But this process has been ignored by the mass media in preference to stories of sport, and entertainment. Now the full force of globalization is striking home and there is anger and confusion among people. They have not been prepared for change.

The lack of political leadership is another source of anger. Politics has become a branch of the television entertainment industry: colourful, superficial and a form of diversion. It is a type of sport, where the political discussion is not so much based on ideas as on who will win. Political parties follow opinion polls. They find out what voters are concerned about and replay their fears back to them (such as the periodic 'law and order' scares). They reinforce old fears rather than provide new ideas.

Politicians tell people what they want to hear – rather than what they need to know. What they have needed to know is that the process of globalization is underway, traditional ideas of the role of national government are no longer relevant and that there is a limited capacity for any government to do much to slow the overall pace of global change. The lack of conventional political leadership has created a political vacuum into which unconventional, extremist leaders have moved.

There is therefore a wave of anger sweeping through many societies. The target is the failure of governments to satisfy the demands of their citizens. This is coupled with a search for scapegoats. Voters are crying out for new ideas and new options. They are not getting them. Politics abhors a vacuum. The lack of leadership from conventional politics is being filled by leaders from the fringes, such as Louis Farrakhan, of the US Nation of Islam, an organization recruiting poor, alienated individuals into Islam. Meanwhile, in Australia the voters are turning to extremist individuals such as the Shooters Party. Much of what they say is nonsense. Not enough has been done by politicians and the mass media to inform people about all the changes through which the world has passed.

Governments can find money to finance sporting events. They ought similarly to conjure up funding to explain to their own citizens just what is going on in the world. Otherwise the right-wing anger will just get worse.

The global justice movement

Free trade is not necessarily fair trade

The Allied governments at the end of World War II wanted to encourage free trade. The erection of tariffs in the 1930s was seen by them as having made the depression even worse. The advantages and disadvantages of 'free trade' provide one of the longest running themes in economic theory. On the one hand, it is argued that free trade is good in that countries get to specialize in what they do best. No human can provide all the goods and services they need (and so have to trade their skills as a way of buying other goods and services) and so similarly no country can ever cope for all its own needs. Therefore, there should be an end to all measures that restrict foreign trade (such as tariffs and import quotas) and allow trade to move freely across national boundaries, as it already does within large federal countries (such as the USA, Canada and Australia) and regions (most notably the EU).

On the other hand, the benefits of free trade are spread across a community but the costs are concentrated. For example, developed western countries used to have a thriving textile, footwear and clothing manufacturing industry. Tariffs and import quotes kept out foreign competition. The prices were high and the choices were limited but at least the industry provided a great deal of employment to local workers.

Then, just over two decades ago, in the interests of furthering free trade, governments began relaxing the tariffs and quotas, so that their citizens can now acquire clothing and footwear from cheaper producers (such as China and south Asia). The good news is that the cost of living has, in theory, gone down because the cost of clothing has gone down and there is a wider choice of clothes and footwear for consumers. The bad news is that many manufacturers have closed down and gone offshore to cheaper producers; these closures have contributed to unemployment problems in western countries.

Thus, the debates over free trade go back and forth without much resolution. At present, governmental opinion in developed countries is very much in favour of free trade. In 1947 the western developed countries agreed to create the International Trade Organization (ITO). The ITO – again reflecting the worldview of the people who had survived the depression and the war – was to promote orderly free trade under the UN's jurisdiction and within its social mandate (including full employment). The new ITO was also to have power to regulate international capital movements. This latter provision – to our current thinking – seems unbelievable but that was how things were done in those days. For example, all British subjects leaving the UK had to list in the back of their passports how much currency they were taking out of the country. Private ownership of gold bullion (as distinct from gold jewellery) was banned in most countries.

The ITO was too restrictive for the USA, which wanted to have control over the post-war international trading system. It did not want to have social considerations incorporated into economic matters. The USA refused to ratify the ITO treaty. Instead, under US pressure, the 'temporary' General Agreement on Tariffs and Trade (GATT) was created. GATT proceeded by a series of 'rounds', in which tariffs were gradually reduced. GATT's ambit gradually increased. The last 'round' was 1986–94.

In 1995 the World Trade Organization (WTO) replaced GATT. It proceeded via a series of 'rounds', and one was held in Seattle, Washington State, in December 1999. But the conference was a disaster. Outside the conference, 40,000 demonstrators suddenly arrived from around the world to draw attention to the dangers of free trade.

Not only that, there was also chaos inside in the conference hall. The EU wanted to have broad-based negotiations to extend the WTO's role into such matters as labour and environmental standards and investment policies. The EU did not share the demonstrators' opposition to the WTO negotiations but it was the closest to their point of view. The demonstrators wanted to stop the WTO's negotiations – the EU wanted the WTO negotiations to continue but to have a greater role in human rights and environmental matters.

The US had a less ambitious agenda but it was still willing to have labour and environmental standards on it. The Clinton administration paid some attention to the demonstrators' point of view – but its corporations wanted the WTO negotiations to go ahead to create even more trading opportunities for them.

Developing countries were opposed to broadening the WTO agenda. They argued that the WTO should stick to its own area of expertise, namely, trade. It should not get involved in other matters, such as human rights and the environment. Those matters could be discussed at UN bodies. Also, the last GATT round (1986–94) favoured the developed western countries. For example, developing countries lose about US$60 billion a year in potential exports because their farmers cannot compete with the heavily subsidized agricultural products in the US and EU countries. Therefore, more has to be done to help developing world countries. Indeed, they wanted to re-open the Uruguay round agreement to get a better deal for themselves.

Governments are now trying to see how the next round of WTO negotiations can be relaunched, with less drama. The problem is that people have now become so sensitized to this matter that the eventual relaunching will attract considerable media attention. Free trade is now very much on the political agenda.

Multilateral Agreement on Investment (MAI)

All the international trade negotiations are done by governments and are implemented by them. But transnational corporations are the driving force behind the agendas of the developed countries. They have convinced the governments that the free movement of trade in goods and services will be of benefit to the governments. The problem for the corporations was that developing countries did not like the increasing power the corporations had over their affairs.

Developing countries used the UN bodies and GATT to voice their concerns about the power of transnational corporations. Developed countries decided to use another vehicle for their free trade agenda: the Paris-based Organization for Economic

Cooperation and Development (OECD). The OECD consists of the 29 most developed countries in the world and is often called the 'club of rich countries'. It was created after World War II to coordinate US Marshall Aid and assist with the recovery of western Europe from the war, and has continued as a forum of those governments, as well as other developed countries (such as Japan).

In 1995 the OECD agreed to create a Multilateral Agreement on Investment (MAI) that would have reduced the power of governments to regulate foreign investment. The MAI project collapsed before completion and so there is no final text but the basic point is that a government would have to ensure all foreign corporations were offered the same terms for investment opportunities as domestic ones. For example, if a government wished to privatize one of its assets, it would not have been able to quarantine some of the investment opportunity to its own citizens and corporations. Anyone (irrespective of nationality) would be able to have the same opportunity.

These negotiations were held in secret until a draft MAI text was leaked by NGOs in 1997. There was widespread opposition to the MAI. For example, in Australia the extreme right-wing nationalist politician Pauline Hanson picked up the MAI issue and suddenly her statements encouraged the media to give MAI more attention. Her criticisms reflected the deepening Australian doubts about the value of free trade, the increasing rate of unemployment and the fact that MAI was being written in secrecy. Her popularity on this issue panicked the Australian government to join with others (led by France and Canada) to withdraw from the negotiations in late 1998. France and Canada were both concerned about what the free entry of US foreign investment would do to their cultures. This was the first time that a trade agreement had been defeated by popular opposition – much of it conducted via the internet.

General Agreement on Trade in Services

GATT concerned itself with food, raw materials and manufactured goods. To use the standard distinction, GATT was very much about what can drop on your foot. Now much more money can be made from 'services' – which can be defined as something you cannot drop on your foot. These include health, aged care, dental care, banking, libraries, publishing, broadcasting, insurance, tourism, environmental protection services and education.

The Final Act of the 1986–1994 GATT round of negotiations is 550 pages long. It was signed in Marrakesh in 1994 by trade ministers from the GATT members-countries. The signing was an act of faith. No one human being can calculate what this collection of treaties will mean for their own country. The ministers put their faith in free trade and hoped for the best.

One of the treaties that make up the Final Act is the General Agreement on Trade in Services (GATS). The WTO members (countries that conduct about 90 per cent of global trade) are now negotiating the specifics of GATS. The overall intention will be to open up national markets in services to foreign providers. The overall trend would be to reduce the role of government in the provision of services and for the private sector to take on that role.

Ironically, this has already been done in developing countries. Those governments that have had debt problems have been pressured by the International Monetary Fund (IMF) to get out of the provision of services and allow more scope for the private sector to provide them. Now developed countries will get the same treatment. This is not due to IMF pressure but because their own governments have put their faith in free trade and are hoping for the best.

One problem with GATS in particular and the WTO in general is the way that trade and finance take priority over social values, such as human rights and environmental considerations. Money is the measure of all things.

Also, the creation of a global 'level playing field' may well mean a lowering of standards and not a raising in them. This could be a race to the bottom. For example, a corporation's lawyers could argue that a country's health or environmental regulations are too restrictive. This has arisen over the introduction of genetically modified crops, which some countries would like to exclude.

Another problem is that governments are cooperating in their own reduction in power because the chief beneficiaries of GATS will be transnational corporations that will be able to expand the global reach of their activities and convert public services into private markets. Thus governments are standing back and allowing corporations to have more influence in their economies.

To conclude, there is a bizarre contradiction among all governments, not least the conservative ones (such as the Bush government in the US and the Howard government in

Australia). On the one hand, these governments are opposed to any expansion of the UN's international protection of human rights in terms of their own practices being reviewed by UN human rights bodies. They have a similarly hostile attitude to UN environmental treaties (such as the Kyoto Protocol on Climate Change). On the other hand, they are willing to surrender their national authority over trade and finance to international organizations. Now they are preparing to surrender public services to the private market. Imagine what the world would be like if governments treated, say, the protection of the environment as seriously as they do international trade, with binding rulings being handed down by international organizations.

Globalization in novels

Finally, there is the reaction against globalization to be found in novels. This genre is indicative of how the reaction taps into the fears that readers have about the sinister forces driving world change and eroding the power of governments. (Of course, for the activists who opposed the MAI treaty, they would say that, in fact, globalization is being done in secret.)

Here is the case of Robert Ludlum (1927–2001). He was one of the most popular novelists in the world, with his books published in 32 languages in 40 countries and selling almost 300 million copies. He left a number of books unfinished on his death and so his novels continue to appear. Four have so far been published posthumously.

All this popularity is an irony because the novels are not great works of English literature. The style is rather tedious, with each novel's excessive length due to the use of quoted speech (so that the novels read almost as dialogue for a movie). There is no lightness of touch and there are no memorable phrases. The characterization is weak and so there is no Ludlum character who stands out in the memory.

Why, then, should the novels sell so well? His popularity says a great deal about how many people view the world and fear what is happening. His novels have several features that resonate with the worldview of many readers. For a start, life is not what it seems. This is the basic element of all conspiracy theories: there is more to this than meets the eye. For example, except as the novels reach a climax, usually a large number of people meet grisly ends in private throughout the pages. Life for bystanders in the novels goes on as normal but beneath this apparent tranquillity, there is a great deal of violence.

Then (from another context): 'the truth is out there somewhere'. An individual or a small group of individuals know the truth but they always have difficulty in convincing others (especially those in authority) of their knowledge. The vast majority of characters in the novels are distracted by sport, entertainment and celebrity gossip. They are missing the major changes going on all around them.

Next, government is not to be trusted. There is always the risk of abuse of power. Established institutions are corrupt and penetrated by evil forces. The individual is best off having no trust in government. Indeed, government is often part of the problem rather than the solution.

Big business is not to be trusted either. Corporations are often the evil force behind governments, bending governments to their own ends. As Ludlum has written: 'Whoever controls a government's economy ultimately controls the government.'

For Ludlum fans, proof of the sinister power of corporations came in February 2006. Jose Bove is a French farmer who acquired international fame by dismantling a McDonald's outlet that was under construction near his sheep farm. He has often since spoken at anti-globalization rallies, including Seattle in November 1999. He arrived in the US in February 2006, only to be advised that he was no longer welcome there and he was sent back to France on the next flight. Only a few days earlier President Bush had endorsed the role of corporations in globalization in his annual State of the Union Address.

Individuals are the key figures. Ludlum's main characters operate outside government and corporations and aim to take them on. They are motivated by high ideals and are individually resourceful: they live on their wits, with little assistance from others. It is almost as though the John Wayne cowboy genre arrived in the late twentieth-century: the silent, alienated, lonely, moody outsider who tackles an evil situation and then moves out towards the sunset.

Therefore, by way of contrast, Ludlum's key figures are not James Bond types. Bond is a proud member of the British Secret Intelligence Service, supported by the full resources of the honourable and well-motivated British government (including scientists who create all types of fanciful equipment at the cost of the British taxpayer). Ludlum has created no 'James Bonds'. Indeed, none of his characters is such a 'hero': they are just ordinary people caught up in extraordinary situations.

Another element is that, life has no endings where all is explained. There is no final scene in a Ludlum novel where all the threads are drawn together. The Ludlum reader is expected to have followed all the twists and turns in the novel. If not, tough. Life wasn't meant to be easy – or explained.

Finally, each novel has a race against time: the individuals have to stop evil deeds but their sense of urgency is not shared by lethargic bureaucrats and law enforcement officials (who may well be part of the conspiracy anyway). This accords with the worldview of some conspiracy theorists that the world is moving towards some grand climax and so they have a sense of urgency that may not be shared by others. The climax may have been (in the Cold War era) a Soviet or Chinese attack; now it may be the threat of Islam or corporations that want to dominate the world through their technology. There is a sense of doom in the bones of many people who fear where the world is heading because of globalization.

Conclusion

There is a widespread reaction against globalization. It has several sources, which are diverse in themselves. There is no single driver of change which is very different from other NGO campaigns in the past. In the old days, there would be meetings among the NGOs to create common policy positions, elect spokespersons and then list 'demands' on government and others.

Thanks to the internet, mobilizations can now take place quickly, with little bureaucracy and hierarchy. Anyone with access to the internet can become her own spokesperson and issue her own statements. Globalization is therefore changing the way in which NGOs and others do business.

Some of the reaction is specifically right-wing nationalist and so anti-globalization is a reaction to the pace of change and 'modernization' in general. The left-wing global justice movement is not so much anti-globalization as wanting to see more done about respecting human rights, protecting the environment and ensuring better living conditions for all.

Questions

1 Do you see globalization as a form of conspiracy?
2 Why have most people paid so little attention to globalization?
3 What can be done to educate people about globalization?
4 How has globalization affected your own life?
5 What should national governments do about globalization?

14 globalization cannot be reversed

This chapter will cover:
- why globalization is here to stay
- the reinvention of government
- the reinvention of nationalism
- ways in which trade knits the world together.

Introduction

The coming era is not one of either/or but of multiple options. Therefore, it is possible that the process of globalization will co-exist with people reacting against that process – or at least using that reaction for their own purposes.

There has been no successful example of a government implementing major policies to reduce the impact of globalization on their country. For example, the US, under President Bush, has withdrawn from some international treaties and refused to accept others. But not even the US can now return to the pre-World War II level of isolationism. The US economy is too enmeshed with the global economy for that to take place. It can no longer, for instance, produce all its own oil and so it has to import most of it. The US has gone from being the world's largest producer of oil to being the largest importer.

Globalization is here to stay

Overall, therefore, the future belongs to globalization. First, the process has moved too far too fast to be stopped. Indeed, governments have been slow to react to what was happening, such as the rise of transnational corporations. The horse is out through the stable door and so it is pointless trying to work out how to close that door (such as national ways of trying to close up the economy to shut out foreign trade).

Then there will be a problem for any extreme right-wing nationalist coming to power (such as Jorge Haider in Austria, Jean Le Pen in France or Pauline Hanson in Australia): the transnational corporations will make life very difficult for them if they were to try to implement their policies. There would be, for example, a 'run' on the currency, whereby foreign holders of the currency will dump it and so drive down the price (and risk inflation at home), foreigners will withdraw their investment and will put in little new investment. The economy will start to collapse. Many of the mass media in that country will be linked to transnational corporations and so they will alert their viewers, listeners and readers to the 'dangerous' policies being followed by their nationalist leaders.

In due course the nationalist leaders will lose their appetite for extreme measures and recognize that they have to go along with the corporations. Even if they remain in office, they will have little influence. Their supporters will become disenchanted with the failure of their heroes and so drop out of politics. They will cease being radical 'citizens' and again become comfortable 'consumers'.

Indeed, it is possible that consumers will not vote anyway for extremist politicians once they have thought through the implications of trying to turn the clock back on globalization. If they were to keep out foreign competition, they would have fewer choices in products and individual cost may be higher. People in developed countries may be worried about the loss of jobs but they do like the broader range of cheaper goods coming in from China and India.

Next, the religious and political extremists may try to arouse the mobs – but their kids want Big Macs, Coke and jeans. This is the problem the high-brow BBC encountered in the 1950s: given a chance, the young listeners preferred entertainment to education – and often so did their parents, really. However much an aesthete may be appalled at popular tastes, the fact is the tastes are popular. If people are to have large disposable incomes, then they will want to spend them on what they want – rather than on what a high-minded central committee or academic elite deem is good for them. The fruits of globalization appeal to many people.

Finally, the opponents of globalization are too fragmented to be effective. They are in too many different groups, with different motivations and different goals. They may be able to bring on some change but the overall trend is towards globalization.

Government has been reinvented

In the early and mid-twentieth century people in many developed countries cared passionately about politics. This was reflected in the size of the political parties and the number of volunteers that could be relied on to help, such as through the distribution of 'how to vote' material. Politicians were then seen as important and fascinating as the Hollywood celebrities of today. Political meetings were well attended and the debates were closely followed. People really did think that the political deliberations were important and that politicians could make a difference.

Now virtually all the political parties in developed countries have much smaller memberships. Politicians are rarely crowd-drawers. To add spice to their public meetings, they try to involve entertainment and sporting celebrities. There is a general air of cynicism, if not boredom about politics among the general public. Half of the American voters do not bother to vote in presidential elections. Australians are forced to vote by government, making it a criminal offence not to do so (a decade ago over 50 people went to prison for not voting).

But the voters are not all that fussed about the declining significance of the political process. They expect little from politicians – and so at least they are not surprised when they fail to deliver.

Meanwhile, governments have reduced their own significance. They are no longer in the business of 'nation-building'. They rarely carryout infrastructure projects, such as roads and bridges. These are now left to corporations, which do them – like any other of their commercial ventures – to make a profit.

Again voters are not fussed. Their living standards have gone up dramatically in recent decades and they are enjoying the products and services of the corporations. They are comfortable consumers so most people are not hostile to the corporations.

Globalization is not riding across the world on a general's stallion. It is not being forced on people. Instead, globalization is embracing the world partly as people seek a better material standard of life. It is enveloping the world in ordinary everyday and practical matters. These are usually ignored by the mass media and so the pace and impact of globalization do not receive the attention they deserve.

The value of nationalism in sport

If nationalism is ceasing to have much prolonged political significance, where is it important? It seems that like so much of the rest of everyday life, it has become commoditized. Nationalism has been recruited to serve the interests of corporations and consumer society. People may not be very nationalist in their political affairs but their nationalism can be mobilized when money is to be made from sport.

Sport in recent decades has become a major financial activity. Sporting teams may make very large sums of money from their activities being televised. They are also part of the 'experience economy'. For example, Manchester United football team makes more money from the sale of souvenirs ('experience economy') than actually playing sport ('service economy').

People are mobilized by sporting activities. The Olympic Games, for example, is one of the most televised events in world history. British people may not feel very patriotically 'British' in politics but they do have nationalist aspirations when it comes to sport. There is money to be made out of sporting nationalism.

As the 2006 Soccer World Cup showed, the business of sport is one of the growing areas of globalization. Events are televised 'live' around the world. Overseas bets can be taken on the events. Fan clubs have global memberships. Sport is bringing the world together – and making money for corporations and players.

Trade knits the world together

The Golden Arches theory of world peace

Finally, there is the role of trade in knitting the world together. This has been called the 'McDonald's Golden Arches theory of world peace'. Countries that sell McDonald's fast food do not go to war against each other. There is nothing special about fast food reducing a person's ability to fight. It is simply that countries that accept fast food outlets are embracing free trade and free trade reduces the risk of war.

As an example, for over 1,000 years, the Franks and Huns, more recently French and Germans, have fought one another. Now they have gone for a generation without a war and it seems unlikely that they will ever have another. 'Why kill those people – they are our customers!' Trade and transnational corporations are knitting the world together.

There are probably as many conflicts underway today as at the height of the Cold War. But there is a new warfare state: conflicts are increasingly internal rather than international. The decline of international conflict has been credited partly to the growth of free trade and democracy. Governments are now committed to free trade and free politics. Capitalism creates a thriving middle class. War is bad for their interests. Middle-class people are more globally orientated and spin webs of affiliation around the world. They create NGOs such as Amnesty International and Greenpeace, as well as transnational corporations. Middle-class people prefer a world where they can travel freely: both to make money and to satisfy their curiosity. Middle classes are less tolerant of prolonged wars. Mrs Thatcher could unite the British in 1982 for the short, sharp Falklands campaign of six weeks' duration but President Johnson could not unite the US for the five years of his Vietnam campaign.

Besides, little is now to be gained by one country invading another. Invasions used to be about the conquest of new territory and resources or the imposition of a religion among new converts. In the new era of information technology, much of a country's wealth is in the heads of its people or in cyberspace. What would a country gain from invading, say, Japan? It has few natural resources. By the same token, Iraq's August 1990 invasion of Kuwait was a bad investment because so much of Kuwait's financial reserves were held offshore.

Of course, old rivalries will remain and there are traditional border disputes. When a country has problems at home it is always tempting to focus attention on an external threat (such as Greece and Turkey, India and Pakistan). But there are few international wars underway at present. Governments are finding that they have more to gain from peace than from war. Even the Indians and Pakistanis, with all their posturing with nuclear weapons, seem reluctant deliberately to have another war.

Global peace is gradually breaking out. Most of the people killed in international war in the twentieth century were killed in the first half of the century. The second half was a much more peaceful time. There were still internal conflicts but most countries had got out of the habit of invading others. Globalization is making the world a safer place.

Peace between China and Russia

It is worth recalling one major war that has not taken place. In March 1969 there was a violent confrontation on the Ussuri River, where dozens of Russian border guards were killed by Chinese soldiers. The Russians retaliated with an artillery barrage. Veteran American journalist Harrison Salisbury wrote a bestseller called *The Coming War Between Russia and China*. He expected this to be the arena of the next big international war. He was wrong.

Almost 40 years later relations are greatly improved and a war now seems most unlikely. There have even been recent joint military exercises between the two countries. There is still scope for accidental violence but overall the situation is much better. There is one fewer international war for the world to worry about.

The border between these two countries is the world's longest. For many decades, it was also the world's most militarized and was three times the length of Europe's 'Iron Curtain'. Three decades ago, the confrontation was absorbing about 25 per cent of each country's military effort.

Geography worked against Russia. The total length of the Russian empire is across ten time zones – almost halfway around the globe. The Russians felt vulnerable about their Asian rear end. Moscow is closer to New York than to Vladivostok.

The military confrontation was no sideshow. Although it cost three times as much to maintain a military division there than it did in eastern Europe, the Russian Asian units received the latest equipment, often before it reached the units in eastern Europe.

The cities and military forces in the area were dependent on the Trans-Siberian Railway, their main surface link with the rest of Russia, for food and military supplies. For 1,500 miles the railway ran ten to 15 miles from the Chinese border. Military movements down the line could have been disrupted by artillery fire. Worse still, the lines could have been cut, isolating the Russian Far East and leaving it at the mercy of a Chinese invasion.

Although Russia and China were both communist allies, they were not good friends. Western politicians exaggerated the extent of the 'unified Red threat' from Berlin to Beijing.

Russia saw itself as the main communist country. Chairman Mao Zedong did not. He largely ignored the advice of Stalin on how to run his country and refused Stalin's request to work with the Chinese nationalists to defeat the Japanese in World War II. He was also critical in 1959 when Stalin's successor, Nikita Khrushchev, tried to improve relations with the US.

The Russians regarded Chairman Mao as an upstart with radical ideas, who was not afraid of launching another world war (expecting that at least some Chinese would survive). They were troubled by his creation of nuclear weapons in 1964 (and he was angry with them because they had not helped him do it).

The major improvement began in 1985, when Mikhail Gorbachev became the Russian leader. He needed money to reform the country and so he needed to reduce its military commitments. He unilaterally removed some of the forces. Then, in 1990, the Soviet Union collapsed.

Russia now wants to develop Siberia and its Far East region. This is Russia's new frontier. Siberia floats on an ocean of gas – the natural gas fields in Siberia are the world's largest. That far end of Russia is also a treasure house of other raw materials: 60 per cent of the country's timber, 60 per cent of its coal and 80 per cent of its water. Gas is called 'blue gold', fur is 'soft gold', coal is 'black gold' and salmon 'red gold'.

But Russia cannot get the wealth by its own means. It is not technologically advanced enough. For example, the ground is frozen as hard as concrete 1,000 feet deep for most of the year. During the summer months the top five feet may thaw and so some vegetables can be grown. Therefore to cope with all these mining and drilling challenges, Russia needs foreign investment and expertise. Foreign corporations need to be reassured there will be no war between Russia and China.

Meanwhile, China also wants more foreign investment and expertise and so it also has an interest in avoiding a war with Russia. Therefore, a thirst for international investment and trade is encouraging an outbreak of peace between Russia and China.

The communists are being united by capitalist ambitions. They can now see some value in globalization.

Conclusion

Globalization is a fixed fact of world affairs. Although there are some critics of it, overall it has too many adherents to be reversed. Indeed, the process has gone too far. The world cannot return to an earlier era of national governments running their own affairs. We need to get used to the new era.

Questions

1 Do you think that globalization is here to stay?
2 How are we to 'reinvent' government?
3 On what occasions do you feel nationalistic?

4 Can you identify the ways in which global trade has been of benefit to you?

5 Have you or your relatives been harmed by globalization (such as by being made unemployed through the loss of work overseas)?

15 making the most of the new era

This chapter will cover:
- world governance
- ways of uniting the people
- world federalism
- the continuing debate over world federalism
- the refusal to change.

Introduction

If the pessimists are to be believed, then the earth is doomed to destruction. Diseases, climate change, environmental destruction, depletion of the oil reserves... there seem to be so many potential causes of catastrophe.

So what is an optimistic interpretation of the current stage of Earth's evolution? Globalization can represent a major leap forward in the way that the planet is governed: from national governments to some form of world government. Of course, even to talk of 'world government' seems, well, out of this world. The driving forces of change can provide us with new opportunities. Globalization may be the bridge to a new era of how earth's affairs are managed.

The UN is the current stage of the evolution towards world government, although it has a long way to go. However, there is no doubt that this is the direction the world needs to go. The choice may be between world government or no world to govern.

This chapter sets out some of the issues about world government. It looks at the different ways to bring people together, along with world federalism and then raises some of the basic questions of uniting the world.

Uniting the people

How are people to be united? There have been various plans for world unity over the centuries. The eighteenth and ninteenth centuries were particularly prolific in such projects, especially the revolutionary period and the Napoleonic wars. Speculation about some form of 'world government' is not, then, simply a recent idea. But the twentieth century (especially since World War I) saw increased urgency given to these ideas and two small attempts (League of Nations and UN) to implement them.

There are three ways of trying to get countries united:

- **The federalist approach** – the deliberate decision by national governments to transfer certain powers (such as maintaining armed forces) to a world government while retaining other powers (such as establishing laws concerning ownership of property) for themselves.

- **The functionalist approach** – the creation of more global agencies (such as the WHO, International Maritime Organization) to handle a particular function (such as health or maritime issues). Experts can cooperate in a less politically charged environment and eventually the globe will be covered by a network of such agencies.

- **The populist approach** – the creation of a grassroots people's movement to establish a democratic world government directly responsible to the people of the world and, in the meantime, to generate ideas for world government and a groundswell in favour of it.

There is a chicken and egg dilemma. We cannot discuss world government because we have no world community to support it. Indeed, the discussion of world government may even retard the development of world community (because of the evil overtones of 'world government' and 'Big Brother') and hence retard the movement towards world government.

Contrariwise, that cautious approach may overemphasize the state of perfection which the world community must achieve before world government can be considered.

An important reason for talking about world government is that nobody knows what it is. Should it aim at limited measures designed to maintain security or is security itself dependent on the pursuit of broader purposes? Should a world state be federal or unitary or should it, perhaps, contain the best features of each? What should be the relation of the world government to the citizens of extant states? What taxing powers shall the world state have and what order of military forces, if any? This list of questions can be prolonged indefinitely and there are countless possible answers to each of them.

World federalism

Principle of federalism

The federal principle is that governmental powers and responsibilities should be divided between levels of government (federal, state and local). Particular matters that cannot be handled satisfactorily on one level should be handled at another. This is also called the 'subsidiarity principle', whereby the decision is made at the political level that corresponds best to its geographical scope. Allied to this is the principle of democracy: that the individual should make as many decisions locally as possible.

The standard example of a federal constitution is the US one, adopted in 1787 – after four years of independence from the UK in which the new confederation failed to come to grips with disputes over commerce and boundaries. Despite some problems, the 1787 Constitution remains one of the world's most visionary legal documents.

World federalism is simply adding a fourth layer of government (to national, state and local). It is not so much about world government as about a governed world. World federalists want the same concerns about law and order within a country's borders to be carried to the global level. A globe of increasing trade, communications, tourism and banking cannot afford to remain in a state of anarchy. There is a need for, among other things, a network of binding treaties, a system of courts to interpret the laws and adjudicate disputes, an executive backed by a police force adequate to enforce the laws and a source of tax revenues to finance all these activities.

The NGO World Federalist Movement is campaigning for one of the biggest global changes ever attempted during the past few centuries. It cannot expect success easily or quickly. What is notable is not that the world federalist movement has failed – but that so many people (often thinking independently of each other) have come to the same conclusion: the need for some sort of world federalism. If the idea has failed – it can also be said to be durable. There is something about it that guarantees its continual existence.

World Federalist Movement

The World Federalist Movement is a movement: it is not an organization or a specific campaign. It should be likened to the women's movement or the peace movement – each of which consists of various organizations, with differing agendas and with tendencies to compete against each other. There is not one, internationally agreed plan for world federation – on the contrary, there are many.

This variety can be explained partly by the usual factors of geography, finance and the personalities of the main activists. These colour any NGO movement. Additionally, individuals may respond to the same event in similar ways at the same time. For example, in response to the rise of Hitler, Clarence Streit (of *The New York Times*) called for a union of the democracies to oppose Nazi Germany in 1939, while three young Englishmen at exactly the same time created the Federal Union organization to campaign for a similar project. Similarly the eventual completion of the UN Charter in 1945 was seen by some people as too conservative and so various campaigns began simultaneously for a stronger UN or a complete replacement of it. The bestseller of this period was written by Winston Churchill's European literary agent, Emery Reves, who wanted a fresh organization entirely (*The Anatomy of Peace*).

A split occurred in 1947 when the federalist movement was divided into the European federalists and the world federalists. The reconciliation did not commence until 1985. The controversy was over how federation should come about: with countries forming into regional federations, thereby creating a global network of regions – or a comprehensive membership of all countries into one global federation? A network of regional federations could eventually create their own form of competition against each other – as has happened with the EU's Common Agricultural Policy, which subsidizes inefficient western European farmers and excludes cheap food imports from overseas. Alternatively, there was a greater hope of achieving some form of regional federation than a global one and so a united Europe could set an example to the rest of the world: half a loaf is better than none. Additionally, a UN, say, coordinating the actions of, say, six regions would operate more efficiently than the present UN with 192 countries of equal membership rights in the General Assembly.

The European federalists have had their own doctrinal problems. Should a 'United States of Europe' be a confederation (an association of independent countries, like the UN) or a federation (involving a specific surrender of control to federal organs of government, such as in the national constitutions of the US and Australia)? NGO opinions were as varied as the governmental ones.

Incidentally, Winston Churchill (who was then out of power) still hoped for some form of overall European federation and he was one of 700 participants at an unofficial conference at The Hague in 1948 that went on to help create the Council of Europe in 1949. It began with ten countries and now has 46 – the 25 EU nations and the other 21 that are not in the EU (it is distinct from the EU but no country has ever joined the EU without first belonging to the Council of Europe). It has promoted the protection of human rights in western Europe and, more recently, commenced a dialogue with eastern European countries with a view to bringing them into the 'European house'. It promotes awareness of a European identity based on shared values.

Federalists have their own 'subsidiarity' problem. This principle means that each decision should be solved at the political level that corresponds best to its geographical scope. The federalists are obliged to tolerate a considerable diversity in fellow federalist organizations. In 1947 they could not, then, insist that the Europeans stop campaigning for a regional body. Neither can the movement lay down a set 'creed' to which all aspiring individual world federalist members should adhere. Consequently, the movement has not been able to create a set focused international campaign. Additionally, there are some basic questions that remain in dispute.

The continuing debate

This section contains certain questions in the various debates over federalism. They do not constitute an exclusive list; neither are they necessarily in any order of priority.

What should the basic unit be?

The present basic unit of international relations is the nation-state – hence the term 'inter-national': transactions between nations. Some federalist proposals are based on bringing countries together.

However, other proposals claim that the individual should be the basic unit. To construct a federal world on existing boundaries would be to entrench old national rivalries within the new system. Additionally, people can be governed; governments cannot. Governments act as they see fit and are very difficult to control if they break international agreements. The more powerful a country, the greater scope it has for mischief on the world stage knowing that it stands a greater chance of getting away with illegal acts.

Consequently, the individual should be the basic unit in a federal world and all people should see themselves as world citizens.

How valid is the nation-state?

Five hundred years ago most of today's countries were pockets of land governed by tribal chieftains, barons or princes. National boundaries are often accidents of history – not something fixed and permanent. Many of today's countries were created by foreigners – such as Africa's borders that are the by-product of European colonialism – and yet people regard national boundaries as a fixed aspect of life. International politics, international law and many schemes for world federalism are all based on them.

What should the role of public opinion be?

All proposals for world federation assume that it can only come about if there is widespread public support for it – either via governments themselves or through world citizens.

Three practical problems are immediately obvious. First, how is a groundswell in favour of world federation to be generated? Nationalism is instilled through, for example, the use of symbols: slogans, anthems, flags, pledges, etc. How could a similar array of symbols be generated in favour of world federation? Who would pay for them?

Second, how would public opinion be assessed? Presumably this would require national referendum. Many countries have no traditions of such referendum. Others which do, have a tradition of citizens preferring to opt for the status quo rather than gamble on a change; Australia is a good example of this conservatism. Would people vote 'no' in a referendum because they feel that they are already unable to influence their own national governments and fear that a global system would be even more difficult to influence? Would they vote 'no' because they would see a world federation as a 'big brother' – rather than as a guardian of human rights?

Finally, how are we to create a global sense of community? How are people to feel that they are all part of a one-world family? Do citizens really care about what happens overseas? They may give some money to help disaster relief – but this is minute compared with what they spend on themselves. Do they really care about what their actions today may result in tomorrow? The consumer boom is based partly on the reckless exploitation of the environment: what has posterity ever done for me?

What is to be done about nationalism?

How is world federalism to be reconciled with nationalism? Nationalism keeps bouncing back. Balkan nationalism helped inflame nationalism elsewhere in Europe in 1914. The League of Nations was based on the assumption that a new sense of internationalism would smother nationalism and so reduce the causes of war. The dictators of the 1930 era, however, were able to mobilize nationalism in the interests of aggression.

A fresh cycle of internationalism emerged in 1945, supported by claims that the world was becoming a 'global village' because of television. In eastern Europe (including the Balkans again), Africa, and even developed countries like Canada (over Quebec), suddenly nationalism is again a potent force.

How valid is the US experience of 1787?

The 1776 Articles of Confederation had been (just about) sufficient to win the War of Independence but not enough to keep the new entity going once independence was achieved in 1783. After 1783, there was chaos in the 13 states; there was not even agreement on the value of the currency. After four years of chaos, a Constitutional convention was held in Philadelphia and, in the words of its chairman, George Washington, a 'miracle' was created.

Americans, with justification, are proud of the 1787 Constitution (which came into effect in 1789). The Philadelphia story colours the thinking of US world federalists. There is a tendency to view the UN Charter as the Articles of Confederation (a non-binding treaty that is ignored when it is convenient to do so) and to yearn for some global constitutional convention.

However, there is little evidence of governments wishing to attend a global constitutional convention. Governments pretend to be able to handle global problems – rather than wanting to surrender their power to an international body. Plagues and pollutions are forcing them to do so – but just how bad are conditions on earth to get before governments are obliged to attend a constitutional convention? Would the planet be in such a poor state that the new federal authority would be unable to redeem it?

Is there scope for another type of federation?

Most federalist proposals are based either on world federalism or a specific geographical region (notably western Europe). The late Henry Usborne (a former British MP and founder of the British Parliamentary Group for World Government in 1946) proposed a 'minifed'. Minifed would be a federal union of the countries of the middle world (which are not superpowers). It would enforce on its members a basic law of weapons limitation – they would not go to war – but they would retain all their other rights. Minifed would possess an efficient federal police force, strong enough to enforce its laws on all its citizens. And, if the union is to be disarmed in the war-making sense, it must allow the UN Security Council in particular and the world's press in general to inspect and verify all its activities.

Instead of proposing an elected federal legislature of the classical type, minifed envisaged something more like a 'treaty of multilateral disarmament' in which the regulations that the 'high authority' would be required to enforce, are all written in detail into the treaty itself. Minifed also proposed that there should be an elected body in the nature of an ombudsman, whose duty is to check the actions of the high authority to ensure that it does not exceed its original grant of powers. This idea went back to the beginnings of parliamentary democracy when, in the Middle Ages, the monarch was accepted as the fount of all law and popular representatives gathered periodically simply to check his or her exuberance.

The minifed proposal was certainly an alternative to other world federalist proposals. However, it ran into the old problem of obtaining support from governments to implement it. Despite all the political friends acquired from Usborne's half a century of distinguished public life, he was not able to get one government to support this proposal.

Do federations last forever?

No. Perhaps part of the hesitancy the UK feels about the EU is derived from its poor record on creating federations. UK-created federations have often failed; why should an EU one succeed? The Canadian and Australian federations have lasted (though there is now a problem over Quebec). But Malaysia (which lost Singapore), Pakistan (which lost Bangladesh) and the Central African Federation (which was established in 1953 and dissolved in 1963) are all examples of short-lived UK-created federations.

Other federations have also been short lived, for example, the USSR (1917–91) and the United Arab Republic (1958–61). The US is more the exception than the rule, in the creation of durable federations.

Why should the EC last forever? What guarantee is there that a world federation would not descend into a civil war?

The idea continues

World federalism is, then, an interesting vision but with immense problems of implementation. But if nationalism keeps bouncing back, so does the idea of world federalism. Just because there are problems with implementation, it does not mean that the current world order is satisfactory. A glance at today's media would indicate that the system of competing nation-states is ultimately self-destructive.

Federalism continues to attract attention – the conversion of the USSR into the Commonwealth of Independent States was done partly through a study of federalism, especially (ironically) examining the lessons of US federalism. Meanwhile the world federalist movement is establishing branches in eastern Europe.

Finally, recent events such as the ending of the Cold War, reunification of Germany and revived interest in UN reform all demonstrate just how rapidly something considered politically unrealistic becomes practical and necessary.

Refusal to change

People can be very stubborn. They prefer to stick with old paradigms that are in trouble, rather than seek better ones.

In 1797 Patrick Colquhoun wrote his *Treatise on the Police of the Metropolis*. This was one of the first attempts to gauge the number of criminals in King George III's London. Colquhoun claimed that about one Londoner in eight lived off crime of one sort or another. As to whether by our standards we would accept that all such people were 'criminal' is a matter of social policy from one generation to another. Definitions of 'crime' vary from one generation to another and from one country to another.

Londoners then thought that crime was rife in their city but they were reluctant to ask the basic questions: what caused it and how could it be prevented? The politicians ignored such questions and, instead, opted for punishment. England had no centralized police force until 1829. Law and order on the street was deliberately left to local authorities and these gave it a low priority. Parish watchmen were employed to do basic patrols and they were usually older men who were not fit enough for regular employment.

The people who had most to gain from law and order were opposed to the creation of a proper police force. The English political culture was based on individualism and privacy: 'An Englishman's home is his castle.' People would rather be robbed occasionally than be subject to the perpetual risk of police visits. This meant that London – one of Europe's most important cities – was particularly notorious for the prevalence of criminal gangs, especially at night. Londoners preferred to stick with what they knew rather than what they did not know. They were reluctant to create a police force because it would mean giving extra power to the government. Two centuries later, this mindset is obvious in respect to most international problems. There are no national solutions to international problems.

Some NGOs have been campaigning for years on the need for some form of global governance. But, like the English two centuries ago, national politicians prefer to stick with the risk of environmental and economic chaos, rather than create an authority higher than themselves. The English were forced to change their attitude because of the crime rate. It remains to be seen just what needs to happen before governments change their minds today.

Conclusion

To sum up, this book has argued that globalization is transforming the world's politics and economics. The globalization process is more than matters of trade (such as cheap labour and sweatshops). It represents the biggest challenge to national governments since the system of nation-states and national governments was created in 1648. It requires us to look afresh at many matters we take for granted.

The current world order has worn well – but it is now wearing out. It is a world order in which national governments had national control over national events. But they no longer seem to be so effective. We are moving from a world with borders to one without.

Globalization is the collective term for the erosion of national boundaries and the reduced significance of national governments. Countries will remain in existence but the process of globalization means that national governments will have to share their power with three other centres of power.

First, governments increasingly have to work together on common problems. Diseases, pollution and climate change do not recognize national boundaries. They have no respect for human-made lines on maps. Therefore, national governments work through intergovernmental organizations such as the UN and EU. Until the recent expansion of the UN's peacekeeping work, about 80 per cent of its expenditure was on economic and social cooperation.

Second, there is the growing importance of transnational corporations. These are now the major driving forces in economic policy. Corporations can, for example, move jobs offshore in search of cheaper workers and fewer unions.

The final form of globalization is the mobilization of people power. This is mainly done through NGOs, for example, Amnesty International, women's movement, peace movement and Rotary. They enable people to work together across national lines for the betterment of humankind.

One implication of this new era of globalization is that many people have lost faith in conventional politics: 'Whoever you vote for, a politician always gets elected.' Governments are rarely able to implement fully their election promises because of the restricting power of corporations and lobby groups (NGOs). But people are still interested in politics. They are cynical about political parties and so they prefer to concentrate on specific campaigns for a specific amount of time through NGOs.

A second implication is that governments have not done enough to warn their citizens about the changes. Hence the rise of the 'politics of anger'. People who see themselves as the victims of globalization and the casualties of change are going to right-wing nationalist spokespersons to get explanations of what is happening. The major gap in politics in most western countries is not between the mainline parties but between the mainstream parties and the alienated, angry people who feel excluded from the political process.

A third implication is that globalization cannot be reversed. It has moved too far too quickly and become too entrenched. Little can be gained by seeking a return to some earlier nationalistic era when life seemed to be easier and better. The 1950s may have been good for the white middle-class males – but there were many other losers at that time.

This book has tried to explain some of the complexities of globalization. It is a complicated subject partly because it is linked to so many other matters. There are no easy answers but it is important that more be done to educate the general public about globalization because it is here to stay and it will have more and more of an impact on all of our lives.

This means that there needs to be more public education on explaining the process of globalization and its implications. Since the public are so sceptical of glossy governmental publications, why can't governments provide funding for NGOs to educate the public about globalization? NGOs know how to produce readable material without high cost.

We will be living with globalization for many years to come. We need to ensure that globalization is *worth* living with.

Questions

1 Are you worried about the evolution of some form of 'world government'?
2 What would be the advantages and disadvantages of a world government?
3 How do you think that a world government could be created (if at all)?
4 Check to see if there is a world federalist/world citizen NGO in your area and investigate the value of joining it.
5 How would you answer all the seven questions listed in the last section of this chapter?

glossary

functional cooperation bringing experts and specialists together across national lines to work on problems of common concern (such as the prevention of avian 'flu)

globalization erosion of the power of the nation-state and national governments

intergovernmental organization an organization with two or more national governments as members (also called 'international organization')

nation a homogenous group of people, with a common sense of history and culture and possibly a flag and anthem (the term may be used, somewhat confusingly, to refer to both a population within a nation-state and an indigenous population)

nation-state an independent territory with a national government (also called 'country')

nongovernmental organization (NGO) an organization of voluntary members that is not controlled by a government and is not run for profit (also called 'civil society organization')

sovereignty the right of a national government to make its own decisions

state the national political, legal and administrative system for governing a nation

transnational corporation a business with ventures in two or more nation-states (also called a 'multinational corporation')

abbreviations

AIDS	Acquired Immunity Deficiency Syndrome
ASEAN	Association of South East Asian Nations
ASOC	Antarctic and Southern Oceans Coalition
BBC	British Broadcasting Corporation
BCCI	Bank of Credit and Commerce International
BIS	Bank of International Settlements
CIA	Central Intelligence Agency
CNN	Cable News Network
DEA	Drug Enforcement Agency
ECOSOC	Economic and Social Council
EU	European Union
FCO	Foreign and Commonwealth Office
GATT	General Agreement on Tariffs and Trade
GDP	Gross Domestic Product
GNP	Gross National Product
ICJ	International Court of Justice
ILO	International Labour Organization
IMF	International Monetary Fund
IMO	International Maritime Organization
INFACT	Infant Formula Coalition
ISD	International Subscriber Dialling
ITO	International Trade Organization
ITU	International Telecommunications Union
MAI	Multilateral Agreement on Investment

NATO	North Atlantic Treaty Organization
NGO	Nongovernmental Organization
OECD	Organization for Economic Co-operation and Development
TNC	Transnational Corporation
UDHR	Universal Declaration of Human Rights
UN	United Nations
UNCED	United Nations Conference on Environment and Development
UNEP	United Nations Environment Programme
UNESCO	United Nations Educational, Scientific and Cultural Organization
UNICEF	United Nations Children's Fund
USSR	Union of Soviet Socialist Republics
WHO	World Health Organization
WTO	World Trade Organization

taking it further

Books

Commission for Africa, *Our Common Interest*, London, Penguin, 2005

Department of Public Information, *Basic Facts about the United Nations*, New York, United National, 2004

Thomas Friedman, *The World is Flat: A Brief History of the Globalized World in the 21st Century*, London, Allen Lane, 2005

Steve John and Stuart Thomson, *New Activism and the Corporate Response*, London, Palgrave Macmillan, 2004

Naomi Klein, *Fences and Windows: Dispatches from the Front Lines of the Globalization Debate*, London, Flamingo, 2002

Naomi Klein, *No Logo*, London, Flamingo, 2000

David Korten, *When Corporations Rule the World*, London, Earthscan, 1995

Kenichi Ohmae, *The Borderless World: Power and Strategy in the Global Marketplace*, London, HarperCollins, 1994

Greg Palast, *The Best Democracy Money Can Buy*, London, Robinson, 2003

Frank Portnoy, *Infectious Greed: How Deceit and Risk Corrupted the Financial Markets*, London, Profile Books, 2003

Eric Schlosser, *Fast Food Nation*, London, Penguin, 2002

Keith Suter, *Global Order and Global Disorder: Globalization and the Nation-State*, London, Praeger, 2003

Rex Weyler, *Greenpeace: An Insider's Account*, London, PanMacmillan, 2004

Websites

Culture Jammers Network/Adbusters Newsletter:
http://www.adbusters.org

Google Earth: http://earth.google.com

Independent Media: http://www.indymedia.org

New Internationalist: http://www.newint.org

One World Trust: http://www.oneworldtrust.org

United Nations: http://www.un.org

United Nations Association of the UK: http://www.una-uk.org

World Development Movement: http://www.wdm.org.uk

index

acid rain 51
advertising 103, 126–9, 141, 180
Africa 28–31, 34–5
AIDS 47, 48–9
Albania 102
Americanization 4
Amin, Idi 61
Amnesty International 146, 162, 170, 211, 227
Andorra 40
anger, politics of 195–8, 227
Antarctica 15, 50, 75, 163
    Antarctic Treaty Environment Protocol 166–70
anti-globalization 187–206
    global justice movement 176, 180, 198–203, 205–6
    in novels 203–5
    and the politics of anger 195–8
    protests 4, 5, 9, 110, 176, 199–200
    and religious fundamentalism 188–95
Argentina 167, 173
armageddon theology 194–5
assessing globalization 9
Association of South East Asian Nations (ASEAN) 89–91
Australia 11, 15, 39, 85, 193, 198
    and ASEAN 91
    economic policies 119

Bakker, Jim and Tammy 193–4
Bank of Credit and Commerce International (BCCI) 58–9
Bank of England 91
Bank of International Settlements (BIS) 91–6, 97
banks, and micro-credit 157–8, 184–5
Basle Accord (1988) 92, 93
BBC (British Broadcasting Corporation) 42
Berlin Conference (1884–5) 30–1, 34–5
Bismarck, Otto von 30–1
Blair, Tony 43, 96

Blinder, Alan 109
Body Shop 181
Bove, Jose 204
brands 179–80
Brazil 95
broadcasting 42–3
Burma (Myanmar) 57, 90–1
Bush, George 37, 42, 89, 109
Bush, George W. 3, 86, 89, 204
Buy Nothing Day 179

Canada 26, 85
Carter, Jimmy 159
Catholic Church 19–21, 22, 182, 191
Chernobyl nuclear disaster 43–4
child labour 132
Chile, and Antarctica 167
China 4, 42, 75, 89, 157, 170
    and ASEAN 91
    and the BIS 95
    and the global economy 102, 103
    and human rights 76
    prison labour camps 132
    and Russia 212–14
    and tobacco 178
    and transnational corporations 7, 101
Chirac, Jacques 89
Christian Brothers Investment Services Inc (CBIS) 182
Christian church 19–21, 22, 28–9, 111, 193–5
    and investment guidelines 183, 184
Churchill, Winston 67–8, 74, 78, 81, 83, 220
civil society organizations see nongovernmental organizations
Clean Clothes Campaign (CCC) 181
climate change 50–1, 166
Clinton, Bill 89, 109–10
clothing
    Clean Clothes Campaign (CCC) 181
    and Islam 191–3

Club of Rome **164–6**
Coca-Cola **102, 104, 106, 189**
Coffee Fair Trade movement **181**
Cold War **2, 5, 6, 211**
    and Antarctica **168**
    ending of the **7, 13–16, 101, 120, 194, 225**
    and the UN **72, 73, 74, 75**
    and World War II criminals **172, 173**
colonialism **9–11, 28–31**
    decolonization **10, 74–5**
    mandated territories **71–5**
    neo-colonialism and the global economy **102**
Colquhoun, Patrick **225**
Commonwealth **85–7**
Commonwealth of Independent States (CIS) **86, 225**
Commonwealth Partnership for Technology Management (CPTM) **86**
communications technology **10, 37, 41–3**
compassion fatigue **62–3**
compulsive shopping disorder (CSD) **129**
consumer boycotts **151–2, 177–80**
consumer relationship marketing **128**
consumer sovereignty **113**
consumerism **13–14, 104, 106, 116, 124–9, 144, 196**
    decline of consumer sovereignty **113–14**
    and developing countries **129–30**
    ethical purchasing **180–1**
    and extreme nationalist politics **209**
    and marketing **126–9**
    and NGOs **149**
    rise of **125–6**
cooperative power **2, 5–6, 176**
corporate power **2, 6–8, 99**
    see also economics; transnational corporations (TNCs)
crime **53–9, 225–6**
    drug trade **53–4, 56–7**
    the Russian mafia **54–6**
    war criminals **172–4**
currencies **28, 84–5**
Czechoslovakia **25, 27, 171**

decolonization **10, 74–5**
democracy **96–7, 170–1**
Deng Xiapong **102**
deregulation **120**
developing countries
    and consumerism **129–30**
    and free trade **132–4**
    NGO projects **150**
    transfer of jobs to **117–18**
Dickens, Charles **132–3**
diplomacy **34–8**
drug trade **53–4, 56–7**
Dubcek, Alexander **171**

Dunant, Henri **153–5**

East Timor **74, 90**
eastern Europe **83–4, 157**
economic depressions **92, 94, 113, 115, 116, 119**
economic growth, and the environment **164–6**
economics **4**
    free market economies **112–14**
    the global economy **101–5**
    Keynesian **93–4, 114–18**
    mercantilism **111–12**
    and national governments **109–10**
    new right 'economic rationalism' **119**
    popular capitalism **121–3**
    privatization and deregulation **120**
    regional economic zones **38–9**
Eichmann, Adolf **173**
employment
    full employment **114–16**
    global workforce **7–8, 105, 106–7**
    as a source of anger **197**
    the workplace as health hazard **136**
environmental issues **4, 15–16**
    and Antarctica **166–70**
    and NGOs **8, 152–3**
    the Club of Rome **164–6**
    pollution **49–53, 190**
    and the UN **76**
ethical purchasing **180–1**
euro currency **28, 84–5**
European Coal and Steel Community **83**
European Commission **84**
European Economic Community (EEC) **83**
European nation-states **17–31**
    and Africa **28–31**
European Union (EU) **4, 5, 81–5, 199–200**
    creation **82–3**
    enlargement **11, 83–4**
    and federalism **220–1, 224**
    problems **83–5**
    and the UK **81–2**
Europeanization **9–12**

fair trade **180–1**
Falwell, Jerry **194**
Farrakhan, Louis **198**
fast food **137, 138–9, 178–9**
federalism
    minifed **224**
    world federalism **217, 218–25**
films, Indian **189**
food production **137–8**
fourth world **12–13**
France
    and the European Union **82, 83**
    and the Group of 8 (G8) **87, 88**
    Islam in **191–2, 193**

free trade **112–14, 130–4, 138, 198–203**
Fugger family **99**
full employment **114–16**

Gandhi, Mahatma **103, 189**
Gates, Bill **110**
GE (General Electric) **177–8, 180**
General Agreement on Tariffs and Trade
    (GATT) **131, 199, 200, 201–2**
General Agreement on Trade in Services
    (GATS) **201–3**
Germany **3, 20, 21, 25**
    and African colonialism **30–1**
    and the BIS **92**
    and the League of Nations **67**
    Nazi war criminals **172–4**
    reunification of **225**
Giscard d'Estaing, Valéry **88**
globalization
    defining **2–3**
    future of **208–15**
    main characteristics of **3–4**
Gorbachev, M. **13, 43, 214**
Grameen Bank, Bangladesh **158, 160, 184**
greenhouse effect **50–1**
Greenpeace **146, 152–3, 211**
Greenspan, Alan **109**
Group of 10 (G10) **93**
Group of 8 (G8) **87–9, 95**

Habitat for Humanity **158–9**
Harris, Paul **155**
Hayek, Friedrich von **119**
health issues **134–44**
    life expectancy **134**
    obesity **136–9, 179**
    pace of life **135–6**
    tobacco **139–44**
    in the workplace **136**
Henry VIII, King of England **21**
Hinduism **189–90**
history and globalization **4**
Hitler, Adolf **27, 67, 92, 94, 115, 195, 220**
Huguenots **61**
human rights **75–6, 91, 103, 195**
    and free trade **133, 203**
    and tobacco control **141**

India **4, 75, 103–4, 105**
    and Hinduism **189–90**
indigenous peoples **12**
Indonesia **90, 132, 170, 171**
Industrial Revolution **29–30, 124, 130**
INFACT (Infant Formula Action Collective)
    151, 177–8
infant formula campaign **151–2, 176**
infectious diseases **47–8**
intergovernmental organizations **4, 5, 66**
    and NGOs **162, 163–4, 176**

    see also European Union (EU); United
        Nations (UN)
Intermediate Technology Development
    Group (ITDG) **150**
International Court of Justice (ICJ) **69–70**
International Maritime Organization **6**
International Monetary Fund (IMF) **202**
International Telecommunications Union
    (ITU) **6**
International Trade Organization (ITO) **199**
internationalism **223**
internet **41, 176, 205**
    broadcasting **43**
    marketing **128**
investment guidelines **183–4**
investments, socially responsible **182–3**
iPod **114**
Iran **106**
Iraq **37, 212**
Islam **42–3, 190–3, 198**
Israel **86, 87**

Japan **10, 71, 91, 133, 172**
Jevons, Stanley **125**
Jews **195**

Kazakhstan **101**
Keynes, John Maynard **93–4, 114–18,
    119, 125–6**
Khrushchev, N. **213**
King, Alexander **164, 165**
King, Martin Luther **176**
Kinshasa Highway **49**
Kiribati **50**
Klein, Naomi, *No Logo* **179–80**
Krieger, Andy **110**
Kroc, Ray **137**
Kuwait **212**
Kyoto Protocol **8, 203**

Latin America **28, 39**
League of Nations **66–7, 72, 73, 74, 148,
    223**
Libya **7**
life expectancy **134**
limited corporations **111–12**
localization **34, 38–40**
Los Angeles **40**
Lu, Annette **170**
Ludlum, Robert **203–5**
Luther, Martin **20, 21**
Luvox **129**

McDonalds **104, 106, 178–9, 204, 211**
Major, John **96**
malaria **48, 139**
Malaysia **42–3, 224**
mandated territories **71, 85–6**
Mao Zedong **213**

marine pollution 52–3
marine resources in Antarctica 168–9
market system and free trade 112–14
marketing 126–9
    and brands 179–80
Martin, Paul 89
media 197
    and NGOs 163, 171
Menem, Carlos 173
mercantilism 111–12
micro-credit movement 157–8, 184–5
Microsoft 110
Middle Ages 20–1
middle class 104, 107, 211–12
    and democracy 170–1
Middle East 3, 88, 116
migrants 11–12, 60–2
minifed 224
Mohammed, Prophet 193
money laundering 53, 58–9
Montenegro 3, 26
Moral Majority 184
Morgenthau, Robert 59
Mozambique 86
Multilateral Agreement on Investment
        (MAI) 200–1, 203
Munich Agreement (1939) 27
music, and marketing 127

Nagy, Imre 171
'nation', definition of 24–5
nation-states 2, 3, 5, 17–44
    characteristics of 22–3
    and colonialism 9–11, 28–31
    and Europeanization 9, 10–11
    minorities within 12
    and technology 40
    and transnational corporations 100
    and world federalism 222
    see also Westphalian system
national boundaries 2, 3, 38, 46, 66
    and tax havens 119
national governments 2–3, 22, 226–7
    and cooperative power 5
    future of 96–7
    and the global economy 109–10
    and NGOs 161–74
    reduction in power 5
    and tax havens 119
national sovereignty 23, 26, 46, 120
nationalism
    in sport 210–11
    and world federalism 223
natural law 22–3
neo-colonialism, and the global economy
        102
Network for Accountability of Tobacco
        Transnationals (NATT) 143
new technology 40–4

new world order 5
New Zealand 85, 91, 110, 119
    and Antarctica 167, 169
NGOs, and national governments 161–74
Nightingale, Florence 153
Nixon, Richard 87
Nobel, Alfred 100, 155
Nobel Peace Prize 155
nongovernmental organizations (NGOs)
        4, 8, 131, 145–60, 211, 227
    and Antarctica 163, 166–70
    and anti-globalization 196, 205
    Club of Rome 164–6
    and community involvement 149
    and community mobilization 148–9
    and consumer boycotts 151–2
    and the decline of party politics 147
    defining 146
    and democracy 170–1
    and the ending of the Cold War 13–14,
        15
    expanding role of 147–8
    Greenpeace 146, 152–3
    Habitat for Humanity 158–9
    and micro-enterprises 157–8
    the Red Cross 153–5
    and research 150
    Rotary International 155–7
    size of 146–7
    and tobacco control 142–4
    and transnational corporations 162,
        175–86
    and the UN 76–7
    and war criminals 172–4
    and the Westphalian system 162–4
    World Federalist Movement 219–21
Noriega, General 57
North Korea 106
novels, globalization in 203–5
nuclear weapons, and consumer boycotts
        177–8, 180

obesity 136–9, 179
OECD (Organization for Economic
        Cooperation and Development)
        200–1
oil issues
    and Antarctica 169
    embargo (1973) 87, 116, 119
    global oilrush 7, 101
Olympic Games 76, 211
ozone layer 51

Palestine 3, 86
Panama 57
Papua New Guinea 71
Pax World Fund 182
peace and globalization 211–14
peace research 148

peasant societies 170–1
Peccei, Aurelio 164, 165
pension funds 181–2, 185
pensions and life expectancy 134
people power 2, 8, 145–60, 170–1
    see also nongovernmental
      organizations (NGOs)
Peron, Juan 173
Petty, Sir William 124
Philippines 170
Pitcairn Island 75
plagues 46–7
Pol Pot 171
Poland 25, 173
politics
    and anti-globalization 197–8
    decline of interest in 209–10, 227
    and democracy 96–7
    and NGOs 147, 163, 196
pollution 49–53, 190
popular capitalism 121–3
positivism 23
power, new centres of 2, 5–8
privatization 120
product placement 127–8
Protestant Reformation 20–1, 41
public opinion, and world federalism 222
Putin, Vladimir 88–9

Reagan, Ronald 15, 89, 194
the Red Cross 153–5
refugees 60–2
religion and the state 191, 193
religious fundamentalism 188–95
Reves, Emery 220
revolution of rising expectations 129
rivers, and national boundaries 66
Robertson, Pat 194
Roddick, Anita 181
Romania 14
Rotary International 155–7, 227
Rushdie, Salman, Satanic Verses 190–1
Russia
    and the BIS 95
    and China 212–14
    and the Group of 8 (G8) 87, 88–9
    Siberia and Far Eastern 214
    see also Soviet Union
Russian mafia 54–6
Ruthenia 25
Rwanda 31, 43, 78

satellite technology 42–4, 103, 190
Say, Jean Baptiste 115
Schröder, Gerhard 89
Schumacher, Dr E.F. 150
Scottish nationalism 84
sea level rises 50
Seattle anti-globalization protesters (1999)

131–2, 199, 204
self-determination 26–8
share ownership 121–2
shareholder activism 181–5
Sierra Leone 43
slave trade 29
Smith, Adam 112–15, 116
smoking
    cigarette advertising 126–7
    tobacco control 139–44
Somalia 43
South Africa 35–6, 85, 183–4
South Korea 91, 95, 170
sovereign equality of states doctrine 36–7
Soviet Union 5, 13, 14–15, 43–4
    and crime 54–5
    federalism (USSR) 225
    and the global economy 102
    and the UN 77
    see also Russia
sport, nationalism in 210–11
SPOT satellite system 43–4
SRIs (socially responsible investments)
      182–3
stagflation 116–17, 119
Stalin, Joseph 13, 115, 171, 213
'state', definition of 24–6
Streit, Clarence 220
subsidiary, and the European Union 84
Suharto 171
Switzerland 26, 34

Taiwan 170
tax havens 119
taxation 118
technological developments 40–4
    and crime 53–4
    and the economy 117
telecommunications revolution 6, 7–8, 15,
      41
television
    advertising 103, 128, 129–30
    broadcasting 42–3
    and compassion fatigue 62–3
    and consumer culture 104, 190
    and evangelism 193–4
    impact of 13–14
Thailand 170
Thatcher, Margaret 120, 121, 169, 212
Third Sector 146
tobacco control 139–44, 178
Tokes, Reverend Lazlo 14
trade unions 121, 122
transnational corporations (TNCs) 2, 3–4,
      6–8, 14, 44, 98–107
    and Adam Smith 113–14
    and anti-globalization 196
    and consumerism 124
    and developing countries 130

and the European Union **84**
evolution of **99–101**
and extreme nationalist politics **208–9**
and free trade **130–4**
and the global economy **101–5**
global impact of **105–7**
and Keynesian economics **117–18**
and national governments **109–10**
and NGOs **162, 175–86**
and taxation **118–19**
transport improvements **37**
Transylvania **14**
tuberculosis **48**
24-hour society **135–6**

Uganda **61**
unemployment **115, 116, 117, 119, 197**
United Kingdom (UK) **10**
    and the Commonwealth **85**
    and diplomacy **37, 38**
    and the European Union **81–2**
    federations **224**
    politics **96**
United Nations (UN) **2, 4, 5, 7, 65–79, 81,
    148, 217**
    achievements **74–7**
    composition **67–72**
        Economic and Social Council
        (ECOSOC) **70–1**
        General Assembly **68, 77**
        International Court of Justice (ICJ)
        69–70
        Secretariat **72**
        Security Council **68–9, 73, 74, 77**
        Trusteeship Council **71**
    continuing problems **77–8**
    and decolonization **10**
    and diplomacy **35–6, 36–7**
    and the fourth world **12**
    and the League of Nations **66–7**
    and localization **40**
    membership **3, 10, 35**
    peacekeeping operations **66**
    and Rotary International **156**
    specialized agencies **70, 77**
    and the Westphalian system **72–3, 78**
United States of America **4, 5, 208**
    Afro-Americans **29**
    Chicago South Shore Bank **184–5**
    and Christianity **193–4, 195**
    and the Cold War **14–16**
    Constitution (1787) **223**
    and corporate power **109–10**
    and the drug trade **56–7**
    economic policies **119**
    federal constitution **219**
    and the Group of 8 (G8) **87–8, 89**
    and the League of Nations **67**

localization **39, 40**
    and NGOs **146**
    and obesity **137**
    and popular capitalism **121–2**
    and Rotary clubs **155–7**
    and South Africa **183–4**
    and transnational corporations **103**
    and white male rage **195**
    and world trade **199–200**
    and World War II criminals **172, 173**
Universal Postal Union **66**
urbanization **39–40**
Usborne, Henry **224**
USSR *see* Soviet Union

Vatican City **36**
Vietnam **103, 170**
vigilante investors **181–2**

wages, downward harmonization of **118**
war criminals **172–4**
Wellington Treaty **169**
Wesley, John **126**
Westphalian system **3, 13, 18, 21, 23–8,
    31, 46, 97**
    and diplomacy **34–8**
    and the European Union **81**
    and the League of Nations **66–7**
    and mercantilism **111**
    and NGOs **162–4**
    and transnational corporations **99, 105–7**
    and the United Nations **72–3, 78**
    see also nation-states
whales **52**
Wiesenthal, Simon **172–4**
Wilson, Woodrow **27, 67, 71**
workforce *see* employment
World Council of Churches **184**
world federalism **217, 218–25**
    basic unit of **221**
    and nationalism **223**
    and public opinion **222**
World Health Organization (WHO) **5–6,
    70–1, 77, 135, 136, 139**
    Framework Convention on Tobacco
    Control **140–2**
    and the infant formula campaign **151–2,
    176**
World Meteorological Organization **6**
World Trade Organization (WTO) **131,
    199–200, 202**
World War I **27, 66, 71, 92**
World War II **10, 27–8, 31, 67–8, 81, 94,
    102, 213**
    hunting down war criminals **172–4**

Yugoslavia (former) **73**
Yunus, Muhammad **158**

From Advanced Sudoku to Zulu, you'll find everything you need in the **teach yourself** range, in books, on CD and on DVD.

Visit **www.teachyourself.co.uk** for more details.

Advanced Sudoku and Kakuro
Afrikaans
Alexander Technique
Algebra
Ancient Greek
Applied Psychology
Arabic
Aromatherapy
Art History
Astrology
Astronomy
AutoCAD 2004
AutoCAD 2007
Ayurveda
Baby Massage and Yoga
Baby Signing
Baby Sleep
Bach Flower Remedies
Backgammon
Ballroom Dancing
Basic Accounting
Basic Computer Skills
Basic Mathematics
Beauty
Beekeeping
Beginner's Arabic Script
Beginner's Chinese Script
Beginner's Dutch

Beginner's French
Beginner's German
Beginner's Greek
Beginner's Greek Script
Beginner's Hindi
Beginner's Italian
Beginner's Japanese
Beginner's Japanese Script
Beginner's Latin
Beginner's Mandarin Chinese
Beginner's Portuguese
Beginner's Russian
Beginner's Russian Script
Beginner's Spanish
Beginner's Turkish
Beginner's Urdu Script
Bengali
Better Bridge
Better Chess
Better Driving
Better Handwriting
Biblical Hebrew
Biology
Birdwatching
Blogging
Body Language
Book Keeping
Brazilian Portuguese

Bridge
British Empire, The
British Monarchy from Henry VIII, The
Buddhism
Bulgarian
Business Chinese
Business French
Business Japanese
Business Plans
Business Spanish
Business Studies
Buying a Home in France
Buying a Home in Italy
Buying a Home in Portugal
Buying a Home in Spain
C++
Calculus
Calligraphy
Cantonese
Car Buying and Maintenance
Card Games
Catalan
Chess
Chi Kung
Chinese Medicine
Christianity
Classical Music
Coaching
Cold War, The
Collecting
Computing for the Over 50s
Consulting
Copywriting
Correct English
Counselling
Creative Writing
Cricket
Croatian
Crystal Healing
CVs
Czech
Danish
Decluttering
Desktop Publishing
Detox

Digital Home Movie Making
Digital Photography
Dog Training
Drawing
Dream Interpretation
Dutch
Dutch Conversation
Dutch Dictionary
Dutch Grammar
Eastern Philosophy
Electronics
English as a Foreign Language
English for International Business
English Grammar
English Grammar as a Foreign Language
English Vocabulary
Entrepreneurship
Estonian
Ethics
Excel 2003
Feng Shui
Film Making
Film Studies
Finance for Non-Financial Managers
Finnish
First World War, The
Fitness
Flash 8
Flash MX
Flexible Working
Flirting
Flower Arranging
Franchising
French
French Conversation
French Dictionary
French Grammar
French Phrasebook
French Starter Kit
French Verbs
French Vocabulary
Freud
Gaelic

Gardening
Genetics
Geology
German
German Conversation
German Grammar
German Phrasebook
German Verbs
German Vocabulary
Globalization
Go
Golf
Good Study Skills
Great Sex
Greek
Greek Conversation
Greek Phrasebook
Growing Your Business
Guitar
Gulf Arabic
Hand Reflexology
Hausa
Herbal Medicine
Hieroglyphics
Hindi
Hindi Conversation
Hinduism
History of Ireland, The
Home PC Maintenance and
  Networking
How to DJ
How to Run a Marathon
How to Win at Casino Games
How to Win at Horse Racing
How to Win at Online Gambling
How to Win at Poker
How to Write a Blockbuster
Human Anatomy & Physiology
Hungarian
Icelandic
Improve Your French
Improve Your German
Improve Your Italian
Improve Your Spanish
Improving Your Employability

Indian Head Massage
Indonesian
Instant French
Instant German
Instant Greek
Instant Italian
Instant Japanese
Instant Portuguese
Instant Russian
Instant Spanish
Internet, The
Irish
Irish Conversation
Irish Grammar
Islam
Italian
Italian Conversation
Italian Grammar
Italian Phrasebook
Italian Starter Kit
Italian Verbs
Italian Vocabulary
Japanese
Japanese Conversation
Java
JavaScript
Jazz
Jewellery Making
Judaism
Jung
Kama Sutra, The
Keeping Aquarium Fish
Keeping Pigs
Keeping Poultry
Keeping a Rabbit
Knitting
Korean
Latin
Latin American Spanish
Latin Dictionary
Latin Grammar
Latvian
Letter Writing Skills
Life at 50: For Men
Life at 50: For Women

Life Coaching
Linguistics
LINUX
Lithuanian
Magic
Mahjong
Malay
Managing Stress
Managing Your Own Career
Mandarin Chinese
Mandarin Chinese Conversation
Marketing
Marx
Massage
Mathematics
Meditation
Middle East Since 1945, The
Modern China
Modern Hebrew
Modern Persian
Mosaics
Music Theory
Mussolini's Italy
Nazi Germany
Negotiating
Nepali
New Testament Greek
NLP
Norwegian
Norwegian Conversation
Old English
One-Day French
One-Day French – the DVD
One-Day German
One-Day Greek
One-Day Italian
One-Day Portuguese
One-Day Spanish
One-Day Spanish – the DVD
Origami
Owning a Cat
Owning a Horse
Panjabi
PC Networking for Small
  Businesses

Personal Safety and Self
  Defence
Philosophy
Philosophy of Mind
Philosophy of Religion
Photography
Photoshop
PHP with MySQL
Physics
Piano
Pilates
Planning Your Wedding
Polish
Polish Conversation
Politics
Portuguese
Portuguese Conversation
Portuguese Grammar
Portuguese Phrasebook
Postmodernism
Pottery
PowerPoint 2003
PR
Project Management
Psychology
Quick Fix French Grammar
Quick Fix German Grammar
Quick Fix Italian Grammar
Quick Fix Spanish Grammar
Quick Fix: Access 2002
Quick Fix: Excel 2000
Quick Fix: Excel 2002
Quick Fix: HTML
Quick Fix: Windows XP
Quick Fix: Word
Quilting
Recruitment
Reflexology
Reiki
Relaxation
Retaining Staff
Romanian
Running Your Own Business
Russian
Russian Conversation

Russian Grammar
Sage Line 50
Sanskrit
Screenwriting
Second World War, The
Serbian
Setting Up a Small Business
Shorthand Pitman 2000
Sikhism
Singing
Slovene
Small Business Accounting
Small Business Health Check
Songwriting
Spanish
Spanish Conversation
Spanish Dictionary
Spanish Grammar
Spanish Phrasebook
Spanish Starter Kit
Spanish Verbs
Spanish Vocabulary
Speaking On Special Occasions
Speed Reading
Stalin's Russia
Stand Up Comedy
Statistics
Stop Smoking
Sudoku
Swahili
Swahili Dictionary
Swedish
Swedish Conversation
Tagalog
Tai Chi
Tantric Sex
Tap Dancing
Teaching English as a Foreign
  Language
Teams & Team Working
Thai
Theatre
Time Management
Tracing Your Family History
Training

Travel Writing
Trigonometry
Turkish
Turkish Conversation
Twentieth Century USA
Typing
Ukrainian
Understanding Tax for Small
  Businesses
Understanding Terrorism
Urdu
Vietnamese
Visual Basic
Volcanoes
Watercolour Painting
Weight Control through Diet &
  Exercise
Welsh
Welsh Dictionary
Welsh Grammar
Wills & Probate
Windows XP
Wine Tasting
Winning at Job Interviews
Word 2003
World Cultures: China
World Cultures: England
World Cultures: Germany
World Cultures: Italy
World Cultures: Japan
World Cultures: Portugal
World Cultures: Russia
World Cultures: Spain
World Cultures: Wales
World Faiths
Writing Crime Fiction
Writing for Children
Writing for Magazines
Writing a Novel
Writing Poetry
Xhosa
Yiddish
Yoga
Zen
Zulu

teach
yourself

politics
peter joyce

- Do you want to understand key political terms and concepts?
- Would you like to consider important political questions?
- Are you looking for an introduction to this fascinating subject?

Politics gives you the background knowledge that enables you to consider important political questions. Focusing on the political systems operating in democratic states, it will give you an understanding of these systems and the key terms, themes and influences. Fully updated to include discussion of the latest developments in politics and international relations, this book is essential reading for all those who want to understand politics today.

Peter Joyce is the Principal Lecturer in the department of Sociology at Manchester Metropolitan University.